Restorative Justice in a Prison Community

Restorative Justice in a Prison Community

Or Everything I Didn't Learn in Kindergarten I Learned in Prison

CHERYL SWANSON

LEXINGTON BOOKS
A Division of
ROWMAN & LITTLEFIELD PUBLISHERS, INC.
Lanham • Boulder • New York • Toronto • Plymouth, UK

Published by Lexington Books
A division of Rowman & Littlefield Publishers, Inc.
A wholly owned subsidary of The Rowman & Littlefield Publishing Group, Inc.
4501 Forbes Boulevard, Suite 200, Lanham, Maryland 20706
www.lexingtonbooks.com

Estover Road, Plymouth PL6 7PY, United Kingdom

British Library Cataloguing in Publication Information Available

Library of Congress Cataloging-in-Publication Data

The hardback edition of this book was previously cataloged by the Library of Congress as
follows:

Swanson, Cheryl G.
    Restorative justice in a prison community : or everything I didn't learn in kindergarten
I learned in prison / Cheryl Swanson.
        p. cm.
    Includes bibliographical references and index.
    ISBN-13: 978-0-7391-2679-0 (cloth : alk. paper)
    ISBN-10: 0-7391-2679-2 (cloth : alk. paper)
    ISBN-13: 978-0-7391-3509-9 (electronic)
    ISBN-10: 0-7391-3509-0 (electronic)
    1. Restorative justice—United States. 2. Prisons—United States. 3. Prisoners—United
States. I. Title.
HV8688.S87 2009
365'.64—dc22   2008047178

    ISBN: 978-0-7391-2680-6 (pbk. : alk. paper)

♾™ The paper used in this publication meets the minimum requirements of American
National Standard for Information Sciences—Permanence of Paper for Printed Library
Materials, ANSI/NISO Z39.48-1992.

Printed in the United States of America

To the men of the W. C. Holman Faith-Based
Restorative Justice Honor Dorm

Contents

Preface

This book has emerged from an ongoing interest in prisons, prison reform, and restorative justice. My experiences with the W. C. Holman Faith-Based Restorative Justice Honor Dorm inspired me to synthesize my observations with other research and writings on the subject. For me, restorative justice and faith-based honor dorms provide hope to the many inmates serving time in our prisons—hope for change, a better life, and the possibility of contributing to their communities. The book is written for students and the public to learn about the possibilities for creating more positive prison communities. This case study is a beginning step.

I want to thank the Alabama Department of Corrections for giving me access to the W. C. Holman Correctional Facility. I am particularly grateful to Warden Culliver for allowing a female college professor to work for an extended period of time in a maximum-security prison. I would like to thank Chaplain Chris Summers for his valuable support, willingness to be interviewed, and openness to academic pursuits. He has provided me with numerous suggestions and feedback on the manuscript. I am extremely grateful to Professor Mary Rogers for her encouragement and her incredible editing talents. She is a true gem. Thanks to Professor John Smykla who introduced me to the honor dorm at Holman. Thanks to the many residents in the honor dorm who trusted me, made individual contributions to the manuscript, and offered invaluable suggestions about the book including the motivation to write it. Thanks to Lexington Books for publishing the book. And finally, love to my husband, Dan, who sometimes not so cheerfully accepted the amount of time necessary for me to spend with my writing.

Introduction

A Blueprint for This Book

Americans are frustrated with prisons. They recognize the need for these institutions, but at the same time, worry whether the money used to build and maintain them is well spent. While very few individuals have toured a prison, those who have recognize them as a tremendous waste of humanity. Men lift weights, watch television all day and night, or just "hang out." Many prisons are dirty, disgusting, and dangerous. The newer ones look cleaner and more orderly, but they are no better in terms of offering inmates opportunities to take responsibility for their crimes, support their loved ones, further their education, learn job skills, and develop positive relationships in healthy, safe, respectful communities.

The restorative justice philosophy offers an opportunity to manage our prisons differently and to achieve positive outcomes. This book provides insight into the philosophy of restorative justice as it is applied to a real world setting—an honor dorm in a maximum-security prison. The book is titled *Restorative Justice in a Prison Community: Or Everything I Didn't Learn in Kindergarten I Learned in Prison*. Most of the people who come to prison never learned the basic tools for living life productively and responsibly. They never thought much about their victims or how their actions affected their friends and family members. They never learned how to get along with others, pick up after themselves, or how to be of service to their fellow man.

Restorative justice applied in a faith-based honor dorm setting offers the possibility for meaningful offender change inside prison.

I researched this book over a three-year period. I was a participant observer, beginning my work while serving as a volunteer instructor in the faith-based restorative justice honor dorm at W. C. Holman Correctional Facility in Atmore, Alabama. While participant observation challenges one's objectivity, I support my observations with inmate writings, surveys, and data complied by chaplaincy programs and the Alabama Department of Corrections. I ground each chapter with literature reviews which inform the reader and place the case study findings in the context of other work in the field. The research is also based on numerous conversations with the chaplain who supervises the honor dorm, the prison warden, corrections officers, and the men in the honor dorm.

Chapter 1 addresses change looking at problems of imprisonment and questions about rehabilitation. It shows how the politics of crime and punishment offers challenges as well as opportunities for change. Chapter 2 lays the foundation for change, introducing the reader to the restorative justice philosophy and how it contrasts with the current way of doing things. To understand the lessons of Holman's honor dorm, it is important to grasp its guiding principles. Chapter 3 introduces the faith-based honor dorm at Holman Correctional Facility where inmates live, learn, and work in a setting that differs from most prison environments.

Major lessons about the honor dorm experience are described in chapters 4 through 8. Many of these lessons are told by the inmates themselves through letters and essays about how restorative justice works in their lives. In some cases data are provided to illustrate a particular lesson. Throughout the book I attempt to place the honor dorm themes in larger context to better understand issues surrounding conflict resolution in prison, offender education, offender accountability, the role of community service, and offender reintegration.

Chapter 4 outlines the lessons of restorative justice for conflict resolution in prison settings. The reader learns how peacemaking circles are organized and used at Holman as well the theory of how they work.

Chapter 5 examines offender accountability from a restorative perspective. It provides insights on the difficult path inmates follow when encouraged to take responsibility for their crimes and the impact they had on their victims' lives. Inmate letters documenting their journey are powerful reading.

Chapter 6 delves into the controversy surrounding prisoner education. It documents the gap between inmate and free world education and examines how it is addressed restoratively at Holman. The reading looks at a variety of reasons why prison education makes sense. The importance of delivering education in a framework tied to the honor dorm's goals and principles is emphasized. The chapter also provides details about the honor dorm's educational structure.

Chapter 7 further explores the restorative philosophy focusing on the concept of community building through service in prison environments. In addition, the chapter describes traditional problems with inmate governance, honor dorm governance at Holman, and conflicts between bureaucratic governance and the restorative approach.

Chapter 8 introduces the reader to the concept of reintegration, contrasting it with rehabilitation. This topic is very timely since an estimated 650,000 prisoners will be released each year in the United States. It considers how honor dorm programming can contribute to successful reintegration efforts.

Chapter 9 deals with how the honor dorms are perceived by corrections officials. Balancing the need for security with reform-oriented policies is an old story with a new twist. Are corrections officers usually opposed to rehabilitative efforts? Do they see honor dorm practices as a challenge to their authority? Interviews with corrections officers at Holman provide answers to these questions.

Chapter 10 speculates on the future of restorative programming in prison. Do the benefits of restorative corrections justify expansion to other prison settings? Will restorative ideals be compromised as its practices are implemented in corrections settings?

This book is not about the dark side of prisons—the drug abuse, gambling, homosexuality, rapes, fights, and murders. Inmates may refer to these kinds of activities in contrast to the more pro-social ones they are trying to develop. Instead, it gives concrete examples, many of them supplied in the words of the inmates themselves, of coming to terms with the things they never learned in "kindergarten." It sends a hopeful message with a prudent reminder that offender change is possible but not easy in a restorative prison environment.

1

Improvement Needed

The history of punishment is in some respects like the history of war; it seems to accompany the human condition almost universally, to enjoy periods of glorification, to be commonly regarded as justified in many instances, and yet to run counter to our ultimate vision of what human society should be.

—David R. Loy, *The Spiritual Roots of Restorative Justice*

Corrections in America is in crisis. It is also at a crossroads. Attitudinal adjustments and political changes are in the wind. Policy shifts occur when evidence shows that current practices don't work, so transformation in crime policy may be imminent.[1] Yet so much in corrections appears to be based on "common sense." To wit, the notion that punishment deters crime and severe punishment will deter crime even more is as widespread a belief as it is difficult to let go.[2]

Embedded even deeper is the idea that the only way to address the harm criminals caused by crime is to inflict pain and discomfort on them. While corporal punishments are no longer officially used in the Western world, pain continues to be inflicted psychologically through imprisonment.[3] The psychological and moral deterioration that occurs in prison is troubling. Prison systems no longer correct the offender but instead are warehouses not unlike the orphanages and mental asylums discredited in the twentieth century.[4]

Statistics on incarceration frequently get attention in the media. For example, in 1980 the number of individuals held in federal and state prisons was 139 per 100,000 population.[5] Twenty-five years later the rate has increased more than 350 percent to remain at an all-time high.[6] High recidivism rates are equally disturbing. In one fifteen-state study, two-thirds of those released from prison were rearrested within three years.[7] Between 1970 and 1995, violent crime decreased, but at a much lower rate than predicted by high incarceration rates.[8] Violent crime is increasing again in some American cities, while prison overcrowding remains a costly problem.[9]

THE POLITICS OF CRIME AND PUNISHMENT

In the 1970s through the 1990s, the best way to assure reelection was to throw a spoonful of "tough on crime" rhetoric into political campaign speeches. State and federal legislators went on record as protectors of the public interest by incrementally increasing sentences for crime. In some states, like California, habitual offenders were sentenced to life without parole for a third offense, even if it was a nonviolent felony. Harsh punishments are associated with the conservative agenda, but liberals do very little to address escalating injustices and costs associated with mass incarceration.[10] Indeed those of the liberal persuasion advocated the repeal of the indeterminate sentence which allowed inmates an opportunity to seek release prior to sentence completion. They believed that the indeterminate sentences gave corrections officials and parole boards too much discretion over the lives of prisoners.[11] An unintended consequence was legislators greatly increased the length of sentences, giving inmates little hope for reprieve.

While Americans are incarcerated at record rates for longer periods of time, programs to help offenders change have been cut back or eliminated. Pell grants for college study are no longer available to incarcerated persons. Today the vast majority of prisoner programs are provided on a sporadic basis by volunteers. Yet the high cost of imprisonment is not inmate programs, meals, or even health care. It is the salaries of large cadre of corrections officers to police and in many cases baby-sit prison populations. Corrections is a labor-intensive enterprise that cannot be automated. In Alabama, for example, corrections officers are the second largest group of state employees.[12] Prison administrators work diligently to economize on food, clothing, utilities, and programming, but guard work is a fixed cost.

In his 2004 State of the Union Address, President George W. Bush asked Americans to consider the 600,000 prisoners released annually who receive no mentoring, job training, job placement, and assistance with housing.[13] This signaled a different message about crime and punishment. In March 2007, the Washington State Senate passed a bill requiring the Department of Corrections to develop detailed reentry plans for prisoners, review state licensing provisions that bar formerly incarcerated persons from holding jobs when a ban is unrelated to their offenses, provide support for obtaining high school degrees, and allow inmates to take college educational courses paid for by the inmate or inmate's family.[14] The ACLU and other organizations work to restore the voting rights of formerly incarcerated felons. Florida is the most recent state to restore civil rights after men and women leave prison with approximately 950,000 disenfranchised ex-offenders.[15] A number of states are instituting sentencing reforms including alternatives to prison for drug offenders and supervision options to reduce the number of parolees and probationers returned to prison.[16]

Criminal offenders are no longer the scapegoats they once were in American elections. In the twenty-first century there is bipartisan support for prison reform. Writing in the New York Times, Chris Sullentrop observes that the political right has a "jailhouse conversion."[17] Faith-based initiatives in prison reform backed by the Bush administration may account partly for this change.

Chuck Colson, an advisor to the Nixon administration, laid the groundwork for prison reform from the right. Convicted for obstructing justice in the Watergate scandal in the 1970s, Colson served a prison term and after release founded Prison Fellowship to reform inmates and prisons. The organization collaborates with all denominations and has become the world's largest outreach organization to inmates, inmate families, crime victims, and former prisoners. Colson's prison reform movement has 40,000 volunteers who work with ministries in one hundred countries. After completing his prison term, Colson promised he would never forget those behind bars. He kept his word.[18]

Today, a number of conservative Republicans associated with the evangelical movement voice a parallel change of heart. Chris Cannon, a Utah conservative says,

I think society has a huge obligation to prisoners. I think that obligation transcends our current view, which is: Lock them up, hide them away, keep my daughter safe, keep my house safe, if he or she burgles, I want that person gone. Out of sight, out of mind. Away. I think that violates the fundamental concepts of who we are as Americans.[19]

Similarly Mark Early, a Christian conservative and former Virginia legislator, reports,

I'm 52 years old, and for the first 48 years of my life, I didn't think much about prisoners. And when I did, it went something like, I'm glad I'm not one, and I'm glad they are where they are. And I really pretty much had the view that prisoners were at the end of the line. That if you were in prison, you had no hope, you'd made a mess of your life and it was better for me that you were there because my family could be safe. I was elected to the Virginia Legislature and served 10 years from '87 to '97, in the Senate of Virginia, and quite frankly, spent most of my time in the Legislature working on how to put more people in jail and keeping them there longer. Virginia, like most states in the '80s, abolished parole, instituted three strikes and you're out, lowered the age at which juveniles could be tried as adults from 16 to 14. . . . [These policies helped increase the American prison population] tenfold in the last 30 years.[20]

These voices for change are welcome to prison reformers. Thus far though, policy improvements focus primarily on the aftermath of prison. What goes on inside of these facilities greatly matters and needs reform, too.

WHAT PRISON DOES TO PEOPLE

How do prisons shape the behavior of inmates? Ideally, prisoners use their time to reflect on their crimes, take responsibility for them, develop an agenda for growth and change, and participate in programs that will help them become law-abiding citizens when released.

The bulk of prison studies, however, suggest this is not the case. The process of assimilating into prison requires that the inmate learn a new set of norms and behaviors, many of which conflict with society's norms.[21] Gambling, homosexual behavior, frequent and open masturbation, fighting, rape, and participation in the underground economy are examples. Alcohol and drugs are commonly available to any inmate who can afford them. Many prisoners respond to oppressive conformity with body art (tattoos). When released from prison their inmate lifestyle becomes a liability. One formerly incarcerated person whose arms are covered with tattoos told me at a micro enterprise conference, "When I go out to bid a lawn maintenance job, I remember to wear a long-sleeved shirt, even in the sweltering heat. If I don't, I scare them."

The inmate's needs for food, shelter, and medical care are provided by the state, and prisoners come to take this state of affairs for granted.[22] Motivation and self sufficiency typically deteriorate. Manipulation and intimidation are strategies used to meet needs. Isolation from "free world" people reinforces the creation of an inmate subculture built around such strategies as well as countercultural values and behaviors. Prisoners understand they are pariahs to the public. To cope with their status, they further withdraw. The result is that prisoners become psychologically and socially crippled, and their ability to reintegrate into society diminishes dramatically.[23] People in prison appear to be defiant, but their insolence hides the recognition that most members of society fear and loathe them. Stepping into the "free world," they are "fish out of water." They feel odd and appear strange to others. Distrust, fear, alienation, and social awkwardness make the development of "normal" relationships difficult. Expectations about the benefits of freedom are unrealistic given the barriers that formerly incarcerated persons face. Technology and the information age leave inmates further isolated and ill prepared for release. A study in the *New England Journal of Medicine* reports that during the first two weeks out of prison, formerly incarcerated persons risk death thirteen times higher than the general public.[24] Many deaths are associated with drug overdose related to transitional stress and reduced drug tolerance levels.

CAN PRISON HELP?

In the 1960s and 1970s reformers argued for community corrections programs to counter the negative effects of prison.[25] Community corrections theory says that effective treatment cannot be delivered in prison environments. The community corrections movement was subsequently abandoned when high crime rates, including serious crimes committed by felony probationers, led to sentencing reforms.[26] The rehabilitative ideal, now viewed as unworkable, was replaced with punitive philosophies based on just desserts, deterrence, and incapacitation.[27] In many states parole was abandoned, longer sentences were instituted, and judicial discretion in sentencing was severely limited.

Whether offender change can occur in prison environments is open to debate. A number of prisoners have told me that they hate to admit it, but prison saved their lives. They surely would have died on the streets but for prison intervention. This observation is confirmed by a Bureau of Justice Statistics study showing that inmates, particularly blacks, live longer than their counterparts outside of prison.[28]

A former warden at W. C. Holman Correctional facility shared with a group of inmates that he was going to keep them until they were old men. While this is offensive to the prisoners, data on aging out of crime supports the warden's approach. The crime-prone years are fifteen through twenty-four, and after that criminal behavior begins to decrease.[29] But mass incarceration is an expensive proposition. Furthermore, risk assessment based on variables such as age is not a science nor does it appeal to parole boards whose members must balance the readiness of a particular inmate to leave with the need to protect society. Men and women who make release decisions might be more confident if prison environments are less criminogenic and more conducive to inmate change.

Budget crises at the state level, a general downward trend in crime rates, and displacement of crime on the national agenda with the Iraq war, health care, and global warming contribute to a new look at incarceration. The will to send large numbers of offenders to prison is waning. Still, prisons will be with us for a long time. Some offenders tell me that they think they deserved some time in prison. However, "some time" may mean ten to twenty years, not life without parole. Ironically, sentencing reform focuses on nonviolent and youthful offenders while older offenders who committed violent crimes sometimes show the greatest capacity for change. Whether they will have the opportunity to change and the life skills to function in society depends not only on their choices, but also on the ability of prisons to function as true correctional settings.

PRISON MANAGEMENT

The warden at W. C. Holman Correctional facility shared that his brother is afraid to visit the prison and never has. This conversation took place during a class fieldtrip. My students conducted interviews with honor dorm inmates, and Warden Culliver asked if they were afraid to participate. The culture of the honor dorm is radically different from that of the general population with respect to violence and disrespectful behavior. I told him after volunteering with the honor dorm, I felt comfortable bringing my students with me. I had communicated this to the class, and they understood that an alternative assignment was available. No one chose the alternative.

Clearly Warden Culliver's brother has legitimate concerns. Between 1995 and 2004, the percentage of state inmates incarcerated for violent crimes increased from 47 percent to 52 percent.[30] Mental health conditions can contribute to instability in prison environments. In a 2005 survey of state inmates, 55 percent of the males and 75 percent of the females had mental health problems.[31] Prison gang affiliation increases the threat of violence and other prison misconduct.[32] The availability of drugs and alcohol is also a catalyst for violence.[33] A survey on sexual violence in prisons and jails shows that allegations of these events increased from 2.46 per 1,000 inmates in 2004 to 2.91 in 2006.[34] President Bush signed the Rape Elimination Act in 2003 to enhance reporting and reduce these incidents.

Other than data collection mandated by law on prison sexual assault, recent data on interpersonal victimization are unavailable. Types of inmate victimization include robbery, sexual assault, nonsexual assault, threats, extortion, theft, and vandalism. While adherence to informal rules once held prisoners together and reduced prison violence, today's prisons are more socially and ethnically heterogeneous. In addition, a culture of individualism has eroded solidarity contributing to a less stable environment.[35]

Poor prison management has thus emerged as one of the major contributors to interpersonal violence and other inmate misconduct.[36] It is more important than prison size and overcrowding.[37] But prisons are less violent if rules are implemented consistently and fairly. Hierarchy and a chain of command can bring accountability, order, and safety to penal institutions.[38] However, the tendency to "overcontrol" needs to be balanced with opportunities for inmate responsibility, if successful adjustment to society is a goal.[39] There is also evidence that providing "opportunity enhancements" reduces rule infractions.[40] These include chances for education and work, skill development, and relationships with family. Even DiIulio, whose research champions the "bureaucratic control" model, argues that "carrots" and well as "sticks" are central to good prison administration.[41]

While prisons provide special management challenges, like most institutions, legitimacy plays a major role in compliance.[42] If a system of taxation is viewed as corrupt and unfair, there is more tax evasion. Likewise, if prison management is lax and unprincipled, rule violations will escalate.[43] In school environments legitimacy, compliance, and learning are enhanced when opportunities for accountability and responsibility are available.[44] Along these lines, some prisons have experimented with community responsibility approaches to grievances and conflicts. Involving inmates and corrections officers in conflict resolution training holds some promise for increasing responsibility and order.[45]

Prisoners cannot reform if they don't know what to expect while living under constant threats to their security. Management perceived as self-serving, arbitrary, and unprofessional further undermines the will to do better. Thus prison administration is a basic ingredient in prisoner change. Lifers at Holman Correctional Facility remember previous administrations when rule violations were tolerated as long as inmates remained more or less peaceful. They prefer the current "by the book" administration because it provides for a living space that is relatively more respectful and decent.

INMATE PROGRAMMING

The ability of inmates to adjust to confinement has implications for inmate behavior within the institution as well as the success of treatment programs. In a study of inmates in Ohio prisons, Wooldredge found that availability and participation in programs, frequent visitation, and safety (experiences with victimization) were related to positive mental attitudes of inmates.[46] Without opportunities for self improvement and some level of social stimulation, inmates become irritable and angry with each other. In spite of these findings, retrenchment of inmate programming and opportunities for social interaction has been the rule rather than the exception.

In early 1970s, sociologist Robert Martinson and his colleagues completed a meta analysis of research on rehabilitation programs.[47] Most academic research does not receive much attention from the public, but Martinson reported his findings in highly readable form in two influential publications opinion leaders read—*The Public Interest* and *The New Republic*. Martinson's study did not find much to recommend the programs he examined, and the catchy phrase "Nothing Works," a twist on "What Works?" part of the title of *The Public Interest* article, spread quickly. Martinson's conclusions inspired politicians to give their constituents, fearful and angry about crime, punishment-oriented policies. In 1989 in *Mistretta v. United States* the U.S. Supreme Court upheld federal sentencing guidelines to remove rehabilitation from sentencing considerations.[48] In a subsequent law review article, Martinson cautioned against giving up on rehabilitation.[49] However, his voice was muffled by the momentum and the strength of the anticrime movement.

Beginning in the late 1980s, a number of researchers systematically studied rehabilitation research to give a more balanced account. This research does not directly address the issue of whether rehabilitation works in prison settings, but the findings shed light on what doesn't work *and* what does work in general. Examples of what doesn't work include the boot camp approach, scared straight programs, psychoanalytic interventions, and programs targeting low self-esteem.[50]

Programs that reduce recidivism target "criminogenic needs."[51] These are factors, based on theory and empirical research, that predict criminal behavior. For example, cognitive behavioral therapies that focus on criminal thinking show promise. However, approaches that do not take into account the *individual* criminogenic needs of the offender—a one-size-fits-all approach—generally fail.[52] Prison bureaucracies are centrally managed and controlled, making them less amenable to individualized treatment, even when resources are available.

Another finding collides with prison practice. Andrews notes that high-risk offenders are responsive to treatment.[53] However, criminal justice sentencing policy labels high-risk offenders as career criminals who deserve long sentences and in many cases life without parole. In turn, prison classification systems move high-risk offenders to maximum-security facilities where they are less likely to receive treatment. Finally, these post-Martinson studies show the conclusion that "nothing works" is premature.

When it comes to prison programming, the public is concerned with *less eligibility*, the notion that inmates should not be provided with opportunities unavailable to law-abiding citizens. But there is also a fear that prisoners will manipulate the system. They will use whatever programming necessary to please parole boards, but then continue with their criminal ways after release. Researchers not only show what is likely to work, but also provide evidence that factors associated with good behavior in prison promote lower recidivism rates.[54]

THE MORAL PRISON

In addition to prison management and sound programming, the philosophy of the moral prison emerged in the late twentieth and early twenty-first centuries. Its predecessor is the nineteenth-century Quaker penitence system, which broke down under the weight of social and economic change. The Quaker experiment reminds us that good intentions can have unintended negative consequences. However, the "good" or moral prison continues to have appeal.

An essay on "The Virtuous Prison" contests the widely held belief that corrections facilities are inherently inhumane.[55] Most criminologists believe that nothing good comes of prisons, and reform will only legitimize an enterprise better discarded. The result is a void in "systematic thinking about what prison should be like."[56] While the virtuous prison is not value free, it can meet standards of accountability by specifying what it is, clearly defining processes for obtaining virtue, and providing the transparency needed for both quantitative and qualitative evaluation.

Cullen and his colleagues suggest that "the goal of the prison experience should be to foster 'virtue' in inmates, which is usually defined as 'moral goodness' or 'moral excellence.'"[57] What this means is that offenders should be held to standards of ethical behavior both in and out of prison, and that these standards are known and agreed upon by most rational people. It is unusual to think of prisons as moral communities. Well-intentioned people think it's impossible. Others believe that those who commit crimes deserve to live in an immoral jungle.

Correctional practice based on "what works" can be integrated with the moral prison. These practices include anti-criminal modeling, effective reinforcement and disapproval, and building caring and respectful relationships.[58] Rather than using the term "rehabilitation," however, the virtuous prison reformer is more comfortable with the term "moral regeneration."[59] The moral prison is favored by progressives who want to make prisons more humane. But social scientists, such as Francis Cullen, also advance this concept. Cullen and his colleagues propose seven general considerations for a virtuous prison. These include

1. Elimination of inmate idleness
2. Providing inmate activities that have a restorative purpose

3. Providing contact with virtuous people such as volunteers from the community
4. Availability of rehabilitative programs based on sound research
5. Providing a humane living environment
6. Participation by correctional officers
7. Screening for inmates who are not suitable for this programming[60]

Many prisons throughout the world include *some* of these components. Two approaches, the faith-based prison and the restorative justice prison are "technologies" to incorporate these components into a systematic whole.

THE FAITH-BASED PRISON AND RESTORATIVE PROGRAMMING

The faith-based prison is founded on religious principles. Most initiatives are Christian, but care must be taken to avoid the establishment of religion in the public domain.[61] The faith-based approach rests on the idea that fundamental change begins with a change in character that reconciles a person with God's will. "This sacred relationship then allows the offender to reconcile human relationships and to embark on genuine, long-term behavioral change."[62]

Many faith-based prisons are linked with chaplaincy programming. Ties with the virtuous prison outlined by Cullen and his colleagues include educational programming and community service projects to target inmate idleness, volunteer participation and mentoring to model virtuous behavior, and classes to restore and strengthen family relationships. Picnics, music, religious services, talks, and other amenities contributed by faith-based groups play a part in creating a more humane and positive environment.

The skeptical criminologist views these activities as a method of social control. A cynical public attaches the label of jailhouse religion—a crutch quickly abandoned after release. These opinions can be verified or rejected through closer observation and evaluation. The longest operating faith-based prison was established at Humaita Prison in Brazil in 1973 by the Association for the Protection and Assistance to the Convicted (APAC). A 1989 evaluation showed a 16 percent recidivism rate compared with the range of 60 to 75 percent in other prisons in the country.[63] Prisoners at Humaita are high-risk offenders and many are serving sentences for violent crimes. Still, those who are capable govern themselves and many are eligible for work release and family visits in a relaxed community setting where meals are even served. After visiting

Humaita, former Texas governor George Bush authorized a similar program at a minimum-security prison in Sugarland, Texas.

Restorative justice supports the moral prison. It focuses on the harm done by crime and places moral responsibility on the offender to make amends. It directs offenders not to hurt others, including their fellows in the institution.[64]

Dr. Andrew Coyle with the International Centre for Prison Studies in London notes that the principles of restorative justice are deeply embedded in all major religions. The title of his book, *The Prisons We Deserve*, suggests that prisons can reach a higher ideal.[65] Dr. Coyle points out that the prison is a relatively new institution with us for less than three hundred years. He asks, "To what extent is the traditional model of imprisonment still relevant at the beginning of the twenty-first century?"[66]

Upon entering prison, inmates are told, often by the chaplain, to use their time in prison positively. However, prisons are places of punishment, not spaces for reform. Coyle argues that the prison we deserve should have four elements:

1. Creating more awareness among convicted prisoners of the impact of crime on victims and programs of direct mediation between victims and offenders
2. Creating a new direction for activities within prisons so that prisoners spend some of their time working for the benefit of others.
3. Remodeling the way disputes are settled within the prison and incorporating restorative principles into grievance and disciplinary procedures.
4. Building a new relationship with the community outside the prison to emphasize the need for prisoners to be reconciled with the wider society and received back into it.[67]

According to Coyle, these elements are best achieved through restorative programming, which is explored in more depth in the next chapter.

IS THIS THE BEST WE CAN DO?

Meanwhile, the fundamental question growing out of this chapter is, "Is this the best we can do?" There is ample evidence that prison is destructive to those who enter. Some argue that the best we can do is try to prevent prisons from making people worse off. The ambition of this book is higher than that. Before we continue our examination of a restorative faith-based honor dorm, we will hear from prisoners about how they experience their incarceration.

The first is an anonymous voice from Rahway State Penitentiary in New Jersey. The inmate experiences the consequences of a corrections philosophy based on punishment and exile.

The Real Prison

The Real Prison is lonliness [sic] that sinks its teeth into the soul of men, emptiness that leaves a sick feeling inside. It is anxiety that pushes and swells, uncertainty that smothers and stifles. It is frustration, filthiness, despair and indifference.

The Real Prison suppresses, deadens and crushes; its walls seem to close in on the inmate. It makes life without purpose. It is all this and more. It is being incarcerated without notoriety; without the traditional storybook's plot and intrigue. The Real Prison is unrecorded and overlooked by the newspapers. It is seldom depicted in books. Likewise the Real Prison is never portrayed on screen.

The Real Prison is where men struggle fervently to find themselves; the place of routine where at times merely living is a task. It is a place rare of hope. The Real Prison is the mute drama of men who have paid debts. For 5, 10, 15 or even 50 years, but know their debts will never be paid in full. So much of the Real Prison is sordidness, indifference, and disappointment. Crowded in the confines of correctional institutions are men who have seen to [sic] many third rate motel rooms in too many cities, or too many cheap smoke-filled gin mills, or too many skidrows, too many days without beauty and too much darkness without light. The Real Prison is more than stone walls, steel bars, fences, and gun-towers. Almost shouted is its contempt for its fumbling and groping humanity. It listens unhearing, unheeding to the cries of the damned.

The Real Prison is cold, harsh, hot and merciless. It is the place of many reasons, causes, excuses, and failures. The place of thousands of untold stories. The Real Prison is the empty feeling that gnaws at a man who waits with anxious anticipation of the letters that never comes [sic], the visits that never happen. It is the place of despair for the youth whose future has been taken away by a demanding and relentless society.

The Real Prison is a place filled with the regrets of men who acted in moments of anger, passion, greed, and downright stupidity. Once the moments were spent they began paying for their crimes, and have paid for them ever since in a thousand different ways. The narrowness of a cell that crushes, that bears down heavily, speaks of the Real Prison. The strains of familiar songs on the radio that stab and torture the memory are a part of the Real Prison. The emptiness of the days and the lonliness [sic] of the nights are repeated endlessly. It is the prison only those who live within its walls will ever know![68]

The next excerpt is written by Jack Abbott, author of *In the Belly of the Beast*. Abbott, a state-raised convict, first entered reform school at age sixteen and spent most of his life in prison. Paroled in 1981, within a short period of time he killed a waiter in New York. Abbot never learned to take responsibility for his crimes and blamed the "system" for them. He committed suicide in 2001. While Abbott was a rebellious and violent inmate, his writing suggests a lifetime in institutions caused significant deterioration.

That is how prison is tearing me up inside. It hurts every day. Every day takes me further from my life. And I am not even conscious of how my dissolution is coming about. Therefore, I cannot stop it.

I don't even talk of these feelings. I never spent much time thinking of them. In fact, I'm only thinking of them now as I write this. I find it painful and angering to look in the mirror. When I walk past a glass window in the corridor and happen to see my reflection, I get angry on impulse. I feel shame and hatred at such times. When I'm forced by circumstances to be in a crowd of prisoners, it's all I can do to refrain from attack. I feel such hostility, such hatred, I can't help this anger. All these years I have felt it. Paranoid. I can control it. I never seek a confrontation. I have to intentionally gauge my voice in conversation to cover up the anger I feel, the chaos and pain just beneath the surface of what we commonly recognize as reality. Paranoia is an illness I contracted in institutions. In is not the reason for my sentences to reform school and to prison. It is the effect, not the cause.[69]

A third writer discusses "the game," a sport that clearly runs counter to the notion of the moral prison. Based on his experience in a Pennsylvania prison, James Paluch Jr. observes

There are many types of games played inside our prisons. Most games require a hustle for material gain or wealth, while others involve spite, violence, or sexual gratification. Material gains involve inquiring [sic] prison money (cigarettes, food, clothing, etc.) among other things. Acts of spite may include snitching on another prisoner, setting another prisoner up for a misconduct report, or spreading rumors about another inmate to cause that inmate trouble. Violence may include robbery, assault, or fighting. As to sexual gratification, prisoners employ psychological schemes to satisfy their desires through acts of coercion, intimidation, blackmail, or promises to "take care of" their intended target.

. . . Unlike other games, the prison game has no rules or regulations and is premised on the concept of doing whatever one has to do to get what one wants, at any cost. Only one unwritten rule exists: No one can be trusted. This ultimately causes conflict among prisoners.[70]

Are we obligated to provide prisoners with an alternative to the game? Advocates of the moral prison would say, "yes." What follows is a description of a philosophy that gives prisoners the opportunity to be virtuous and corrections institutions the opportunity to do better.

NOTES

1. Howard Zehr, *Changing Lenses: A New Focus for Crime and Justice* (Scottsdale, Penn.: Herald Press, 2005), 91.

2. Anthony N. Doob and Cheryl Marie Webster, "Sentence Severity and Crime: Accepting the Null Hypothesis," *Crime and Justice* 30 (2003): 143–96.

3. Gresham M. Sykes, *The Society of Captives: A Study of a Maximum Security Prison* (Princeton, N.J.: Princeton University Press, 1958).

4. John Irwin, *The Warehouse Prison: The Disposal of the New Dangerous Class* (Los Angeles: Roxbury Publishing, 2005), 57–84.

5. *Correctional Populations in the United States, 1997* (Washington, D.C.: Bureau of Justice Statistics, 2000), available at www.ojp.usdoj.gov/bjs/abstract/cpus97.htm (accessed 3 May 2008).

6. William J. Sabol, Heather Couture, and Paige M. Harrison, *Prisoners in 2006* (Washington, D.C.: Bureau of Justice Statistics, 2007), available at www.ojp.usdoj.gov/bjs/abstract/p06.htm (accessed 3 May 2008).

7. Patrick A. Langan and David J. Levin, *Recidivism of Prisoners Released in 1994* (Washington, D.C.: Bureau of Justice Statistics, 2002), available at www.ojp.usdoj.gov/bjs/abstract/rpr94.htm (accessed 3 May 2008).

8. Marc Mauer, *Race to Incarcerate* (New York: Free Press, 1999), 83.

9. Marc Mauer, "What Wave?" *The American Prospect 2007*, available at www.prospect.org/cs/articles?articleId=12601 (accessed 3 May 2008).

10. Chris Sullentrop, "The Right Has a Jailhouse Conversion," *New York Times*, available at www.nytimes.com/2006/12/24/magazine/24GOP.t.html (accessed 24 December 2006).

11. Francis T. Cullen, Jody L. Sundt, and John F. Wozniak, "The Virtuous Prison: Toward a Restorative Rehabilitation," in *Contemporary Issues in Crime and Criminal Justice: Essays in Honor of Gilbert Geis*, ed. Henry N. Ponetell and David Shichor (Saddle River, N.J.: Prentice Hall 2001), 265–86.

12. Warden's Commentary, "The Key" (Atmore, Ala: W. C. Holman Correctional Facility, 30 March 2007), unpublished.

13. George W. Bush, "Transcript of State of the Union, January 20, 2004," CNN.Com, available at www.cnn.com/2004/ALLPOLITICS/01/20/sotu.transcript.7/index.html (accessed 15 January 2007).

14. Editorial, "A Smoother Re-entry," *New York Times*, available at www.nytimes.com/2007/03/27/opinion/27tue4.html?_r=1&ex=1175659200&en=a83a3e7f547c8cef&ei=5070&emc=eta1&oref=slogin (accessed 27 March 2007).

15. Abby Goodnough, "In a Break with the Past, Florida Will Let Felons Vote," *New York Times*, 16 April 2007, available at www.nytimes.com/2007/04/06/us/06florida.html?ex=1176523200&en=a94a840f40d89ca0&ei=5070&emc=eta1 (accessed 27 March 2007).

16. Ryan S. King, "Changing Direction: State Sentencing Reforms 2004–2006," *The Sentencing Project Releases: News Report*, available at sentencingprojectorg/Admin/Documents/publications/sentencingreformforweb.pdf (accessed 14 March 2007).

17. Sullentrop, "The Right Has a Jailhouse Conversion."

18. "Inside Prison Fellowship," available at www.pfm.org/Bio.asp?ID=43 (accessed 13 May 2007).

19. Sullentrop, "The Right Has a Jailhouse Conversion."

20. Sullentrop, "The Right Has a Jailhouse Conversion."

21. Donald Clemmer, *The Prison Community* (Boston: Holt, Rinehart, Winston, 1940).

22. Clemmer, *The Prison Community.*

23. John Irwin and James Austin, *It's About Time: America's Imprisonment Binge,* 2nd ed. (Belmont, Calif.: Wadsworth, 1997), 78–79.

24. Ingrid A. Binswanger, Mark F. Stern, Richard A. Dayo, Patrick J. Heagerty, Allen Cheadle, Joann G. Elmore, and Thomas D. Koepsell, "Release from Prison—a High Risk of Death for Former Inmates," *New England Journal of Medicine* 356, no. 2 (January 2007): 157–65.

25. Belinda R. McCarthy, Bernard J. McCarthy Jr., and Matthew C. Leone, *Community-Based Corrections,* 4th ed. (Belmont, Calif.: Wadsworth, 2001).

26. Joan Petersilia, Susan Turner, James Kahan, and Joyce Peterson, *Granting Felons Probation: Public Risks and Alternatives* (R-3186-NIJ The Rand Corporation, 1985).

27. Robert Martinson, "What Works? Questions and Answers about Prison Reform," *Public Interest* 35, no. 4 (Spring 1974): 22–54.

28. Christopher J. Mumola, "Medical Causes of Death in State Prison, 2001–2004," Bureau of Justice Statistics 2007, available at www.ojp.usdoj.gov/bjs/pub/ascii/mcdsp04.txt (accessed 4 May 2008).

29. Alfred Blumstein, Jacqueline Cohen, and David Farrington, "Criminal Career Research: Its Value for Criminology" *Criminology* 26, no.1 (February 1988): 1–35.

30. "Prison Statistics, Summary Findings," Bureau of Justice Statistics 2008, available at www.ojp.usdoj.gov/bjs/prisons.htm#publications (accessed 4 May 2008).

31. Doris J. James and Lauren E. Glaze, "Mental Health Problems of Prison and Jail Inmates," Bureau of Justice Statistics Special Report 2006, available at www.ojp.usdoj.gov/bjs/abstract/mhppji.pdf (accessed 4 May 2008).

32. Mark T. Berg and Matt DeLisi, "The Correctional Melting Pot: Race, Ethnicity, Citizenship, and Prison Violence," *Journal of Criminal Justice* 34, no. 6 (November–December 2006): 631–42.

33. James A. Inciardi, Dorothy Lockwood, and Judith A. Quinlan, "Drug Use in Prison: Patterns, Processes, and Implications for Treatment," *Journal of Drug Issues* 23, no. 1 (Winter 2003): 119–29.

34. Allen J. Beck, Paige M. Harrison, and Devon B. Adams, "Correctional Violence Reported by Correctional Authorities, 2006," Bureau of Justice Statistics Special Report 2007, available at www.ojp.usdoj.gov/bjs/abstract/svrca06.htm (accessed 4 May 2008).

35. Irwin, *The Warehouse Prison*, 45–46.

36. Ross Homel and Carleen Thompson, "Causes and Preventions of Violence in Prison," in *Corrections Criminology*, ed. Sean O'Toole and Simon Eylands (Sydney: Hawkins Press, 2005), 101–8.

37. John J. DiIulio Jr., *Governing Prisons: A Comparative Study of Correctional Management* (New York: Free Press, 1987).

38. Charles H. Logan and Gerald G. Gaes, "Meta Analysis and the Rehabilitation of Punishment," *Justice Quarterly* 10, no. 2 (June 1993): 245–63.

39. Michael D. Reisig, "Rates of Disorder in Higher-Custody State Prisons: A Comparative Analysis of Managerial Practices," *Crime and Delinquency* 44, no. 2 (April 1998): 229–44.

40. Homel and Thompson, "Causes and Prevention of Violence," 101–8.

41. DiIulio, *Governing Prisons*.

42. Anthony Bottoms, "Compliance and Community Penalties," in *Community Penalties: Change and Challenges*, ed. Anthony Bottoms, Lorraine Gelsthorpe, and Sue Rex (Devon, U.K.: Willan Publishing, 2001), 87–116.

43. DiIulio, *Governing Prisons*.

44. Cheryl Swanson and Michelle Owen, "Building Bridges: Integrating Restorative Justice with the School Resource Officer Model," *International Journal of Restorative Justice* 3, no. 2 (September 2007): 68–92

45. Homel and Thompson, "Causes and Prevention of Violence," 101–8.

46. John D. Wooldredge, "Inmate Experiences and Psychological Well-Being," *Criminal Justice and Behavior* 26, no. 2 (June 1999), 235–50.

47. Douglas Lipton, Robert Martinson, and Judith Wilkes, *The Effects of Correctional Treatment: A Survey of Treatment Valuation Studies* (New York: Praeger, 1975).

48. Jerome G. Miller, "The Debate on Rehabilitating Criminals: Is It True that Nothing Works?" available at www.prisonpolicy.org/scans/rehab.html (accessed 4 May 2008).

49. Robert Martinson, "New Findings, New Views: A Note of Caution Regarding Sentencing Reforms," *Hofstra Law Review* 7, no. 2 (Winter 1979): 243–58.

50. Edward J. Latessa, Francis T. Cullen, and Paul Gendreau, "Beyond Correctional Quackery: Professionalism and the Possibility of Effective Treatment," in *Correctional Contexts: Contemporary and Classical Readings*, 3rd ed., ed. Edward J. Latessa and Alexander M. Holsinger (Los Angeles: Roxbury Publishing, 2006), 337–47.

51. Don A. Andrews, "The Principles of Effective Correctional Programs," in *Correctional Contexts: Contemporary and Classical Readings*, 3rd ed., ed. Edward J. Latessa and Alexander M. Holsinger (Los Angeles: Roxbury Publishing, 2006), 253.

52. Andrews, "The Principles of Effective Correctional Programs," 253–54.

53. Andrews, "The Principles of Effective Correctional Programs," 252–53.

54. Paul Gendreau, Claire E. Goggin, and Moira A. Law, "Predicting Prison Misconducts," *Criminal Justice and Behavior* 4, no. 4 (December 1997): 414–41.

55. Cullen, Wozniak, and Sundt, "Virtous Prison," 266.

56. Cullen, Wozniak, and Sundt, "Virtuous Prison," 267.

57. Cullen, Wozniak, and Sundt, "Virtuous Prison," 268.

58. Latessa, Cullen, and Gendreau, "Beyond Correctional Quackery," 340–42.

59. Cullen, Wozniak, and Sundt, "Virtuous Prison," 268.

60. Cullen, Wozniak, and Sundt, "Virtuous Prison," 279–80.

61. Neela Banerjee, "Court Bars State Effort Using Faith in Prisons," *New York Times*, 4 December 2007, available at www.nytimes.com/2007/12/04/us/04evangelical.html?ex=1197435600&en=f5bb0d0a68340127&ei=5070&emc=eta1 (accessed 4 December 2007).

62. Cullen, Wozniak, and Sundt, "Virtuous Prison," 281–82.

63. Center for Justice and Reconciliation, "Growing Interest in Innovative Prison Management System," *Prison Fellowship International News* 2006, available at www.pficjr.org/newsitems/apac1/ (accessed 17 April 2007).

64. Cullen, Wozniak, and Sundt, "Virtuous Prison," 277.

65. Andrew Coyle, *The Prisons We Deserve* (London: Harper Collins, 1994).

66. Andrew Coyle, "Restorative Justice in the Prison Society" (paper presented at the International Prison Chaplains' Association Conference, Drubergen, Holland, May 2001), 3.

67. Coyle, *The Prisons We Deserve*, 8.

68. Anonymous inmate, Rahway State Penitentiary, undated and unpublished letter.

69. Jack Henry Abbott, *In the Belly of the Beast* (New York: Random House, 1981), 4–5.

70. Jack Paluch Jr., *Life without Parole: Living in Prison Today* (Los Angeles: Roxbury Publishing, 2004), 93–94.

2

Restorative Justice
in Prison Communities

Life does not exist for concepts, but the concepts exist for life. It is not logic that should postulate what happens, but life, contact, the sense of right, whether it is logically deducible or impossible.

—Rudolph von Jharing, *The Mirror of Justice*

Living the values of restorative justice is an individual choice that has the potential to create a restorative society. It is a challenging road to take, as it expects much of individuals, interpersonal relationships, and society as a whole. But men and women in prison can help to lead the way.

—Barb Toews, *The Little Book of Restorative Justice for People in Prison: Rebuilding the Web of Relationships*

The spirit of the first quotation cuts through legal abstractions to rest on a more human foundation. Just as legal sociology reacted to legal positivism early in the last century, repairing relationships may be an alternative to assigning blame and punishment in the current one.

Restorative justice is not a new philosophy, but a revival or rebirthing of past traditions. These include the practices of small communities before modern justice systems were introduced, the practices of indigenous peoples, and spiritual traditions including but not limited to Islam, Christianity, and Buddhism.[1] Some people argue that restorative justice can stand on its own and that tying restorative to premodern justice distorts or romanticizes the past.[2]

However, the important question is, can these premodern frameworks contribute to greater justice, fairness, and satisfaction with our criminal justice system today?

What characterizes these premodern frameworks? First, they were highly decentralized and community based. Second, they focused on the harm caused to people and relationships. Third, they were informal and discretionary. Fourth, they focused on making things right or restoring the imbalance caused by the offense to the previous "good" order. Fifth, individuals who were a party to the conflict were encouraged to take responsibility for their actions. And finally, those who perpetrated the offense and those directly affected by it were asked to participate directly in the process of making things right.[3]

The conditions that coexisted with compensatory justice were tightly knit, interdependent communities and economies; an absence of a formal system of laws; and no formal criminal justice system (police, courts, prisons). If a farmer was victimized by someone in the village, the impact of the crime was clearly perceived by its members. The farmer's contribution to the community was necessary to its successful functioning, and his loss was the community's loss. Justice was dispensed in a way that was highly responsive to the needs of those affected by the crime and by the circumstances surrounding the act itself. Furthermore, it was important for offender and victim to repair their relationship so that village life could proceed as before. That crime was seen in more personal and experiential terms makes sense within the context of the times.

During the eleventh century a major paradigm shift occurred in the way crime was dealt with among English-speaking populations. The shift was from crime seen as a conflict between people in the context of community to the framework we know today. This was brought about in England when Henry I issued a royal degree proclaiming that certain offenses such as murder, robbery, and theft were crimes against the king's peace.[4] While the modern criminal justice system developed over many centuries, the action of Henry I was a turning point because crime was no longer seen primarily as a harm to people and relationships but instead took on the more remote, abstract quality of being a violation against the state.

A restorative approach to crime is also evidenced in the traditional practices of indigenous peoples in North America, New Zealand, Australia, Africa, and parts of the Middle East.[5] These practices emphasize compensation to the victim and restoration of community peace rather than law-breaking and punishment. While the offender must take accountability for the wrongs he committed, he is encouraged to make amends to the victim, and the community is encouraged to take the offender back into the community once the offender's obligations are met. Today, some native groups are reviving these traditions, particularly for their use with juvenile offenders.

Finally, restorative justice is linked to spiritual traditions. Judeo-Christian values, for example, embrace care of the outcast, providing for those in need, and the intrinsic worth of all human beings. These values are evident in restorative initiatives.[6] Let's take a closer look at how the principles of restorative justice are found in a variety of beliefs.

SPIRITUAL ROOTS

The link between restorative justice and spiritual traditions makes it an attractive framework for prison work, since prisons allow greater accommodation for religious programming. When an inmate is not allowed to practice his or her religion, the burden of proof is on the state to show that the institution's need to maintain security outweighs the inmate's "preferred right" to freedom of religion. Case law shows that when prisoners claim their religious rights, they are on more solid ground than when they challenge institutional practices that allegedly violate their right to free speech and protections against illegal search and seizure.

What place should religion have in the criminal justice system? Case law gives the basis for religious freedom for prisoners but cautions against practices that could be interpreted as the establishment of a single religion by the state. Because restorative justice is not connected to a particular faith, its importation to the prison environment does not violate First Amendment freedoms.

Christianity is the most frequently practiced religion in American correctional settings. The biblical notions of healing, reconciliation, and forgiveness have motivated individual Christians and churches to start restorative justice programs. For example, Prison Fellowship International has a strong restorative component. Some Christian organizations challenge the state's claim to divine authority to justify its approach to crime and punishment. For example Allard and Northey boldly assert that, "Rightly understood, the words 'punishment' and 'retribution' have no place in Christian vocabulary."[7] Legal historian Herman Bianchi suggests that punitive Roman law was incorporated into Christian culture after the fall of Rome so that the Christian teachings of ideal justice had little impact on the Western legal system.[8]

Howard Zehr, a catalyst of the restorative movement in the United States, maintains that restorative justice is not primarily about forgiveness and warns against further harming crime victims by admonishing them to forgive in order to be right with their faith traditions.[9] However, practice suggests that when an offender takes responsibility for his crime and offers a sincere apology to the victim, the victim is more likely to experience freedom from the obsessive resentment that often accompanies severe victimization.[10] This freedom becomes the goal of *therapeutic forgiveness.*[11] Furthermore, the Christian principles of redemption and personal transformation are highly compatible with restorative notions of healing and making things right for both victim and offender.[12]

In the United States, Islam is the nation's largest minority religion with an estimated 6 million members. In jails and prisons, approximately 10 to 12 percent of the African American population is Muslim. The biggest failure of restorative justice in Islam is the treatment of women as equal participants in the criminal justice system. However, Islam allows for meetings between victim and offender, the practice of restitution, and healing. Indeed it is being practiced in many Muslim communities today for certain types of crimes.[13] A prisoner at Holman Correctional Facility who practices Islam commented that the reason he is attracted to restorative justice is because its principles are compatible with many of those central to his faith. While in the minds of the public, Islamic criminal law is associated with the frequent use of executions with limited appeals and other severe punishments, these practices may be better understood in the context of the socioeconomic and political environments of many Islamic nations where income inequality, lack of education, and oil politics prevail.[14] References in the Qur'an to forgiveness, mercy, and reconciliation, and the fact that the Qur'an is not "obsessed" with crime and punishment, support the aforementioned prisoner's perception that the restorative justice philosophy resonates with his spiritual beliefs.[15]

Aboriginal understandings of justice are also congruent with restorative philosophy and practice particularly with respect to its holistic nature and spiritual foundations that stress the interconnectedness of all things. Legal expert Val Napoleon observes that in Aboriginal cosmology,

Human beings are part of an ongoing cycle of interactive relationships with each other, the land, and nonhuman life forms. All events, including crime, are a responsibility because they arise out of relationships. When misfortune occurs, people are responsible for determining the cause of the breach and for correcting it.[16]

Arthur and Meredith Blue observe that a source of confusion for First Nations' people is the conflict between their culture, spiritual beliefs, and understandings of justice and the Western legal system.[17] When the media focuses on Native American practice in prison, underlying spiritual principles are overshadowed by sensational coverage that focuses on the legitimacy of prisoners owning peace pipes or convening in sweat lodges within the prison complex. The use of ceremonies to help the offender understand his relationship to the community in the past, present, and future and particularly to understand his or her responsibility to the community is lost in the drama of conflict between prisoner and correctional institution.[18] Many of the practices associated with restorative justice such as sentencing circles and healing circles draw from aboriginal understandings of justice.

While Buddhism is not widely practiced in prison communities, its similarities with the general direction of restorative justice are striking. There is no one Buddhist faith as it has taken numerous paths in different cultural settings. However, a central thrust is the nature of personhood which is viewed as imperfect but capable of further enlightenment. Punishment has no purpose unless it is to educate or correct.[19] Rather than black and white concepts of guilty or innocent, the offender is seen as a person with "unwholesome mental tendencies," which, while deeply ingrained, do not necessarily define the essence of that person or reflect where that person will be the rest of his life.[20] Thus compassion is required for those who err on their life's journey, and nothing is seen as static or permanent. Rules are not viewed as rigid requirements but rather a guide to the good life intended to help the individual gain enlightenment.[21] Buddhism does not necessarily share the relational views of restorative justice, but the individual capacity for change, transformation, and healing are values common to both world views.

Religion is important to prisoners because it allows them to deal with their guilt and feelings of unworthiness.[22] In many cases it provides a path for personal transformation, and for those with very long sentences, it offers the gift of hope. Invoking restorative justice in prison communities is not a difficult task from the perspective of inmates because it works toward their needs for healing and peace and can be understood within the context of their individual spiritual beliefs. Furthermore, justice is one of those concepts that seems to bridge the secular and the spiritual.[23] Notions of the nature of personhood, our relationships to one another, and our concepts of what is right, moral, and good and how we become so are intertwined in both domains.

THE MOVEMENT

Restorative justice, which seeks peaceful ways to resolve conflict based on compassion and active concern for everyone involved when someone hurts another, is a movement that does not fit neatly into politically charged labels of conservative or liberal. Indeed, it seems to transcend these categorizations. It was introduced in North America in the early 1970s with the creation of the Minnesota Restitution Center in 1972 and the introduction of victim offender reconciliation programs (VORPs) in Kitchener, Ontario, in 1974 where a probation officer urged young offenders who had broken into several peoples homes to make amends to their victims in person, and to develop a plan that would address the harms done and serve as a basis for law-abiding behavior in the future. The term "restorative justice" was coined somewhat later, and is attributed to an article written by Albert Eglash in 1977.[24] It has grown into an international movement with its principles best known in the practices of the Truth and Reconciliation Commission in South Africa. New Zealand has institutionalized restorative justice in its juvenile justice system and restorative practices have become more widespread in Australia, Canada, Britain, and the United States.[25]

While victim-offender mediation is only one example of a restorative practice, its growth has been fairly well documented. Since 1990, the number of victim-offender mediation programs has grown eight times to over 1,200 throughout the world.[26] As the movement has matured issues of standards, ethics, and where restorative justice fits within the conventional criminal justice system have emerged. A number of countries such as New Zealand, Australia, and Britain have passed the United States in the institutionalization of restorative justice. In the United States its practice varies from programs that are fairly marginal to the criminal justice system to those that have a more prominent role.

It is difficult to pinpoint how the restorative justice movement developed. Fredericksen notes that restorative justice emerged in different contexts.[27] Van Ness and Strong identify several movements whose criticism of the status quo contributes to restorative justice thought.[28] Each context or movement identifies a particular problem as well as a critique of the current way of doing things, particularly in criminal justice settings, but also in schools and other venues. Restorative justice challenges the thinking that underlies "justice as usual" and provides a common set of values and principles as a substitute or at least as an improvement.

One critique surfaced in the 1970s expressing a lack of confidence in the formal legal system. The concern is that people serve the legal system rather than the legal system serving citizens.[29] The legal system is characterized as abstract and inaccessible, dominated by paid professionals who speak a language not easily understood by their "clients." From this perspective, the law and its practice does not help people solve their problems. Nils Christie, often quoted in the restorative justice literature, argues that the state has in essence "stolen" conflicts from its owners.[30] This *informal justice movement* argues for more access to the law, increased citizen participation, deprofessionalization, and decentralization. Crowded court dockets and ideas related to informal justice are associated with mediation in civil cases becoming a more standard practice, gaining popularity in divorce cases, for example, where parties to marital conflict often said that they had little or no control in the formal legal process over matters of great concern to them.

The *restitution movement* began in the 1960s and continued to gain momentum in the 1970s and 1980s as a response to prison and jail overcrowding and the belief that in many cases imprisonment is not an appropriate response to the nature of the offense committed. Restitution is seen as a way to directly benefit the victim, hold the offender accountable, and reduce the costs and stigmatization of incarceration. Restitution could take the form of direct remuneration or symbolic restitution such as an apology or community service.[31]

The *feminist movement,* which also reemerged in the 1960s, took a number of directions all focused on equality for women. One concern, equal pay for equal work, is a bread-and-butter issue. Within the criminal justice arena feminists argued for changes in a system that revictimized rape victims.[32] The lack of protection for victims of domestic violence became a major concern in the

1980s. Broader justice issues concerned feminist scholars such as M. Kay Harris who argued that the criminal justice system should be reformed to include feminist values such as caring and the importance of relationships.[33] Along with Harris, *peacemaking criminology* led by Hal Pepinsky and Richard Quinney focused on reconciling the criminal justice system with issues related to social justice.[34]

The *victim's rights movement* gained momentum in the 1970s and 1980s. Victims argued that their needs were not adequately met in the criminal justice system, and that the needs and rights of offenders took precedence. As a result of this movement, judges and legislators became more aware of the need for restitution and victim compensation, a majority of states and the Federal government passed victim's rights legislation, and the office of victim advocate became a standard fixture in local law enforcement and state attorney offices.[35] Providing a more central, inclusive role for the victim in the criminal justice system was the major thrust of this movement.

Reforms related to *juvenile justice* have also contributed to a restorative focus. The juvenile justice system that was created in the late nineteenth century was intended to be separate from the retributive adult system and used a social welfare or rehabilitative model. The "tough on crime" attitudes that prevailed in the 1970s and 1980s moved the juvenile justice system closer to the retributive model. Prosecutors used their discretion to try juvenile cases in adult court in response to criticism that the juvenile system coddled young people and did not adequately deter delinquent behavior. Alarmed at the prospect of juvenile offenders being permanently harmed by the adult justice system, the restorative approach appeared promising with its focus on offender accountability to the victim and the community using processes less draconian than the prison alternative.[36]

Reforms to better the *plight of Aboriginal peoples*, particularly in Canada, Australia, and New Zealand, have also helped shape the restorative justice movement. For example, Aboriginal people are overrepresented in Canadian prisons, and when surveyed they showed considerably more disaffection and alienation from the criminal justice system than non-Aboriginals.[37] To address this problem, in the late 1990s and early twenty-first century, Canadian practice began to recognize the restorative values that were part of Aboriginal culture including reconciliation, healing, and restitution. These practices contrasted with the adversarial retributive features of the Western criminal

RESTORATIVE JUSTICE IN PRISON COMMUNITIES

justice system. The practice of using sentencing circles to process criminal cases was endorsed by the Canadian Supreme Court.[38] In the 1990s New Zealand adopted Maori traditional practices in its juvenile justice system so that now, all juvenile cases with the exception of murder offenses are addressed through a family group conferencing.[39]

A common set of principles and ideas has emerged to address a wide variety of concerns with the modern criminal justice system. Restorative justice requires that we look at the problem of crime and justice through a different set of eyes.

THE RESTORATIVE PHILOSOPHY: THE BASICS

Early in the twentieth century, members of the so-called Free Law school argued that the particular circumstances in any given case were more important than written legal norms and that the judge should feel free to ignore positive law altogether, or to fill in its gaps, by applying his sense of right and wrong to the realities of the case before him.[40]

The restorative philosophy sees crime as a violation of people and of interpersonal relationships. Thus, it can't ignore particular circumstances in any given situation when identifying harms and repairing the damage. This philosophical foundation allows restorative justice to be applied to a wide variety of settings.

These settings include schools, churches, families, and work places. It has been most actively used as a reform in the criminal justice system, predominantly to address nonviolent juvenile offenses where the focus is on the harm caused by criminal behavior. In its wider application, restorative approaches address the harms caused by conflict such as the problems that occur between a teacher and students who create a disturbance in the classroom.[41] Getting to the underlying causes of the problem is a strength of restorative justice that has the potential to provide more lasting and satisfying results.

How is restorative justice different from the way we do things now in the criminal justice system? In his *Little Book of Restorative Justice*, Howard Zehr provides a simple and straightforward account of the premises of restorative justice.[42] First, *crime is a violation of people and of interpersonal relationships.* In our current system crime is a violation of the law and the state. This has come to mean that the victim's role is limited to that of witness and that his or her pains, fears, and anxieties can be summarized nicely in a standardized legal code. The legal code, which is intended to vindicate the victim, in fact marginalizes him or her. Economic, emotional, and psychological needs are addressed in a limited way, if at all. In contrast, restorative justice is a victim-centered approach to the crime problem.

A second premise of restorative justice is that *violations create obligations*. These obligations, above all, center on the offender's obligation to take responsibility for his or her crime and to make things as right as possible for all those affected by the offense—primarily the victim, but not exclusive of the victim and offenders' family members and the larger community. Restitution is the most familiar way to make amends. But sometimes symbolic restitution—in the form of an apology or community service—is equally satisfying to the victim.

The larger community may also have obligations to address conditions that contribute to crime and to assist crime victims and offenders with their efforts to reintegrate back into the community. Contrasting with the restorative perspective, our current criminal justice system views criminal violations as creating the need to assign guilt through a set of formal procedures defined by law. The process ends when punishment is imposed.

The third premise of restorative justice is an extension of the premise that violations create obligations. That is, *justice involves victims, offenders, and community members in an effort to put things right*. Restorative justice promotes engagement and participation from *all* stakeholders in the crime. The criminal justice system limits participation with rules of evidence and the formal roles assigned to judge, defense attorney, and prosecutor. The professionals provide the definitions and meaning of the crime. Clearly a great deal of "data" are left out in the interest of equity, efficiency, and fairness. A fair trial means that everyone should be treated equally and that no extraneous or biased information that could contaminate a fair trial is introduced. However, these "contaminants" are the real "stuff" of how the crime was experienced and that remains unaddressed in our current system.

The *central focus* of restorative justice is victim needs and offender responsibility for repairing harm. The central focus in criminal justice is offenders getting what they deserve.[43] These contrasting foci can be illustrated with examples from our current justice system. In the very few cases where accused offenders go to trial, they are encouraged to plead not guilty, even if they have in fact committed the offense. If found guilty, offenders meet their obligation for the harm done through a prison sentence or another form of punishment. In the majority of cases where offenders enter a plea bargain, they are *not* assuming an obligation for what they actually did. They are participating in a bureaucratic process that is designed to benefit all but the victim, that is, move a case quickly and efficiently through the criminal justice system.

Offenders who have participated in this process and have been sentenced to prison report that at no time during the legal proceedings were they encouraged to think about the harm they had done to the victim or their own families. Saving their own skins or getting the minimum sentence possible was their primary concern. Taking responsibility for what they did was the furthest thing from their minds. Even after entering prison, offenders indicate that surviving in a new and dangerous environment dominates their thinking. While offenders do indeed experience discomfort and pain in prison, the present system does not encourage accountability and the obligations that derive from it.

A restorative justice scenario brings willing victims and willing offenders together. Family, friends, and community members can be included in the process. Victim needs for information, telling their stories, empowerment, restitution, and vindication would be addressed directly.[44] Offender needs for accountability and encouragement to change would also be addressed. This is only one example of how restorative justice might be realized. It does not rule out the possibility of restraint (imprisonment) when circumstances justify it.

Putting the whole package together, we can envision the core of restorative justice as "making things right." It focuses on harms and needs, addresses obligations, uses inclusive collaborative processes, and involves stakeholders including victims, offenders, and communities.[45] The glue that holds the package together is *respect*. Facilitators of restorative processes are trained to balance concerns for all parties and to use practices that encourage respect even among so-called enemies.[46] With these points in mind, Claassen and his colleagues provide a succinct definition of restorative justice. It is "a response to conflict, misbehavior, and crime that makes things as right as possible for all those affected."[47]

RESTORATIVE JUSTICE IN CUSTODIAL SETTINGS

Restorative practices are most frequently used at the front-end of the criminal justice system, particularly for juvenile offenses. They take place in the "free world" where personal choice and responsibility are cultural norms. The introduction of restorative justice into prison environments is more challenging and less widespread. It is important to recognize the inherent conflicts between prison organization and culture and the restorative paradigm. Several elements of prison organization are in conflict with restorative values:[48]

Security

Punishment

Offender focus

Separation from community

Authoritarian and hierarchical decision-making

Rule based

In addition, prison culture mitigates against honesty and accountability essential to the restorative philosophy. Given these organizational and cultural obstacles, on what basis can restorative justice catch hold within the prison environment?

Less recognized, but, nevertheless, part of the prison mission are the following elements which are more fully embraced by the restorative philosophy:

Safety

Respect

Purposeful activity such as educational and training programs

Reintegration into society

While not fully realized in many prison settings, respect and purposeful activity contribute to the safety of officers and the inmates.[49] The personal qualities of fairness and respect are seen by some officers as more important to securing compliance from inmates than the legitimate or formal positions of authority they hold or the use of force.[50] In the prison world, interpersonal relationships are just as important as they are in the free world. Thus, relationships between prisoners and their captors are unavoidable. They can be based on corrupt practices that undermine trust, fairness, and responsibility, or they can be based on respect, honesty, and communication.

Finally, the United States leads the world in rates of incarceration with 2.26 million of its population in prisons or jails.[51] This is a 500-percent increase over the past thirty years. As prison costs escalate and recidivism rates remain high, state and federal agencies are looking for new ideas about how prisoners might be more successfully reintegrated into society. The holistic nature of restorative programs holds promise as these efforts are pursued more seriously.

Introducing restorative justice into custodial settings is challenging. Yet, a number of programs have been used in prison. The following list derives from Van Ness who categorizes restorative programs according to their objectives and degrees of ambition.[52]

The first is *programs that attempt to develop offender awareness of the impact of their crimes as well as offender empathy for their victims.* From a restorative standpoint, true accountability begins with offenders owning up to what they did and recognizing, perhaps from a deeper, emotional level, the impact of their actions. Some state correctional institutions in Illinois and New Hampshire, for example, have victim impact curricula that cover a wide range of crimes. These curricula are similar to college-level victimology classes in that they introduce the "student" to the harms caused by crime and the needs created as a result.[53] Empathy classes include offenders writing a hypothetical apology letter to their victims.[54] Other forms of victim awareness include victim impact panels, where groups of like victims tell stories of their trauma and healing.[55] Others organize conversations between prisoners and surrogate victims.[56] It is noteworthy that some programs, while keeping the primary emphasis on the victim, also encourage offenders to recognize their own victimizations. Data showing a correlation between victimization and subsequent offending support this type of effort.[57]

A second category of programs is *making it possible for prisoners to make amends to their victims.* This process is more challenging because it involves changing laws and regulations that prohibit offenders from contacting their victims. In some states amend letters are made available in the district attorney's office and victims are notified that the letters are available. Offenders can also make restitution from their prison paychecks or make indirect restitution by doing community service.

A third category is *facilitating mediation between prisoners and their victims.* Given the seriousness of the offenses committed by incarcerated individuals, these mediations are voluntary and it is suggested that they be victim initiated. This restorative practice requires more resources in terms of time and preparation. For example, victim-mediation programs in Texas and Ohio have lengthy preparation times.[58]

A fourth type of restorative program is *developing relationships between prisons and the communities where they are situated.* This differs from indirect restitution at the individual level because it involves breaking down the isolation and separation of prisoners from the free world. These kinds of projects could include groups of prisoners providing a community service that is valued by their neighbors. This objective involves overcoming what Zehr refers to as the "mystification" of criminals as totally evil human beings who have nothing to contribute to society.[59] The mystification of crime contributes to community fear and isolation and the inability of inmates to function successfully when they are released.

A fifth type of restorative practice is *developing a culture in prison where conflict is resolved peacefully.* Examples of these practices include teaching inmates in conflict resolution courses, training inmate mediators to recognize and resolve conflict, and using peacemaking circles as an alternative to formal grievance and disciplinary procedures.

The final and most ambitious type involves *creating an environment in which the prisoner is offered the opportunity to be transformed.* This approach includes a range of activities, including many of those already listed. Restorative justice is introduced as a philosophy informing all aspects of the inmates' activities. It also includes support for the offender when he or she completes a sentence

Although these types of programs are not common, they have been implemented in prisons in countries such as Canada, the United States, England, Germany, Switzerland, and Brazil. The Focus on Victims Program in Hamburg, Germany, for example, helps offenders think about victimization in general as well as those they personally know who have been victims. Another example is the Sycamore Tree Project run by Prison Fellowship in a number of countries that use a surrogate victim approach. A program in Pennsylvania makes offender apology letters available to victims. The states of Minnesota, Texas, and Ohio have developed programs where crime victims or survivors meet directly with their incarcerated offenders. Formal evaluations in both states show very positive results for victim and offender satisfaction.[60] The Restorative Prison Project in England uses public awareness activities, recruitment of volunteers, and community service projects to strengthen the ties between prisons and their communities. Among other programs, the Quakers have introduced Alternatives to Violence Workshops into a maximum-security prison in New York. And finally, the faith-based restorative justice honor dorm at the W. C. Holman Correctional Facility in Atmore, Alabama, attempts to create a space for inmate transformation based on restorative values.

CREATING RESTORATIVE COMMUNITIES IN PRISON

The fifth and sixth objectives of restorative programs in prisons involve the ambitious task of creating a restorative culture as an alternative to the traditional prison culture. A large part of what Newell describes as the "cultural web" of the prison, is its power structure, which is at odds with the principles of the restorative philosophy.[61] At the same time, prisons can never become moral places unless individuals are given the responsibility to make moral choices.

Significantly, restorative justice challenges the power structure of the separate subcultures in prisons. It does so by involving prisoners in taking personal responsibility for their offending and seeking to make reparation. All of this counters some of the culture of secrecy and close camaraderie. It implies a degree of overt power sharing that can be very different from the expectations of many staff. It challenges the stereotyped perception that prisoners are not capable of exercising such personal power; it challenges the assumption that they remain in the role of offender through denial, rather than break out from it through becoming responsible citizens. It also challenges the separation between staff and prisoners that is often a psychological survival necessity in systems of coercion and overload of numbers. The dynamic of a conference setting or circle in which all participants are considered able to make a contribution to the solving of the dispute challenges the normal approach of prisons in which management subconsciously seeks to develop dependency in prisoners so that they fit into the system of the institution.[62]

Doing restorative justice requires taking calculated risks. Maintaining the delicate balance of power that provides stability in an environment where large numbers of individuals are held against their will is daunting. Any attempts to change the power structure will likely be met with resistance, not only by skeptics of restorative justice but by those who desire to make the system function smoothly.

Some restorative scholars question whether there can be a restorative prison. For example, Toews observes that if a prison was totally restorative, it would no longer be a prison as we know it.[63] However, *restorative spaces* that are built on a restorative foundation can be introduced into prisons for the purpose of meeting the goals of peaceful conflict resolution and personal transformation. Examples of these spaces might be realized in a particular cellblock set aside for that purpose such as a prison honor dorm. However, in the context of restorative justice, a restorative space is not limited to a physical location. It also includes spaces that are relational or emotional in nature.[64] Therapeutic communities that promote personal responsibility among drug addicts or sex offenders is one example. Family nights, where offenders share a meal with their family members in a more comfortable and "normal" setting than the prison cafeteria, is another. Programs that promote parenting relationships between inmates and their children are a third example. Church services and religious studies also provide a sanctuary from a stressful prison environment. Thus, settings and practices that use relationships to promote accountability and healing can be classified as restorative spaces.

The restorative justice definition of crime as a violation of people and relationships that creates obligations to make things right illustrates the importance of people engaging with one another to achieve justice. In a prison environment, the language of restorative justice with its emphasis on positive, healing relationships may at first seem like a foreign language.

The Quakers, who were involved in early penal reform in America, understood the importance of relationships. When creating Eastern State Penitentiary in 1829, the first true penitentiary in the world, the Quakers sought to isolate offenders from *negative relationships*. For them, the true path to reform involved removing the prisoner from criminogenic influences so that his only relationship was a positive one between him and his higher power. The prisoner slept, worked, and exercised alone. No human contact through sight or sound was permitted. He was encouraged to take responsibility for his crime and eventually repent.

People debated the effectiveness and compassion of solitary confinement. Due to prison overcrowding, the Pennsylvania System eroded. What followed were the prisons that we know today where prisoners interact and survive in crowded facilities creating subcultures that are more deviant than pro-social. Relationships that more closely typify law-abiding ones in the free world are put on hold.

Building relationships in prison that contribute to personal change and prepare the inmate to more effectively function in the community requires changing the way that prisoners interact with one another. It involves "acting one's way into right thinking" rather than "thinking one's way into right action." Toews refers to this process as *restorative living*.[65] The restorative philosophy which emphasizes respect, particularly respecting the rights and needs of the victim, by implication means that all individuals deserve such respect, including those that live and work in the prison community. Restorative living asks that when an inmate is faced with disrespect or wrongdoing, he acts in such a way as to avoid physical confrontations and resolve the matter in a peaceful fashion. The inmate might use facilitated mediation or a peacemaking circle within the prison community. It involves replacing the "tough guy" image with honesty, understanding, kindness, and caring. It replaces the "blame game" and minimizing the effects of one's crimes with personal accountability and empathy. It stresses relationships and mutual responsibility over "minding your own business." And it replaces the value of "survival" with personal change. Such a cultural change seems monumental. It can be achieved one step at a time, and one inmate at a time, by providing restorative spaces which promote values such as interconnectedness and relationship to others, mutual responsibility, personal accountability, nonviolence, honesty and trust, personal healing, safety, creativity and positivity, and productivity and constructiveness.[66]

APPLYING THE RESTORATIVE RELATIONAL MODEL TO CUSTODIAL SETTINGS

The remainder of this book focuses on using restorative interventions in custodial settings with particular attention given to relationship-building. The case-study method is used to illustrate the opportunities and challenges associated with this approach. The prison case involves a restorative community where inmates are encouraged to solve conflicts peacefully and experience personal transformation. Pranis elaborates on the concept of restorative community, describing it as a learning community "that learns about itself from those who have been hurt and those who have caused hurt, and uses that learning to improve community life for all."[67] Several inmate residents from the Holman Faith-Based Restorative Justice Honor Dorm volunteered to share their reflections on the meaning of restorative justice in a prison community. These inmates do not represent the views of the entire honor dorm as each member is at various stages in learning about their environment. The volunteers who wrote these essays have permanent party status—that is, they have been members of the honor dorm for at least two years.

Reflection 1

When first introduced to restorative justice, I was shown how restorative justice was different from retributive justice. This was something that I could understand because I was part of the system of retributive justice. I had experienced first-hand the assigning of guilt and blame. I was serving the time (punishment) and the time had itself certain built-in punishments in addition to just being separated from the rest of free society. But restorative justice in a prison community opened up the possibilities for an entirely different way of living in prison.

Restorative justice teaches me that I am a stakeholder in the justice process along with the victim and the community. It focuses on the harms that were caused to all the stakeholders, the victim first, but nevertheless, all the stakeholders. So by focusing on the harms to my victims, I was able to learn about empathy and gain a greater sense of the harm that I caused.

Restorative justice also teaches me that the right thing to do is to try and repair the harm I caused or try and make things as right as possible. Sometimes this is hard to do in prison with your victim because of being out of touch with them. However, this same concept can be applied in prison as a way of life that is an alternative to the normal routine. Restorative justice has helped me in prison to place a greater value on people and the relationships that I have with them. So, if I have a problem with someone, my education of restorative justice has conditioned me to have empathy, identify the harms, and try to repair the relationship. This gives me more choices and more freedom right where I'm at in prison.

The meaning of restorative justice for me in a prison community is that restorative justice has given men an entirely different outlook on life. It offers the kind of justice that I would desire for myself so I try to practice it in my personal life with everyone around me so that one day maybe I will be treated the same way by others.

Reflection 2

Restorative justice has had a very lasting effect on the way that I see things. When I read Howard Zehr's Changing Lenses, *I was excited. I began to see how people in my environment (prison) had left so many unanswered questions and unresolved feelings for victims. I myself have done irreparable harm to my community. The current justice system, in my layman's opinion, has only exacerbated the harms done by crime. It is taboo even to think of reaching out from behind the wall to just write a letter of apology.*

Upon learning that RJ was relational in its application as well, I began to apply it to situations of conflict that occur here. I never knew how important it is to really hear someone out. For many people it contributes to their healing to be allowed to tell their story uninterrupted. There isn't always a speaking object, so there has to be something, some principle in place to insure that a person can speak uninterrupted. I use the principle of mutual/collective respect. Respect for the next person's right to be heard. In many instances, with people who are cooperative, it works.

In this environment, whether it is a dispute about the television or stealing from another person, I have found the principles of RJ to be effective. It has really helped me out in my own interpersonal relations. My conversations seem to carry more weight now. So, whether on the basketball court, in the television room, or on the weight pile, I have an effective way of resolving petty or valid disputes that could end in resentments, fistfights, or violence with weapons involved. Who would've thought that RJ could be effective in a maximum-security prison?

Reflection 3

Restorative justice for me is a way of life in that it can be applied no matter what the setting or situation. It has given me more choices when it comes to conflict or everyday life situations. It has transformed my personality from one who is reactive to one who is proactive.

Restorative justice has opened my eyes and my heart to what others feel and has given me tools to be a positive participant who takes responsibility when warranted and allows others the latitude and opportunity to grow even if it doesn't benefit me. Lastly restorative justice, because of its foundation, tenets, and processes, has reaffirmed my spiritual beliefs.

Reflection 4

In my opinion it means culture change. It establishes and sets the bar for an entire institution, but only if facilities stay true to the five pillars of restorative justice. Prisons all over the world are full of people that hurt others. The implementation of restorative justice is an opportunity to address not only the conflict they have brought upon the victims and their families/communities, but also a chance to confront and deal with the conflict within. Once you embark upon that mission, it creates an avenue by which that cycle of dead living can be dealt with.

Restorative justice in maximum-security prisons allows offenders an opportunity to work toward being equipped in such a way as to be able to positively take responsibility for what they have done and begin the process of healing for the victim(s) and their families and the offender. Victims have real needs that the current criminal justice system is ill equipped to meet, and tragically fails to address. It's also an opportunity for offenders to prepare themselves for a life of restoration while still incarcerated and "make zero days count," and a chance to get free from the conflict and go beyond it and similar conflicts.

Normal prison culture is based on the convict code. If you cross the line and get in someone's business then one can expect a violence response; there ain't no talking, there's gonna be some turning going down.

But when restorative justice is given a chance then it provides an environment where people are safe to express themselves in a positive way without fear of violent retribution. It allows people to sit down with a group of committed and concerned people who want to make a difference. This is my opinion based on some of my own experiences with restorative justice in a maximum-security prison.

Reflection 5

Restorative Justice will be a subject I need to learn and talk about. I have a strong feeling that a person or convicted felon must be very sincere about trying to help him and know his victim. Most victims never want anything to do with us as felons, but I hope it will be entered into the Alabama Prison system and applied where people are sincere.

I have a goal now to learn more about R.J. and to try to pick up as much as possible to have a better understanding of how this program will help me or others like me.

As I've mentioned to Dr. Swanson I'd hate to think that I traumatized a victim so badly, I ruined the rest of their lives or their relatives. I'm referring to

Stephanie, a student of Dr. Swanson's, who was a victim. I doubt I'll ever forget the story of Stephanie. So after hearing the damage that was done to her during a robbery, it bothered me a lot. I now wonder if I've ever left a victim so badly traumatized, to the point of needing doctors or nut doctors to help her come out of it. So I will try to learn more of R.J. to see if I'll ever be able to help someone heal and learn to do better.

NOTES

1. Michael J. Hadley, "Introduction: Multifaith Reflection on Criminal Justice," in *The Spiritual Roots of Restorative Justice*, ed. Michael L. Hadley (Albany, N.Y.: State University of New York Press, 2001), 1–30.

2. Gerry Johnstone, *Restorative Justice: Ideas, Values, Debates* (Worchester, U.K.: Willan Publishing, 2002), 37.

3. Howard Zehr, *Changing Lenses: A New Focus for Crime and Justice*, 3rd ed. (Scottsdale, Pa.: Herald Press, 2005), 97–125.

4. Mark S. Umbreit, Betty Vos, and Robert B. Coates, "Restorative Justice in the 21st Century: A Social Movement Full of Opportunities and Pitfalls," *Marquette University Law Review* 89, no. 2 (Winter 2005): 255.

5. Daniel W. Van Ness and Karen Heetderks Strong, *Restoring Justice: An Introduction to Restorative Justice*, 3rd ed. (Cincinnati, Ohio: Anderson Publishing, 2006), 14.

6. Van Ness and Strong, *Restoring Justice*, 109–10.

7. Pierre Allard and Wayne Northey, "Christianity: The Rediscovery of Restorative Justice," in *The Spiritual Roots of Restorative Justice*, ed. Michael L. Hadley (Albany, N.Y.: State University of New York Press, 2001), 135.

8. Allard and Northey, "Christianity," 127.

9. Zehr, *Changing Lenses*, 49.

10. Zehr, *Changing Lenses*, 47.

11. F. LeRon Shults and Steven J. Sandage, *The Faces of Forgiveness: Searching for Wholeness and Salvation* (Grand Rapids, Mich.: Baker, 2003), 21–23.

12. Allard and Northey, "Christianity," 120.

13. Nawal H. Ammar, "Restorative Justice in Islam: Theory and Practice," in *The Spiritual Roots of Restorative Justice*, ed. Michael L. Hadley (Albany, N.Y.: State University of New York Press, 2001), 178.

14. Ammar, "Restorative Justice in Islam," 166.

15. Ammar, "Restorative Justice in Islam," 167.

16. Val Napoleon quoted in Hadley, "Introduction: Multifaith Reflection," 13.

17. Arthur W. Blue and Meredith A. Rogers Blue, "The Case for Aboriginal Justice And Healing: The Self Perceived through a Broken Mirror," in *The Spiritual Roots of Restorative Justice*, ed. Michael L. Hadley (Albany, N.Y.: State University of New York Press, 2001), 64.

18. Blue and Blue, "The Case for Aboriginal Justice," 69.

19. David R. Loy, "Healing Justice: A Buddhist Perspective," in *The Spiritual Roots of Restorative Justice*, ed. Michael L. Hadley (Albany, N.Y.: State University of New York Press, 2001), 87.

20. Loy, "Healing Justice," 82.

21. Loy, "Healing Justice," 91.

22. Todd R. Clear, Patricia L. Hardyman, Bruce Stout, Karol Lucken, and Harry R. Dammer, "The Value of Religion in Prison: An Inmate Perspective," in *Behind Bars: Readings on Prison Culture*, ed. Richard Tewksbury (Upper Saddle River, N.J.: Pearson Prentice Hall, 2006), 333–35.

23. Loy, "Healing Justice," 81.

24. Douglas J. Sylvester, "Myth in Restorative Justice History," *Utah Law Review*, no. 1 (2003), 471–72.

25. Johnstone, *Restorative Justice*, 36–37.

26. "Restorative Justice FAQ," Victim Offender Mediation Association, available at voma.org/rjfaq.shtml (accessed 6 May 2008).

27. Erica A. Frederiksen, "Rethinking Justice in a Post Colonial World" (paper presented at the annual meeting of the Canadian Political Science Association, London, Ontario, June 2–4, 2005), 1–2.

28. Van Ness and Strong, *Restoring Justice*, 12–19.

29. Van Ness and Strong, *Restoring Justice*, 13–14.

30. Van Ness and Strong, *Restoring Justice*, 13–14.

31. Van Ness and Strong, *Restoring Justice*, 14–15.

32. Andrew Karmen, *Crime Victims: An Introduction to Victimology*, 5th ed. (Belmont, Calif.: Wadsworth/Thomas Learning, 2004), 5.

33. Van Ness and Strong, *Restoring Justice*, 18–19.

34. Harold E. Pepinsky and Richard Quinney, eds., *Criminology as Peacemanking* (Bloomington: Indiana University Press, 1991).

35. Karmen, *Crime Victims*, 4–7.

36. Gordon Bazemore and Lode Walgrave, eds., *Restorative Juvenile Justice: Repairing the Harm of Youth Crime* (Monsey, N.Y.: Criminal Justice Press, 1999), 1–6.

37. Fredericksen, "Rethinking Justice," 17–18.

38. Fredericksen, "Rethinking Justice," 20–21.

39. Van Ness and Strong, *Restoring Justice*, 29–30.

40. Theodore Ziolkowski, *The Mirror of Justice* (Princeton, N.J.: Princeton University Press, 1997), 215–16.

41. Cheryl Swanson and Michelle Owen, "Building Bridges: Integrating Restorative Justice with the School Resource Officer Model," *International Journal of Restorative Justice* 3, no. 2 (September 2007): 68–92.

42. Howard Zehr, *The Little Book of Restorative Justice* (Intercourse, Pa.: Good Books, 2002), 19–41.

43. Zehr, *The Little Book*, 21.

44. Zehr, *The Little Book*, 17.

45. Zehr, *The Little Book*, 34.

46. Zehr, *The Little Book*, 36.

47. Ron Claassen, Charlotte Tilkes, Phil Kader, and Douglas E. Noll, "Restorative Justice: A Framework for Fresno," Center for Peacemaking and Conflict Studies, 2001, available at peace.fresno.edu/docs/ (accessed 7 May 2008).

48. This list is compiled from observations from Daniel Van Ness, "Restorative Justice in Prisons" (paper presented at the Symposium on Restorative Justice and

Peace, in Cali, Colombia, February 9–12, 2005), and Tim Newell, "Restorative Practice in Prisons: Circles and Conferencing in a Custodial Setting," Restorative Justice On-Line, available at www.restorativejustice.org/search? SearchableText=Newell (accessed 7 May 2008).

49. Frank Schmalleger and John Ortiz Smykla, *Corrections in the 21st Century* (New York: McGraw Hill, 2005), 474.

50. Cyndi Banks, *Criminal Justice Ethics* (Thousand Oaks, Calif.: Sage Publications, 2004), 139–40.

51. William J. Sabol, Heather Coulture, and Paige M. Harrison, "Prisoners in 2006," available at www.ojp.usdoj.gov/bjs/abstract/p06.htm (accessed 3 May 2008).

52. Van Ness, "Restorative Justice in Prisons."

53. William G. Doerner and Steven P. Lab, *Victimology*, 4th ed. (Cincinnati, Ohio: Lexis Nexis Anderson Publishing, 2005).

54. Barb Toews, "Restorative Justice: Building the Web of Relationships, Resources for Restorative Justice in Prison," Pennsylvania Prison Society, available at www.prisonsociety.org/progs/rj.shtml (accessed 7 May 2008).

55. Jennifer M. Allen, "Planning and Design in Restorative Justice: A First Look at Four Victims of Crime Impact Panels in the Midwest," *American Association of Behavioral Social Science On-Line Journal*, 2004, available at aabs.org/journal2004/AABSS_76-88.pdf (accessed 7 May 2008).

56. Simon Feasey, Patrick Williams, Rebecca Clark, "An Evaluation of the Prison Fellowship Sycamore Tree Programme," Sheffield Hallman University, 2005, available at www.restorativejustice.org.uk/rj_&_the_CJS/pdf/Sycamore_tree_evaluation.pdf (accessed 7 May 2008).

57. William R. Lindsay, Jacqueline Law, Kathleen Quinn, Nicola Smart, and Anne H. W. Smith, "A Comparison of Physical and Sexual Abuse: Histories of Sexual and Non Sexual Offenders with Intellectual Disability," *Child Abuse and Neglect* 25, no. 7 (July 2001): 989–95.

58. Mark S. Umbreit, Betty Vos, Robert B. Coates, and Katherine A. Brown, *Facing Violence: The Path of Restorative Justice and Dialogue* (Monsey, N.Y.: Criminal Justice Press, 2003).

59. Zehr, *Changing Lenses*, 57–59.

60. Umbreit, *Facing Violence.*

61. Newell, "Restorative Practices in Prison," 2.

62. Newell, "Restorative Practices in Prison," 3.

63. Toews, *Little Book for People in Prison,* 75.

64. Toews, *Little Book for People in Prison,* 76–77.

65. Toews, *Little Book for People in Prison,* 79.

66. Toews, *Little Book for People in Prison,* 76.

67. Kay Pranis, "Restorative Justice, Social Justice, and the Empowerment of Marginalized Population," in *Restorative Community Justice: Repairing Harm and Transforming Communities,* ed. Gordon Bazemore and Mara Schiff (Cincinnati, Ohio: Anderson Publishing, 2001), 289.

Restorative Justice Goes to W. C. Holman Correctional Facility

Prisons should be considered moral institutions and corrections a moral enterprise. Inmates should be seen as having the obligation to become virtuous people and to manifest moral goodness.

—Francis T. Cullen, Jody L. Sundt, and John F. Wozniak, *Contemporary Issues in Crime and Criminal Justice: Essays in Honor of Gilbert Geis*

W. C. Holman Correctional Facility is a maximum-security prison located in southwestern Alabama in a rural area fifteen minutes north of the small town of Atmore. Even though it lies only two miles from Interstate 65, the prison is isolated. It is categorized as a level-five prison by the Alabama Department of Corrections, the second highest security level in the system.

The building design is telephone-pole architecture—a prison style common in the 1960s when Holman was built. The gray cement building consists of a long hallway with inmate housing located within the "arms" that cross it. The prison is surrounded by barbed wire fencing, with four guard towers outside the fence on each corner of the rectangular compound. In addition to the honor dorm with its 174 residents, 800 other men live at Holman. They live in open dorms, in segregation, and on death row.

Before considering the living arrangements in the honor dorm, let's look at a special event for its residents. In the summer of 2006, I conducted a survey that indicated honor dorm residents thought there was room for a great deal of improvement with respect to health issues. While the inmates have little control over the health services outsourced to a private firm by the Alabama Department of Corrections, a group of inmates met and agreed that they did have some control over preventive measures. With this in mind, the inmates and I organized the First Annual Honor Dorm Health Fair in October 2006. The men stayed up into the early hours of the morning implementing the plan. The following is my recollection and impressions of the event when I entered the honor dorm the morning of October 13.

I walked into a large, brightly lit room excited about the first annual health fair. A whiteboard near the entrance listed the day's events—a group stress reduction exercise, a speaker on HIV and Hepatitis C, a computer-assisted health diagnostic sponsored by the University of West Florida, presentations on cardiovascular disease and stroke, and a visual meditation. In the center of the room was a choice of health drinks—ginseng tea, mango tea, and Gatorade. Nearby was a display titled "alternative approaches to mental, spiritual, and physical health," which included books ranging from those written by Emmette Fox to the Qur'an to Buddhist practice. It resembled a new age bookstore but included the old and the new. Two people browsed through a book that looked like an oversized Webster's dictionary. On closer inspection, it was a health encyclopedia filled with descriptions and treatments for every ailment imaginable. I overheard one of the men comment, "I never heard of gout before." The other man replied, "My grandfather had gout. His big toe used to swell up, and he was in a lot of pain. He said it was from eating too much red meat or something like that." He added, "I think I might have the beginnings of it. Let's see what the book has to say about gout."

Around the room's perimeter were numerous booths decorated with brightly colored tissue and labeled with letters cut from construction paper. A booth on heart disease was accented with Valentine hearts sprinkled with glitter. The booth on Eastern spiritual practices had a continuously running DVD on yoga exercises. Other booths provided information on cancer, stroke, CPR, arthritis, and Alzheimer's disease. A number of benches were placed in a circle for people to listen to guest speakers scheduled throughout the day. I heard one person ask another, "What time is the presentation on stress management? I heard it was going to be led by a family therapist from Florida." Near him I noticed a computer station where people could test their knowledge on various health issues. I thought, "Maybe I'll try that later."

A group of my volunteer friends and acquaintances from Alabama, Florida, and Georgia had arrived by now and some of them were milling around the room and starting to mix with people manning the booths. The atmosphere was warm and relaxing.

The room looked like the typical health fair sponsored by a hospital, local mall, high school, or college. But it wasn't in a health facility, a shopping center, or an educational setting. It was in a faith-based restorative justice honor dorm in a maximum-security prison. And the individuals sponsoring the event were not hospital employees, community volunteers, or students. It was created by prison inmates at Holman Correctional Facility.

Clearly, the health fair and the honor dorm where it took place contrasts with Holman's stark institutional image. How is it possible, that a group of men serving long sentences for very serious crimes could have the capability and be trusted to organize such an event?

WHAT IT IS AND HOW IT WORKS

In 1999 former corrections commissioner Mike Haley mandated that all major correctional facilities in Alabama create a faith-based honor dorm. The purpose of the decree was to provide inmates who wanted to improve their lives a separate space to do so—one removed from the everyday challenges of prison life. The honor dorms vary according to programming. The honor dorm at W. C. Holman Correctional Facility rests not only on a faith-based foundation but also on restorative justice values.

The faith-based focus of the Alabama honor dorms is as an approach that emphasizes spiritual principles such as dedication, integrity, and discipline.[1] This contrasts with the one-size-fits-all approach long associated with the failed rehabilitation movement.[2] Likewise, restorative justice emphasizes principles over a particular blueprint so that programs can be developed that best match a particular setting and clientele. In discussing why he introduced the restorative philosophy to the honor dorm at Holman, Chaplain Chris Summers says, "It added a coherent framework for encouraging offender change that was theologically, sociologically, and penologically sound."

The Holman Faith-Based Honor Dorm (HFBHD) began in 1999. Originally housed in one of the four open dorms in the main building, today the honor dorm is in a large detached structure that resembles an airplane hanger. Inmates designed the dorm that includes a sleeping area, showers/bathrooms, computer lab, library, and an open space furnished with donated church pews used for community meetings, classroom, and TV viewing areas. There is no cable television, and TVs are for educational materials in addition to broadcast programming. Computers, books, televisions, and other educational materials are donated by free world groups.

The HFBHD has its own administrative structure. Part of this structure is integrated with the prison administration with the warden situated at the top of the hierarchy, and various correctional staff who have specific responsibilities as part of the Honor Community Administrative Review Committee. The honor dorm's internal administrative structure consists of community representatives (liaisons with the prison administration), senior coordinators (oversee the operations of the honor dorm), coordinators on duty, department heads (such as education and audio visual), and crew members (work various jobs in the honor dorm). A set of standard operating procedures outlines the responsibilities for occupants of these positions as well as behavioral expectations for community members. Serious rule violations can lead to dismissal from the honor dorm, although an inmate who leaves under these circumstances can reapply for admission at a later date.

The organizational hierarchy of the dorm facilitates responsibility. It gives inmates an opportunity to learn skills such as supervision, report writing, program implementation, rule application, data entry, and working with others. Some components of the dorm focus more directly on the restorative philosophy emphasizing peaceful conflict resolution, inclusiveness, accountability, respect, and integrity. These include *circles, education,* and *mentoring.*

Several types of circles are used ranging from conflict resolution and disciplinary matters to community planning. The *peacemaking circles* are described in detail in the next chapter. In addition to circles that focus on conflict resolution, all residents are assigned to a family circle that meets weekly to discuss topics of relevance to the group. Recently a leadership class taught by a free world volunteer evolved into an "innovative thinking" group that has been working on projects that will benefit local charities and strengthen ties between the honor dorm and the nonprison community.

For the restorative justice approach to work effectively in any setting, capacity-building needs considerable attention.[3] Thus, working toward a GED is required for remaining in the community. In addition, a rigorous four-semester curriculum, set in a context of twenty six-week semesters, has been developed. It continually and repetitively exposes the residents to the principles and values of restorative justice. These *educational efforts* develop competencies in verbal expression, ability to listen, ability to respect others, and openness to creative problem-solving. Also, through restorative justice programming offenders learn to take ownership of past crimes and work as much as possible to repair the harms of their crimes. While the programming does not currently have a victim-offender mediation forum, it is a goal for the future. In the meantime, many offenders make amends by acknowledging the crimes they have committed and living more productive and positive lives. Crime impact and empathy classes are integral to this process.

Mentoring is the third forum. Residents learn mentoring includes more than showing a student how to work math problems or how to participate in peaceful conflict resolution. A mentor's role also entails inspiring, encouraging, and befriending those under their care in every aspect of life. As an example, mentors help mentees prioritize daily schedules so students and residents will have time for schoolwork, dorm responsibilities, and personal activities. In this context, mentors stress the importance of timely discipline in the process of achieving goals.

Mentors gain valuable experience that will hopefully influence their own lives and those of the mentees as well as other members of the HFBHD community. In this way emphasis on building relationship skills is practical and daily. These skills are essential to a positive, responsible environment. They are also a foundation for community reintegration. Lessons about relationship-building are addressed in more detail in subsequent chapters.

CHALLENGES

A tremendous amount of work went into creating a unit organizationally and culturally distinct from the average prison. Yet the only formal requirement to enter the honor dorm is that an inmate be disciplinary free for six months. Needless to say, people who apply for residence have diverse motives and different levels of commitment to making the changes necessary for personal growth and transformation and contributing positively to the honor dorm community. For example, one crewmember with bookkeeping responsibilities was caught trading coffee for course credits. In the fall of 2006, for the first time in its seven-year existence, two honor dorm residents were involved in a stabbing in the dining hall. Some honor dorm inmates continue to use drugs, gamble, or run stores. Occasionally racial slurs are exchanged. However, the following comment from a ranking correctional officer best describes the vast majority of honor dorm residents: "The rules they choose to live by are more difficult than I could live by. They are rougher on each other than we (corrections officers) are."

In 2006 I conducted a survey among all honor dorm residents to assess their *expectations* for the HFBHD community. An inmate focus group selected a set of values, and residents ranked each one according to its importance to them. Figure 3.1 shows the items the respondents would most like to see realized in the dorm. The survey also asked residents to assess how close the honor dorm comes to meeting their expectations. Figure 3.1 shows that the gap between expectations for the dorm and their actualization is not large. A convenience sample of inmates in the general population took the same questionnaire. The latter not only had lower expectations for quality of life values, but also indicated that they are experienced to a lesser degree (see figure 3.1).

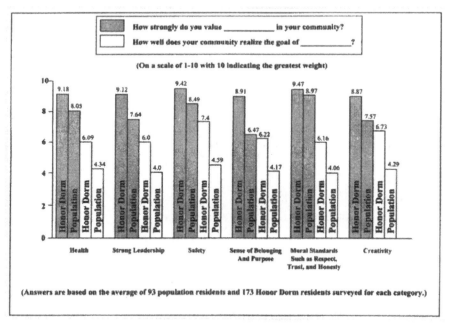

FIGURE 3.1.
Survey Results on Community Expectations and Perceptions Comparing Holman's General Population to the Honor Dorm

While residents seem to thrive in the honor dorm environment, they put on their "game faces" when they enter the exercise yard and eat their meals in the dining hall where they share space with inmates from the general population. They must negotiate between two worlds that contrast much more dramatically than is experienced outside of prison when we, for example, transition between work and family life. Furthermore, while HFBHD residents enjoy benefits in their environment, they are deprived of the income that general population inmates earn in the underground economy. In that sense, the life of the honor dorm inmate more closely approximates that of the free world "resident" because he is required to balance making a living with educational and community responsibilities.

ESSAYS AND GOALS

Following an orientation period, HFBHD residents begin four semesters of required courses. While completing core requirements, inmates write both an essay and a goal statement. Most of the inmates have never done anything like this before. Some are afraid and hide their fear by referring to the task as just another "Mickey Mouse" requirement. Those with more schooling enjoy writing an essay about themselves or something with which they are familiar. The head of the Honor Dorm Education Department reads the essays. He finds that he learns more about his fellow inmates because sometimes they are willing to open up more in an essay and say more about themselves. He sees this exercise as a capacity-building process where the residents get in touch with who they are and where they are and also begin to work with language and communication. The following sample of writings provides insights into the men's life experiences, their experiences in prison, their hopes and dreams, and their perceptions of the honor dorm.

Essay 1: Untitled

On March 25, 1978, I was convicted of capital murder and received an automatic death sentence. Upon conviction, death was mandatory. The judge made the jury stay out till around 11 p.m. that night to reach a decision and this was a Saturday. The next day was Easter Sunday, and the judge told them if they didn't reach a decision they would be back on the holy holiday until they reached a decision. March 25 was my birthday and I just turned 24 years old. I got locked up January 29, 1977, and was only 22 years old.

The judge held a hearing to determine if my death sentence should be reduced to life without parole. It was already ironic that I was convicted and given a mandatory death sentence on my birthday. When the judge let stand my death sentence and made up his own aggravating circumstances, that was even more ironic and vengeful on the judge's part. The only way a mandatory death sentence could remain was if you had the required aggravating circumstances listed in the Alabama Code of Law. I didn't even have another felony on my record, much less meet any of the requirements of the aggravating circumstances listed in the Alabama Code law book.

I had gotten married when I was fifteen years old and my wife was already five months pregnant. I had another child the following year, two children by the time I was seventeen years old. I was a family man struggling at my young age to support my family. I was no criminal or prior felon, or out wild running the streets and breaking the law.

I was arrested in Houston, Texas, where I had been living for over five years. I spent about six months in the county jail there before I was extradited back to Mobile, Alabama. The jail in Houston was a shock but in no way could it have prepared me for the horror and filth and depravity I came into upon arrival at the Mobile County Jail. People were crammed into tiny cells and had to sleep on the floors. You couldn't hardly get to the bathroom at night because of bodies lying everywhere, including all around the toilets. There was only one shower for 80 to 90 inmates. Everything was filthy and the food actually stank so bad you couldn't eat most of it no matter how hungry you got. If you didn't fight for your tray you starved or existed on scraps. I seen so many young guys get raped it was unreal. I just could never imagine that fellow human beings could treat one another so savagely, nor could I imagine cops and public officials treating its citizens so horribly. I had been taught by good, decent, and loving parents. I knew in my mind what human and public decency should be, but that did not exist in the Alabama Penal System, or the courts.

When I arrived at Holman prison in December of 1978, death row was also a pig sty. There was trash and food all over the floors and green slime leaking down the walls. I was put in a five-foot by eight-foot cell with a heavy logging chain and padlocks. The cell had a bare light bulb in the back that you had to screw in to turn on and off. At the end of the bunk by the bars was a small table and there was a sink in the back. The strangest thing was this large block of concrete under the sink that had a round hole in it that I found out was the toilet. The smell was pretty rough but at least I had a private cell and a large mattress made from raw cotton balls with seeds still in them. The food was quite an improvement compared to Mobile County Jail. You might find a pig teat with hair on it in your soup or a pig ear or pig eyeball now and then but for the most part it was edible. I got milk and eggs, beef, and cereal for the first time in two years.

We were allowed to go outside two to four times a week, we were strip-searched in the cell and handcuffed behind our backs before leaving the cell. We kept the handcuffs on behind our backs until we got back in our cells and only had a small cage to walk around in for about thirty minutes. We had no TV's until about eight or ten months later. We were allowed a small radio with a speaker. The best part was the packages we were allowed to get in each month. Anyone could send you one food package and one incentive package per month. In the food packages we were allowed to get anything you could buy or cook. In the incentive packages you could get in clothing such as underwear, T-shirts, blue jeans, denim shirts, sheets, bedspreads, games, novels, and etc. That was all stopped around 1980 and the food took a drastic turn for worse. They took up all the jeans and denim shirts and issued total white clothing. I was one of the first hall runners on death row. I was allowed out of my cell for nearly eighteen hours a day to feed the other death row inmates three meals a day and pass out coffee, milk, some kind of drink, ice, and hot water. It was also my job to sweep and mop after each meal and let the death row inmates clean their cells. I also painted on occasions. A few years later we finally got the handcuffs taken off during the exercise period and as death row grew in population they had to allow us to go outside on a small yard in groups for exercise. Eventually we got a law library and were allowed out there once a week for six to eight hours in groups. We could also play games such as cards, dominos, checkers and do research in the law books. They also provided two typewriters. We also started having church in the law library two or three times a week. There were free world people coming in to preach, teach, and fellowship by the late 1980s. Around 1980, we were allowed to have contact visits as the population did, once a week, because of a lawsuit. The contact visits each week helped me to survive all the other hardships and ordeals I was facing daily. I was very fortunate and blessed that my family only lived about sixty miles away in Mobile and my family was here to visit every week. We could each sit around a table and talk, eat sandwiches, drink cokes, and eat snacks for up to six hours per visit.

The worst part about death row for me was when an execution would take place. You would get to know these guys and their cases and they didn't deserve to be put to death, executed, by the state in your name. For the most part, there are lots of worse cases out in the general population than death row. Depends on whether you were from a poor county and they couldn't afford a capital trial, or had some ambitious district attorney running for re-election or higher office, or a white person was killed. There are so many wrongful capital convictions in the state of Alabama, illegal evidence, lies, perjured testimony, false testimony, and prosecutorial misconduct and judicial misconduct run rampant across this state. The whole judicial system is in a very sad state of flux in Alabama and behind times with the rest of the United States.

About thirteen years later I finally got my case reversed on prosecutorial misconduct. In 1989 the appeals court said there was no aggravating circumstance in the Alabama Code to give me a death sentence. I was retried in 1990, convicted of capital murder under a revised stature allowing lesser-included offenses. The jury recommended life without parole unanimously 12-0. The judge overrode the jury's recommendation and sentenced me to death again. One year later the appeals court reversed my case again for prosecutorial and judicial misconduct. I was finally able to get rid of my judge and was given a new judge for my third trial in 1993. I was once again convicted of capital murder and once again the judge overrode the jury's 12-0 recommendation of life without parole. The old judge had given my case to his friend and followed in his footsteps. This trial was full of prosecutorial misconduct, however, the appeals court did not rule on any of those issues. I was given a reversal in 1996–1997 because, jury misconduct had occurred at the start of trial and no other issues were considered. I went on trial again for capital murder in 1999, before a new judge. The first trial judge had taken the case from the third trial judge and given it to a lower district court judge whom he was supporting for a Federal judgeship. This judge had no jurisdiction to even try my case, never tried a murder case much less a capital case. A district court judge does not have authority to try criminal cases before a jury in Alabama. They handle only arraignments, misdemeanors, divorce, and juvenile proceedings. In the middle of my trial the Governor appoints this district court judge to fill a vacant circuit court judgeship. I was convicted of capital murder, and the 12-0 jury recommendation was overrode and I was sentenced to death again.

The Alabama appeals courts have upheld my appeal, but did reduce my sentence to life without parole, I'll be filing my Rule 32 appeal to the trial court next Friday, I've never been this far on appeal before. My last trial was also full of prosecutorial misconduct, same prosecutor I've had since 1977 and he is known statewide for gross misconduct. The sad fact is, he's been an assistant attorney general for over 26 years, which is unheard of. Never before has anyone been an assistant attorney general for over 26 years. He was seen at my trial tampering with the jury while they were in deliberations in 1999. I will prove this soon and hopefully remove this monster from office. That should put me on the streets when that happens. So I await the outcome of my Rule 32 appeal.

I came to population in 2004 and it seemed like a step back in time when I first went to the Mobile County Jail. It was very overcrowded and filthy. I wasn't used to being around people and having to get in line and wait on my food, store, or medical. Some of the horrors I'd only heard about I was now seeing. The drugs and killings are not nearly as bad as in years past. The sex deviants and homosexuals were everywhere. I did have more freedom outside but nothing to look forward to.

I signed up for the Honor Dorm. I'd heard good and bad things about it, but I wanted more than general population had to offer. About seven months later I was accepted into the Honor Dorm. It is by far a lot cleaner, quiet, and inmates are more respectful. There are two libraries, five TV's, five CD players (which I'd never heard before), and around twenty computers with all kinds of programs on them. There are self-improvement classes, faith classes, and even computer and Spanish classes. You can do arts and crafts work out here and there are picnic tables on the side of the building. A professor teaches a victimology class and we get religious visitors out here. I've been in here about a year now, and it's by far a better place to live than population. It gets crowded at times with 174 people, but self-improvement in the Honor Dorm is unlimited.

I'm even learning how to type and work on and build my own computer. I signed up for the computer class and the Spanish class. I only have about two weeks left of my second semester. In about another year I'll be a permanent party and eligible for the family eat out.

From death row to the Honor Dorm is a definite improvement in my life. It will help me to prepare for freedom one day. I hope that will be soon. . . .

Essay 2: Population to the Honor Dorm

I have never written an essay. But I hope to show the positive things that have happen [sic] to me since I have moved out here in 5 (honor) dorm.

Where to start? Let me go back to about 4 years ago when I first remember Capt. P. coming into 2 cell on a Sat. morning about 8:00 a.m. calling out a bunch *of people's name [sic] and telling them to get ready to move to 3 cell that the honor dorm for Holman was fixing to start up. I believe that is how I remember it starting*

I also remember seeing who was moving out of 2 cell and seeing that most of the people moving out were child molesters, rats, catch-outs, and most of the weakest class of people here at Holman who usually had a hard time living in population. Also notice that I said almost everyone that was moving was a rat, catch-out, child molester. Not everyone, just almost.

And also, I never knew or could conceive that these same people who I considered weak and beneath me [sic]. I never knew that 4 years later that I would be living out here in the honor dorm with these same people and thanking God that I am out here with these people.

I have been in prison for over 29 years. If I had known how good this honor dorm was I would have been with those first people who pioneered the honor dorm here at Holman. Prison will not be any better than this honor dorm. Especially for life without parole. It's quiet, clean, no dick-jackers to contend with. You don't have to worry about someone stabbing you in your sleep. Or having to stab someone else for disrespecting you 20 different times a day. My spiritual life is 100 percent better. I love these classes, thinking for a change—real good. Overall having to be in prison won't get any better than the honor dorm.

The whole Holman prison itself has changed. Like Warden Culliver said, Holman Unit has gone through a complete culture change. And the honor dorm has helped do it. Less stabbings, sandwich shop, irons, and ironing boards.

That's another thing, my opinion and attitude toward Mr. Culliver has changed from one of believing him to be a racist, sorry-ass warden. My attitude has changed to one of respect for Warden Culliver. He has a good plan for us here at Holman. He is a smart administrator. And from the newsletters that I read, Warden Culliver has a spiritual side to him. Hence, his administrating ability.

I am just amazed at how I used to think about things a year ago. I moved in the honor dorm Jan. will be 1 year. Today is 12/21/03. And as I sit here writing this essay, I am just amazed. And I thank God for being here. When I first learned that I had to write a 2,000-word essay. I was intimidated. But, once I checked into it, I found out it didn't have to be perfect or formal. Cause this is the first time in my life that I have wrote [sic] an essay. And I find that it is therapeutic as I write and think on what to write.

I can really see the Lord out here. We have our religious TV. What a blessing. We have spiritual classes. One on or really two on Mon. One Muslim class on Mon. morning and one Catholic class in the evening. There is plenty of private places to pray at. Especially these TV rooms out here. They have plywood partitions separating TV room A, B, and C. Which makes it real private. Especially comparing it to regular population. . . .

Check this out: As I write this essay right now, I can pause and look around out here in the honor dorm and see 3 TV's on: two muted and one play out. And hear how quiet it is. That is a blessing. Especially when I compare it to how it would be inside the TV rooms inside the camp: loud, very loud. Man. This is only some of the things that I am grateful for. . . .

Me and Big A met about 7 years ago. We have been up together about that long. There is no doubt about it I would not have made it out here in population this long without me having Big A to care for. And man, how I have grown in the Lord by having a big brother–little brother relationship with Big A and for the last 2 years my little brother Ray.

But back to Big A first: Man when I first met him he was so little in size; I mean little! 5 foot 6 in., 110 lb., 21 years old. He looked like a 14-year-old kid. And God! In a world like this prison [main population] Big A was gator bait to the homosexuals here. . . . And I remember telling him then 7 years ago, "Brother, we won't last 2 months together here in population. The odds are stacked up against us. So be ready. Cause the first stinking S.O.B. who puts his hands on you or disrespects you. You are going to have to make your stand as a man. And stab him or them whoever it is. . . ." So on we went surviving in a mad world full of insane people. The Lord being our guide while we faced danger everyday. . . .

Anyway the above is just a hint at the blessings that the Lord has given me with Big A. We have been in the honor dorm almost one year. Big A has gained 15 to 20 pounds. He weighs 165 lbs. and gaining. I am so thankful to the Lord for Big A and very proud of him to see and hear him and listen to him and thank the Lord for letting him grow in to a good strong man who has a personal relationship with Jesus Christ and has a sound mind and good spiritual inner man. Me and Big A talk more about the Lord out here than we ever did in regular population. Again it is the peaceful environment that the Lord has placed me and Big A in that allows us to worship Him and be thankful. Yes! Thank you Lord for Big A in my life and for us being in the honor dorm so that we do have a better environment to worship you. . . .

The inmates writing the first two essays have been sentenced to life without parole. Over half of the honor dorm has this sentence. Life without parole in Alabama and most other states *means* life without parole. An inmate at Holman once told me that this punishment is like being buried alive in a coffin. For these men, prison is their home.

Both inmates have been in prison over twenty-five years. This is longer than many readers have spent in their respective communities. The men compare and contrast life inside and outside the honor dorm. Drug and alcohol abuse, homosexual intimidation, and violent relationships are common in general population. The kind of safety and security we have in our own residences are absent there. They write that the honor dorm is an oasis where they find protection.

Both men describe opportunities for self-improvement in the honor dorm. The ability to practice one's faith in a quiet and peaceful space is valued. Personal advancement by taking classes and developing computer skills is appreciated. But more importantly they portray changes in attitudes toward people and transformation in interpersonal relationships. Before entering the honor dorm, the inmate in the second essay saw its inmate founders and the warden in negative terms—one group is weak and at the bottom of the inmate pecking order. The warden is a racist. In the honor dorm the inmate's attitudes change. He is thankful that the inmate founders are part of his community. He sees the warden as a smart and talented administrator. The relationship between this inmate and his friend Big A in general population is based on survival and escape through drugs, but in the honor dorm, they have an opportunity to explore a deeper friendship based on mentoring and shared values

The first essay is distinct because the writer lived on death row for twenty-six years. Jail and early prison conditions, particularly death row, are deplorable. He is exasperated and cynical about Alabama courts. He does not speak of his crime, and he has not experienced the meaning of justice.

The inmate in the second essay gives details about his spiritual beliefs. His writing is agitated when he talks about the God he turns to for protection in general population. In the honor dorm he turns to spiritual teachings for personal growth. Do you think these two inmates are the same men who arrived in prison over twenty-five years ago?

Now let's see what two other residents wrote.

Essay 3: Untitled

This essay will be about my life to date in general. I remember growing up in Titusville, Fl. around the age of five. What stands out most in my memories is Cape Canaveral and the Kennedy Space Center. I remember not only visiting the Kennedy Space Center on school field trips, but also being blessed enough to see the shuttle a minute or two after launch clear the trees on the horizon. My family and many neighbors used to take lawn chairs on our roofs to watch the shuttle launch. We couldn't have been more than forty-five miles away. We could even see the American flag painted on the side of the shuttle because it was so big and we were so close. I was able to see three or four launches over a five- or six-year period from about 1980 through 1986. Some time in 1986 we moved to south Florida. I was in the fifth grade, elementary school, and the Challenger space shuttle was about to launch, with Christa McCullough, the first schoolteacher to attempt a space flight. We were watching the take-off in our classroom when the Challenger exploded, killing everybody on board. I will never forget the sadness that all of us felt. Especially me who had an intimate attachment to the space shuttle and the space program in Florida in general. For me, life was no longer a perfect thing. Life didn't always turn out good. Bad things could happen. I think that might have been the first time as a child that I realized that.

It wasn't long after that that I entered the sixth grade and started middle school. I went from one teacher for all subjects to a different teacher for each individual subject. I was unable to adjust to that type of schedule. To further complicate matters, my dad, because of work, was forced to move us a couple of times a year, every year, for several years on end. It seemed impossible to stay focused on school when I knew I would not be there long. It seemed like I would just get settled in socially and we would be doing it all over again. After failing the seventh grade it was time to do something about it. . . .

I voluntarily entered military school in Melbourne, Fl. The name of the school was Florida Air Academy. I stayed there for seventh and eighth grade and other than some minor rebellion, I was making average grades and doing good overall. It was everything I needed except for one small problem. It was an all boys' school and I just turned fifteen in my eighth-grade year. I could have entered high school and stayed at Florida Air Academy until I graduated the twelfth grade. Because I had a choice I naturally chose to go back to public school where the girls were. It has proven to be one of my all-time stupidest decisions ever made. I was now living in Texas, Corinth to be exact, and that is where I started my ninth-grade year back at public school. Needless to say I failed my ninth-grade year. Then we moved to Birmingham, Alabama, in the summer of 1989. I started my ninth-grade year again in public school. By 1991 I was sixteen years old and failing so badly that my dad offered for me to withdraw from school if I would get a job. I quickly agreed. I never ended up with a job and I slowly but surely began hanging out with other kids that were rebellious. I was doing nothing positive with my life. Dropping out of school was beyond stupid. I continued doing drugs, partying, getting in fights, and doing stupid things in general. After a couple of years of this I finally decided to get my GED. I succeeded at that and finally got a meager job. I was eighteen years old, engaged to be married, had a job, and had a small apartment of my own. Life seemed to be slowly but surely shaping up. Wrong! My past would soon come back to haunt me. . . . My "friends" were still stopping by and trying to get me to go out. More and more I was turning them down. Then one night a young fourteen-year-old girl my fiancée and I knew called us saying five guys had raped her. When she told us who they were we realized that they were some people we used to be friends with. I decided I was going to take matters into my own hands like a damn idiot. I was going to make them pay.

To make a long story short, I rounded up some friends and got a gun. Then I went to confront them. After a short confrontation in a parking lot, in which insults were hurled back and forth, everybody seemingly dispersed. Totally unaware, I was faced with the biggest decision of my life. Do I leave it at that or do I let them know that they raped the wrong girl? So, faced with the biggest decision in my life, I chose wrong. I decided I was going to shoot in the apartment they were staying in and scare the hell out of them. And scare them I did. One of them was even killed. In a few seconds I went from a reckless teenager to an eighteen-year-old kid facing capital murder charges and the possibility of the death penalty. It would be years later before I truly realized the extent of my actions. . . . Even as I write this essay I am serving a sentence of life without the possibility of parole. It is amazing that if no one had been shot that I would still have been just a reckless teenager. But someone was shot and died. So now I am a violent criminal. What do you think?

It's 1993, I'm eighteen-years-old, and in the county jail awaiting trial for capital murder. Because of our justice system, I had no time to reflect on what I had done, as I mentioned earlier, and instead I was immediately forced to find a way to avoid guilt. I mean sure, I knew I was guilty, and if taking responsibility had been accepted, I would have. The system forced me to fight instead. Not that it did any good, mind you.

I ended up at twenty years old going to Kilby for six months, then West Jeffer-son for three months, then St. Clair for twelve months, and Holman for the last seven years and counting. I immediately started losing weight and letting depression take control of my life. I basically let my mind and body slowly deteriorate.

When I arrived at Holman I immediately started doing marijuana and mor-phine. I can only say that God led me through somehow, some way. Through seven years of doing drugs and standing up for myself in prison I never got a dis-ciplinary or a citation. I am writing this essay because God finally led me to the honor dorm. Since I have become an honor dorm member I have not done any drugs for over eight months, I quit smoking six months ago, and my life is more spiritually oriented. And you know what? I have never felt better or freer. I was a slave to my habits and addictions. Every week that goes by in the honor dorm sees me as a more mature individual. . . .

It is amazing how many blessings appear in your life when you give up self and try your best to submit your will to God. I mean my dad and I are closer than we have ever been, and I have a new mom and a new little sister. My other sister just moved closer to me with her husband and my niece and nephew. My cousin and I have become best friends. I have a girlfriend who has two beautiful kids. I have some of the best friends a man could have right here at Holman prison. I have gained sixty-five pounds. I am becoming more mature, more responsible, and closer to being a mentor.

The only thing left to a person in my circumstances is to strive to grow and ma-ture into a better person. To learn from my mistakes in the past and not let them define who I am today or tomorrow. I imagine that this is every person's goal, but I am just beginning to realize that it is mine. . . .

I don't think that any man is truly whole or complete until he has a wife and children. At least that is what I pray for. That is the loss I feel more than any other loss. It is almost akin to a physical loss so painful it is. I can't even begin to ex-plain just how painful it is. . . .

If per chance someone is actually reading this essay, I can only hope that I have succeeded in painting some kind of picture for you, however vague. Maybe you will gain at least a general idea of my life up to now. I'm sure you are bored enough if you have made it this far so imagine if I would have really gone into detail. You would have probably never made it this far.

I only lack 209 words to finish this essay so please give me a little more of your precious time. After all I have said I must wonder how you view my circumstances.

Do you think that I should spend the rest of my life in prison? If I would have made a different choice when I committed my crime would I have eventually committed some other crime?

Please make no mistake—of course I think about the life that is lost. The family of the victim. The community that was shocked with a violent crime. My family's loss. But it is hard for me to feel the level of remorse I know I should, because I never saw anybody get shot. My memories are dramatic, but not as dramatic as if I would have seen the effects of my actions. I didn't see the victim get shot. I didn't see any blood. I didn't see him die. What I did see was a window with the blinds down. Then a couple of hours later I saw the police pulling guns on me and arresting me. They say, "You just killed someone." And my mind could not comprehend that because I never saw the results of my actions. So it is hard for me to think I should never have a second chance. Even being 100 percent honest with myself I think I should be able to earn a second chance. For now I can't. . . .

Essay 4: Enhancing Growth and Development

Throughout my entire bid, I've noticed a change in a majority of my ways and actions. Not just a normal change, but also a change for the best.

I've been practicing self-discipline a lot due to the fact of my current situation, and my hunger to become more mature and better educated.

Being a young black male, from a violent neighborhood, a low-income family, and negative peers, has caused many of whom I encountered myself with to develop doubt about me, and stereotype my character. Maybe it was because of a character that I presented, I don't know. But I do know that I got tired of being told that I wasn't able to do this or that.

After getting kicked out of school in the eleventh grade, I never put up a fight to try to go back because I felt like I knew enough. But in reality, I didn't really know shit. All I did know was how to run the streets, rob, sell drugs, and cheat on women. My ignorance caused me to lose focus on the right path in life.

After two and a half or three years in the state prison, reality set in on me again. I sat down in my cell here at Holman Correctional Facility's Segregation Unit, and realized that it was time for me to make a change in my life. I had to humble myself and swallow my pride. I learned to accept knowledge and wisdom from individuals that I never thought would exist in my circumstance.

I invested a lot of my spare time in reading and writing. This helped me develop a better understanding about life, people, places, and the reason they exist.

Once becoming conscious of life, I developed a thinking pattern that was zero tolerant to foolishness. I acknowledged the fact that I didn't have any room left to take anything for granted. I realized that life was more serious than I thought it was. And in order to survive life in prison, you have to realize that life out of prison still exists.

I was determined to become a better person as well as a better influence on people that looked up to me. I read all of the books that I am able to comprehend. And try my best to share the knowledge with everyone that I encounter myself with. I take all of the positive advice that I can and apply it to my daily activities. Trying my best, and doing all that I can to try to become a better person not just to others, but to myself as well. Because even I got tired of looking into the mirror everyday and seeing the same dummy.

So after doing my reading and studying everything that caught my attention, I felt different, I felt the thrill of wanting to test my intellect. I got to the point where I would pull up on almost anyone and just start asking questions. I felt so strong in the mind and and in my heart. I felt like I knew everything again.

That's when it happened. I knew everything but the right thing at the right time. I ran into a point in my life that I now remember as the "great depression." It was about a month ago, but I can still remember it like it was yesterday. It was the first time in my life that I had the opportunity to take my GED test. From the first second I sat down in front of that test till the last second before I got up; I just knew that I had passed it without a shadow of a doubt. But when I received my results, my whole life changed again. I failed, by only three points.

After doing an introspection very carefully, I realize that I wasn't humble enough. I still had my pride in my mouth and hadn't swallowed it yet. So now I'm back in the lab again, working even harder on my growth and development.

Maybe somewhere in my near future, I'll be proud of myself, and many others will be proud of me as well. Because one thing I know for sure is that positive education always creates elevation.

Essays three and four are by two people from very different backgrounds. One grew up in a middle-class home and the other in poverty. Both had trouble coping with school and became high school dropouts. The honor dorm provides an opportunity to continue their education in order to retrieve what they didn't learn in "kindergarten."

The inmate in the third essay refers to the accountability component of restorative justice and how it contrasts with retributive justice. The writer notes that given the adversarial nature of the judicial system, he had little if any opportunity to think about the harm he caused to the victim and his surviving family. Furthermore, the restorative environment, with its emphasis on repairing relationships, gives this honor dorm resident the opportunity to build strong positive bonds with his own family members. It may bother you that he has the opportunity to build a relationship with his father, while the parents of the young man he killed do not have this prospect. If this inmate could, however, he would do anything possible to reduce the tremendous pain experienced by his victim's loved ones. Research shows that for some family survivors, information about the circumstances surrounding the crime that only the offender knows provides a degree of comfort and relief.[4]

The last essay is a description of another type of relationship—the relationship that inmates in the honor dorm have with their pets. This relationship entails both responsibilities and rewards.

Essay 5: The Honor Cats

Lady and Tom are the honor cats, Lady a black and white house cat approximately eight months old and about twenty pounds. Tom is a black and tiger-striped gray, the same age as Lady and about five pounds heavier. Both cats are approximately the same age, being born sometime in September of last year. These two felines have been quite an addition to the Honor Dorm. It seems that everyone has accepted the cats as the dorm pets. It was first thought that the administration would get rid of them, but they have prevailed and now seem like part of the Honor Dorm fixture. They are all over the yard at any time of the day and night, they have a box in the utility tunnel they enter and exit through a hole in the wall.

The two people that seem to have the most control over the cats are Tim C. and Darryl S. They are the ones who train, feed, and doctor on the cats when it's necessary. The cats' diet consists of just about anything, egg, milk, spam, chicken, anything served in Holman's chow hall and even some things brought off the store and the sandwich line. They do not lack being pampered. The cats are growing older with each day and they are beginning to range away from the dorm, a little farther each day. At night they seem to hang closer to home. Tom had an incident recently with some razor wire, the razor wire won. Tom had a hole in his side, his ear almost cut off and his long tail has changed shape. Tim C. doctored on him, stitches and all, duct-taped him, and turned him loose. Tom looked a sight with duct tape wrapped around his head and neck. He's looking better now, but still has a way to go. Lady seems like she is in heat, I mean a lot of other cats have been making late night visits; Tim C. has started locking her up at night. I think it's possible that in the near future, we will be writing about honor kittens. Lady and Tom seem to be good for me and the other guys, because they are so frisky and playful and anybody can pet them. They are used to humans and unafraid of them. The whole camp seems to have accepted the "Honor Cats" and everyone likes to play with them. Darryl S. will whistle and the cats will come, he's the only one that they will do that for. The cats thrive on attention and they get plenty of that.

The cats have been trained not to roam the dormitory area; they have been to that area once or twice, but after a couple of spankings by Tim C. they figured out that the dormitory area was off limits. They now only come to the front lobby and at time easing a step or two into the TV room. Their favorite place seems to be the information desk chair. They jump up on the chair and sleep, sometimes both at the same time, sometimes we'll pet them while they are there. The cats seem to be good for everyone. People just sit and watch the cats play chase and catch bugs. The cats eat pretty good. They sometimes get sandwich shop food, canteen food, and they get regular meals of egg and milk from the kitchen every morning. It is remembered when you could hold the cats in the palm of your hand. Watching them grow up is something. The cats sometimes play stalking games with mice and birds. Lady made her first kill to our knowledge. She batted a bird out of flight, pounced on him and then carried him to Tom to finish him off, but someone took the kill and put it out of reach. I am sure that there will be others.

Both of the cats have fleas; there is talk of trying to get some medication. One of the keepers will find a way. Some people think that the cats should not be out there; some people think that we need more of them.

It is surprising that the administration has not had any real input concerning the cats. I am sure that in the future, some rule or another will affect the Honor Cats. Lady is showing signs that she is going to have kittens. No telling how many kittens that she will have and the effect it will have on the status of their present habitat.

There are plenty of cats at Holman. The Honor Cats are the only ones that humans can get close to. The other cats are wild and run at the approach of any humans. They usually ravage the garbage when they get the chance. These cats seem *to know when mealtime is and when the garbage will be taken out. We have been told that the cat population is close to a hundred, and they roam over the whole camp, mostly at night. Cats have just about eliminated the mice and rat population here. They're still here but they are no way as plentiful as they used to be. Someone said that the administration has plans to get rid of some of the cats; the method of elimination is undecided.*

I don't think that Lady and Tom have anything to worry about. They have made everyone love them, and I think that they have made a home. There they are now running and chasing each other and all eyes are on them, "The W. C. HOLMAN HONOR CATS."

Prison contributes to life without goals where an inmate experiences depression and is suspended in limbo. Alternatively, it can lead to unrealistic goals such as a prisoner with a sixth-grade education who thinks he can be a surgeon after his release. The goal statement is one of many tools used in the honor dorm to meet the inmate's need for discipline, direction, motivation, and a sense of reality. It gives the inmate structure and the opportunity to be accountable by stating simple goals and achieving them. During the third and fourth semesters inmates complete a goal accomplishment sheet. After becoming a permanent resident, inmates write a goal summary every six months. These goals charts and summaries are reviewed by a three-member accountability panel. Most turn out well, but if the requirement is not taken seriously, the resident is asked by his fellows to redo the assignment. The following examples are gleaned from goal sheets and summaries on file in the honor dorm.

Goal Statement 1

1. *To better myself.*

   The main thing that I've been doing to accomplish this goal is going to classes, looking to get something out of them and to apply it to my everyday life. Some of them has [sic] been very helpful such as crime impact. That class has made me look at my own situation differently.

2. *To better my relationship with my kids.*

   I've written my daughters to apologize for not being there for them. I also write them once a month even when they don't write me back until later on. I stress to them that I love them and I'm here to listen to anything that's on their mind. Some times are better than others in our communication, but I feel that it's pretty good now. This has been a long-term goal that I'll have to continue to work on while I'm in this place.

These are my short- and long-term goals that I think that I'll never accomplish but can always get better.

3. *Be the best mentor that I can be.*

With the mentoring program we've started I have become much closer to my mentee by spending time with him in study hall and outside it. We have good understanding and talk about other things than him getting his GED. I do homework myself to keep it on a level that it can be done and sometimes we do it together. If nothing else, I believe that we've become good friends.

Goal Statement 2

My initial goals were: 1. Re-establishing better contact with my family and friends on the outside. 2. Return to writing home more often. 3. Break associations with the prison friendships I had formed (the ones rooted in homosexuality, drug use, and drinking). 4. Return back to work in the hobby shop with the attitude of not allowing it to become a God worshiping experience. 5. It was and remains that these changes would help me in my prayers and efforts to challenge myself to change for the better.

Now, nearly three years later I am happy and encouraged to say, my relationship with my family and friends on the outside has improved much. I try to call home at least twice a month and I respond more promptly to my mail. Plus I am presently in contact with a nephew and niece I haven't seen in over twenty years.

On another note I am happy to say I haven't had a homosexual experience with another person here since coming to the Honor Dorm. It wasn't easy, but I feel good about not giving in to the feelings when they occur.

I am yet wrestling with hurt feelings in regards to how some of the Honor Dorm residents who were in leadership positions attempted to take my confessed past in this area and paint me to be a person who lives and breathes homosexual thoughts. In that I was much hurt.

Financially I have been blessed with more. I try to use my blessings now for healthy giving.

With drinking and smoking pot, I have made some good gains. I have taken an occasional drink, but nothing like before coming to the Honor Dorm when I used to drink every chance I got. Plus smoke pot.

I see shooting dope now as crazy and I am happy to say I haven't did [sic] that since coming to the Honor Dorm.

Most of my gains came when I found the strength to come to the Honor Dorm and cut my contact with a lot of my old friends I used to hang out with.

I am not as popular among them now, but I don't really care. In fact I like it. I just won't share that with them.

I'm working more in the leather shop and am seeing a lot of good as a result. But now I feel I need to better my work hours with a healthy balance, because I feel I am working too much. So I am working on that.

All in all, the Honor Dorm has been a life-changing blessing for me, and even in light of the up and down and disagreements along the way, I still feel like these are the best group of guys I have lived with since my incarceration of nearly twenty-four years. I look forward to continuing with the experience of this program.

Goal Statement 3

Better communication with my son and ex-wife.

I finally got a letter and pictures from my wife, but still have not heard from my son. My wife will write every so often and I haven't been able to get any-thing out of my son. I'm still trying to make it work.

Supporting myself.

I am doing more and more in the leather shop to try to add to my tag plant pay. It's a slow process, but it is moving along. I am doing a little work for oth-ers up there to help me and them.

Better communications with dorm residents.

I am doing a lot better in this area. I talk to more than I did but I don't think it is possible to get into being friends with everyone.

Better relationship with God.

As I have written before, this is a hard one. I still pray but don't get into the Bible the way I should. I'm not sure that I will totally accomplish this goal.

Organizations and individuals in the free world make goals to help them advance toward a desired state. Rarely do we think of inmates having goals.

The goals of honor dorm residents are simple and straightforward but by no means easy to achieve. They require discipline, diligence, and new ways of thinking. Better relationships with friends, family, and a higher power are often priorities. Giving up old behaviors and relationships that inmates think are unhealthy are cited such as drinking, drugging, smoking, and in some cases homosexual behavior. Interestingly, one inmate struggles with being a "workaholic." Many of the following goal statements address similar themes as the men express their struggle to overcome a "prison mentality."

Goal Statement 4
Goals were and remain:

1. *Establishing better communication with my family and friends (on the outside).*
2. *Challenge myself to stop using drugs and participating in homosexual activities.*
3. *Put a sincere effort into re-establishing my relationship with God and his will for my life (in prison or out).*
4. *Disassociate myself from the peoples and negative activities I was hanging around with in the general population.*
5. *I also sought a break from spending so much time in the leather shop chasing money to afford drugs and homosexual activities.*

It's nearly five years later now since I came to the Honor Dorm and took on the challenge of the above-mentioned goals; in the area of establishing better communication with my family and friends (on the outside), thanks to God, that desire, and the efforts I have put into it, I'm happy to share that those relationships are much better. I'm back in touch with my family and friends and since starting the effort I have been blessed with first time contact with four additional family members out-of-state. In short it's better than five years ago.

Concerning my number two goal, "challenge myself to stop using drugs and participating in homosexual activities," boy! I really had to give those two to God, because alone the challenge was too much for me. But I'm thankful to say now five years later "they were foolish activities of my past." . . .

Concerning my third goal, "Putting a sincere effort into re-establishing my relationship with God and his will for my life (in prison or out)," it has been a walk with challenging myself and my interaction with others. I don't feel, no let me put it this way, it's impossible to seek God or allow yourself to be susceptible to his will, if you are dishonest about it, so to speak.

With dishonesty travel a lot of negativities as with truth travel a lot of positives, God being one of those positives. So in short, it has been rewarding and a good friend traveling in that spirit in my thoughts and actions.

Concerning my fourth goal, "disassociating myself from the peoples and negative activities I was hanging around with in the general population," being in the Honor Dorm has made it easier for me in that area. Because here the entire dorm is centered around positive change. The guys here are not sitting around drinking, getting high, or doing whatever comes to mind, so to speak. All of which is good and a friend to a person who is trying to get away from the prison life of yesterday, so to speak.

So in making the decision to come to the Honor Dorm, I also decided that if my associates weren't about to try something different in a positive sense I could do without their company.

It wasn't real hard, because the lifestyle we were living had nearly killed me. So nowadays I try to encourage them to give the Honor Dorm a try, but I have no desire to live with them or go back through all the craziness we went through. No way.

Concerning my fifth goal, "getting out of the leather shop chasing money to afford a crazy prison life". That's in the past, like breaking free from one hold helped me to break free from another, so to speak. I'm not into the activities of my past, so I don't need the money to afford them. It's just that simple. . . .

Goal Statement 5

Upon entering the honor dorm I hadn't created an agenda for some specific goals. Praise be to Allah the honor dorm made goal-setting a part of its curriculum. This caused me to zero in on some specifics. I selected enhancing my knowledge of the Arabic language, concentrating more on my honor dorm teaching skill, and bridging the gap between my ex-wife and son.

Well it seems as if I've been successful except the gap between my son and I. I write him and send cards. I get indirect responses through Susan (my ex-wife). I don't feel as if I have failed. I feel as if the task is more complicated than I expected. I will never abandon the effort to rekindle a love my son and I once shared. My Arabic has greatly improved and this I attribute to the computer pro-

gram Alim we got in sometime ago. My teaching efforts I personally feel have also greatly improved and this is due mainly to giving it more attention, increasing the amount, and praying for a stronger teaching performance. My advancement in knowledge since entering the honor dorm has strengthened me all the way around. The rewards are many in this dorm if a person can see them and capitalize from them. . . .

Goal Statement 6

My goal this semester is to try to be the best Community Manager I can be. Also to try to implement the positive attitude myself and the other Community Managers along with all the department heads and assistant have been going over with each other.

I see my road to this accomplishment as having to go through different avenues. Such as being available to all residents as the need *occurs. There are going to be times when the chain of command will have to be set aside when the greater good of the community is served.*

Also, we as Community Managers are going to have to keep informing the dept. heads, Sr. Coordinators, that some decisions are theirs to make, just to keep us updated on situations. By doing this we give the other residents in leadership positions the opportunities they need to grow into their positions and share responsibilities.

And most important, from all points is to try not to become over-frustrated to the point where we lose sight of the main goal: to move the dorm forward in a positive manner. Hopefully, if we keep lines of communication open we will continue to make progress toward the goal of a safe, harmonious, and honorable place for people to grow.

Goal Statement 7

 # 1—Learn typing skills.
 # 2—Learn how to operate a computer.
 # 3—Social skills.
 # 4—Communication skills.

What decided me to become a member of the Holman Unit Honor Dorm, was after a move from Dorm 3 out to Dorm 5, members were talking about all of the computers they had. Prior to the move, I was tempted to enter the Honor Dorm almost from the start back in October 1999, but I held back because I wanted to learn and observe what the Honor Dorm was going to be like. This is due to years of being incarcerated, and still "stuck" on the prison mentality. Anyway, I did observe some good advantages of being an Honor Dorm member and made the move.

Since I've been in the Honor Dorm from May 2003 to the present, November 2005, I got on the computers and I am able to type, at least more than I knew before. The basics are easy, it's just a matter of time before I'll know all of the ins and outs. In the process of getting to the typing program on the computer, I have learned more on how to operate a computer, yet I still got a ways to go to become totally literate with computer skills. I'm waiting to see if the hours change on the class that —— teaches on computers, cause right now the time conflicts with my assigned DOC job. It'll work out.

My social skills have gotten better, due to my duty as a coordinator, because for at least six hours a week, I have to work with other members of the Honor Dorm in a "head-of-the-household" type of position, which takes tact and diplomacy dealing with other "convicts," and not be too controlling making sure the dorm runs smoothly, such as: workers on duty getting their jobs done; quietness; any kind of conflicts between members; plus working with a DOC officer if they need a member to go somewhere and/or make announcements.

All of the above have bettered me on communication skills, and working with others that I can leave prison with and use out in society. I am grateful for being able to get this opportunity to become a member of the Honor Dorm here at Holman, which all-in-all will make me a more sociable and productive member of society, instead of a person with the low-down prison stinking thinking.

LIVING WITH HONOR

Some of the men in the honor dorm grew up learning how to live with honor, but sometimes teachings fall by the wayside, perhaps under the influence of peers or drug and alcohol addiction. Others due to their upbringing don't have a clue. The honor dorm offers inmates an opportunity to regain a sense of discipline, respect, and honesty. Restorative values such as accountability, healing, relationship building, and responsibility to community provide a framework for building the capacity to live with honor.

Honor is a subjective term. Some people associate it with heroic figures. In the general prison population an honorable person is a "stand-up guy" who keeps his own council, is not a pushover, will lend you a hand when needed, and can be depended on. Loyalty and solidarity are part of the prison honor code.

In the honor dorm the situation shifts so that each individual is given the opportunity to explore what it means to live with honor. This is done in a structured environment, but nevertheless one that leaves the resident a substantial opportunity to grow personally. The honor dorm is not unlike a college or university honors program where additional resources (albeit donated in Holman honor dorm) are offered to a unique population to enable its members to access special courses and facilities for enhanced learning.[5] In the honor dorm character-building is part of this process and starts at the most basic level.

Living with honor is not a stagnant concept at Holman. It will change with the resident's level of development. There is no one blueprint, but there is a philosophy and programmatic element designed to promote living with honor.

Let's look at some examples of what living with honor means to a few dorm residents. For one man it means doing something that is meaningful and seen as worthy by others. Given the isolation of prison, this is not easy to realize. To another resident it means living a life where you always give more than you receive. For another it means going as much as possible beyond the call of duty. In his words, it also involves "establishing a presence and setting a precedent." Others equate honor with being true to yourself, trust, respect, and integrity.

Some of the men equate honor with their living arrangements in the dorm. This consists of respecting the rules of the community, contributing to the community, sharing what they have learned, living in an environment where the inmates govern themselves, and resolving issues in a peaceful manner. No residents I talked with specifically mentioned repairing harms to their victims as a sign of living with honor. Perhaps this is because inmate-victim contact is forbidden in the Alabama corrections system. Education that focuses more directly on the relationship between victim and offender has been a relatively new development in the honor dorm and will be discussed in more detail in chapter 6.

An inmate told me that his life before coming to the honor dorm could be described by a tattoo he saw on the arm of a biker. It read, "Sworn to Fun and Loyal to None." Many honor dorm residents accept the challenge of moving from a self-centered approach to life to living in relationship with others in community. The circle process described in the next chapter explains a mechanism for doing this.

NOTES

1. "Standard Operating Procedures," Holman Correctional Facility, Faith-Based Restorative Justice Honor Community, November 15, 2004, unpublished, 2. For a description of the evolution of faith-based prison units, see Jonathan Burnside with Nancy Loucks, Joanne R. Adler, and Gerry Rose, *My Brother's Keeper: Faith Based Units in Prisons* (Devon, U.K.: 2005).

2. Paul Gendreau, "The Principles of Effective Intervention with Offenders," in *Choosing Corrections Options That Work: Defining the Demand and Evaluating the Supply*, ed. Alan T. Harland (Thousand Oaks, Calif.: Sage, 1996), 117–30.

3. Maria R. Volpe and Staci Strobl, "Restorative Justice Responses to Post-September 11 Hate Crimes: Potential and Challenges," *Conflict Resolution Quarterly* 22, no. 4 (Summer 2005): 527–35.

4. Howard Zehr, *Changing Lenses: A New Focus for Crime and Justice* (Scottsdale, Pa.: Herald Press, 2005), 46–47.

5. Bridget T. Long, "Attracting the Best: The Use of Honors Programs to Compete for Students," 2005. (Chicago: Spencer Foundation. Eric Reproduction Service No. ED465355), 1–25.

4

Learning to Play with Others

This peacemaking circle is recommended to resolve a conflict between two residents. Tom allegedly disrespected Larry at the drinking fountain.

—*Example of a conflict in Holman Faith-Based Restorative Justice Honor Dorm*

Learning how to get along with others is part of life. It holds true whether you are five or fifty years old. Conflicts commonly arise in families, the workplace, and communities, and if conflict-resolution skills are not used, the situation quickly deteriorates. Many Holman residents are in prison because a disagreement escalated into a violent conflict. Furthermore, most of them have long prison sentences for using violence to get what they wanted, whether it was money, sex, or revenge. Conflict resolution skills can be learned, even in a maximum-security prison. In fact, corrections facilities are more in need of nonviolent problem-solving skills than any other institution in America.

In prison settings, small conflicts frequently arise because men are confined to close quarters and deprived of their freedom, privacy, and autonomy. Prisoners with poor dispute-resolution skills often resort to physical violence. If apprehended they are sentenced to lock-up (segregation) for a period of time and released to general population where the cycle begins again. At Holman Correctional Facility, inmates released from segregation sign a form agreeing not to resume the conflict. However, since the underlying causes of the problem are not addressed, resentments often resurface and lead to another assault.

Restorative justice offers principles for peaceful conflict resolution. The honor dorm uses the restorative approach to prevent nonviolent conflicts from escalating into violent ones. The dorm's core curriculum conceptualizes and contextualizes restorative principles of respect, connectedness, mutual responsibility, and healing. The curriculum of four six-month semesters applies these concepts to different situations, particularly those relevant to a prison environment. While conflicts that become physical are grounds for removal from the dorm, the residents have a well-developed structure for handling nonviolent disputes, including those when another honor dorm resident has been victimized.

Peacemaking circles are used to resolve honor dorm conflicts, and are at the heart of restorative practice in the unit. In an atmosphere of respect and concern these circles bring men together to talk honestly about difficult issues. The circle uses a structured format adopted from aboriginal practice and today it is used in a variety of criminal justice settings. In Canada Judge Barry Stuart introduced circles to sentence juveniles. Judge Tracy McCooey runs sentencing circles for adults in Montgomery, Alabama. Circles of support help formerly incarcerated persons adjust to the community. However, it is unusual for prisons to use circles for conflict resolution.

Honor dorm peacemaking circles at Holman originated with peer review boards. The peer review boards fit the self-governing concept of the faith-based honor dorm where inmates hear cases and impose sanctions on rule violators. With an increasing commitment to restorative justice and a growing awareness of peacemaking circle processes, the dorm's meetings took on the nature of peacemaking circles and began to address behavioral problems and conflicts within the dorm from a restorative perspective.

Eventually the dorm created a department headed by an inmate to organize and implement peacemaking circles. Today peacemaking circles are organized to address conflicts every weekday if needed.

A CULTURE OF VIOLENCE

A major goal of the honor dorm is to create a community based on caring relationships and other pro-social values. This involves building a culture distinct from the prison at large (general population). Prisons vary in their levels of violence. Given prison conditions, it is remarkable that individual and collective violence do not surface more frequently. However, the amount of overt violence, while serious, is overshadowed by the subtle, implied violence that one man communicates to another when he tries to collect a debt, straighten out a homosexual relationship, or feels disrespected. Threats and verbal abuse are daily occurrences, and many times threatening someone with violence is the preferred way to approach a situation. Even the most sophisticated interaction between men carries overtones of violence. Implied violence pervades conversations with the understanding that a violent outcome awaits an unresolved problem. This contributes to a stressful and fearful environment.

A typical event occurred in 2006 in the prison cafeteria. Bert entered the front of the chow line for a second helping instead of taking his place at the end. Another prisoner, Emile, told him this was the wrong thing to do, particularly given the religious beliefs Bert frequently professed to others. Insulted, Bert called Emile "a snitch," an inflammatory and dangerous label in prison. Emile told Bert if he did not apologize he would get a knife and stab him. Bert refused to apologize, repeating the insult. Following through on his threat, Emile left the cafeteria, returned with a homemade weapon (shank), and slit Bert's throat. A number of men witnessed the confrontation, tried to break it up, and got pepper-sprayed when corrections officers arrived on the scene. Fortunately the injured inmate survived.

This is the first and only stabbing involving honor dorm residents in the dorm's seven-year history. Honor dorm residents eat with men in general population. Luckily the stabbing did not take place in the honor dorm or there might have been serious repercussions from the administration. At the time of the assault, Emile lived in the dorm for less than one month and exhibited the convict mentality. Bert lived in the honor dorm for a longer period of time but other residents described his attitude and behavior as irritating—a self-righteous, bullying religiosity. After the incident, an honor dorm resident, Paul, said he wished he had taken Bert to a circle because he saw the problem coming. Bert's behavior seriously irritated Paul on numerous occasions. Paul recognized his responsibility to the help the community prevent violence and knew there was a structure to address the problem. Furthermore, a week after the assault, men in an honor dorm leadership class discussed how similar incidents might be prevented. The residents identified Bert and Emile as "at-risk" individuals and said programs might be developed to give this category of individual special attention. While the assault is tragic, the dorm residents responded positively, emphasizing community responsibility for conflict resolution and violence prevention. According to the dorm's standard operating procedures and prison rules, Bert and Emile were removed from the dorm.

CONFLICT RESOLUTION IN THE HONOR DORM

When men move from the general population to the Faith-Based Restorative Justice Honor Dorm they are exposed to a different culture where respect, accountability, and responsibility are experienced, expected, and modeled. Peacemaking circles are part of an integrated effort to use restorative practices in the dorm. They offer residents an alternative means of resolving conflict and complement an emphasis on community and relationships. The peacemaking circle process is an educational tool as well as a pragmatic means of mediating conflict. It teaches the offender alternatives to violent problem-solving in a hostile environment like prison.

The circle encourages all stakeholders to take responsibility. This includes the immediate parties to the conflict and the circle members representing the dorm community. Practicing respect for all parties is essential, not only for the integrity of the circle, but also as a model to teach respect to others, particularly newcomers. Through dialogue and participatory decision-making, inmates learn how to work with others in the community to peacefully solve their problems. They discover that their actions not only affect those directly involved with the conflict, but also the well being of the entire honor dorm. Dorm residents have shared how they spent most of their lives thinking only of themselves. Realizing how their behavior affects others is a powerful learning experience.

The quotation at the beginning of this chapter introduces us to Tom and Larry, who encounter each other at the drinking fountain in the honor dorm. Larry is angered by his perception of Tom's disrespectful and hostile behavior and completes a form provided by the inmate coordinator on duty. The form explains the incident and "invites" Tom to a peacemaking circle to sort things out. Tom prefers not to attend a circle, but as a requirement for joining the dorm he signed a contract committing to circle attendance should a conflict occur. The peacemaking circle department head reviews the request and decides a circle is warranted. The goal is to confront the problem as quickly as possible before it escalates. There are five permanent circles consisting of four to five inmates appointed to hear conflicts for different days of the week. The offense occurred late Wednesday afternoon so the circle that meets on Thursdays receives the case.

The keeper of the circle is responsible for familiarizing himself with the situation. He summarizes the facts of the case when the circle convenes, but he is not a "judge" or a "lawyer." The participants to the conflict are asked to tell their stories about what happened and how it affected them. Larry reports that it was a very hot day and Tom "pulled up" on him while he was drinking water at the fountain. Tom tugged at his arm and said, "Hey, man. I want some water." Larry got angry. He didn't like Tom "grabbing at his arm" and thought the behavior was disrespectful. Larry responded with, "That's it. I'm gonna take you to a peacekeeping circle, man."

It was Tom's turn to tell his story. He had a different perspective but agreed that it was really hot. He was tremendously thirsty and thought that Larry was taking an awfully long time at the water fountain—"just standing there." He said he simply touched Tom's arm to let him know he was waiting. "Hey, I thought he was gonna take a swing at me." After the two parties tell their stories, five inmates who represent the community in the circle take turns making comments or asking questions. One inmate, Bill, tries to get a better understanding of the situation. "Hey Tom, had you been exercising a lot before you came to the drinking fountain?"

Tom and Larry are then asked to reflect on the situation and suggest what could be done to repair it. Tom immediately apologizes to Larry saying, "I didn't mean you no harm. This is me, 'Tom.'" Larry suggests that since he and Tom share the same spiritual beliefs, they get together for a couple of little prayer meetings. Tom agrees this is a good way to make things right between them.

The circle members take turns suggesting what they think should be done. They like the prayer arrangement, and one community member thinks both men should apologize to the dorm at a weekly community meeting since others witnessed the altercation and talked about it. Both men agree to apologize. The keeper of the circle ends the meeting with a nondenominational prayer. The men shake hands and some trade hugs. The circle secretary records the terms of the agreement and follows up to make sure they are met.

This account shows how circles work as a pragmatic and restorative way to resolve conflict and prevent its escalation. Feelings of anger and frustration are expressed. Seasoned and savvy community members like Bill ask questions rather than give advice. Communication is open but is guided by principles such as respect. Each person in the circle has an opportunity to speak as often as needed, but dominance is avoided. Decisions are made consensually rather than autocratically. Repairing harm and understanding how a "violation" affects another individual and the community as a whole replaces retributive values.

The circle story also illustrates how the process educates. Permanent party residents (those who have completed the honor dorm curriculum over a two-year period) model restorative principles and practices for men entering the circle as participants. According to several men I spoke with, circles vary in quality. When circles function best, their members are nonjudgmental, outcomes are not punitive, storytelling and perspective-taking are used instead of lecture and pontification, and understanding and problem-solving are promoted. Men are encouraged to take responsibility for their contribution to the conflict, to understand how the conflict affects them and others, and to link their behavior to the well-being of the honor dorm community. Most importantly, they learn to use nonviolent communication skills to resolve conflict. Thus when circles function properly, they build the capacity to form relationships and to repair damaged ones.

TYPES OF CONFLICTS

The conflict between Tom and Larry is based on a role-play created and recorded by inmates for a presentation at a national conference.[1] However, the nature of the conflict and the process for resolving it are real. This conflict is typical of most reported to circles because there is no clear victim and offender. In other words, the conflict is the result of a misunderstanding, one that is coproduced by the individuals involved. The drinking fountain incident might not be taken very seriously in the free world. However, in a non-air-conditioned prison environment with ninety-five-degree temperatures, it is best to address the situation immediately. In this case, the circle becomes a possible lifesaving intervention.

Other inmates in the dorm, including dorm supervisors (senior coordinators) can report a conflict. If a conflict involves a clear rule violation, it can result in a point deduction in the dorm demerit system. The demerit system was installed when the honor dorm began. It is more retributive than restorative because it is imposed for a rule violation, rather than being an outcome of the circle process. When a rule violation is reported by way of a statement of facts form, it can lead to a demerit. When a complaint is delivered through an incident report, demerits are not involved. However, the system evolved to where conflicts and alleged rule violations originating through the use of either form may enter the circle process.

The following are examples of Group II write-ups during one week in the honor dorm taken from the statement of facts form of the complaining resident. This category of write-up, in contrast to the more serious Group I violation, is referred to peacemaking circles:

Description of Violation:	Negative behavior
Description of Behavior:	I observed David along with Theodore arguing in the dorm and using profanity calling each other n——rs and saying f—— you and walking up on each other. I have pulled these two up in the past about their behavior problems.
Description of Violation:	Negative behavior
Description of Behavior:	I asked Gaines if he had a light so that I could go outside and smoke. He said for me to get out of his face and to "kiss his a——."
Description of Violation:	Negative behavior
Description of Behavior:	Jones commented to Nelson, "I heard you were going to drop a bomb-shell on someone." Nelson responded "f—— you!" So Jones responded back, "f——!" Then Jones was restrained by other residents and Nelson shouted out "bitch." Then Jones responded that Nelson was a "rat."
Description of Violation:	Unbecoming behavior
Description of Behavior:	I was standing by the smoking area looking toward the "camp" when Mr. O. walked up to my face and asked me,

"What the hell I was looking at" I told
him that I didn't like him, and to get
away from me. His actions are con-
trary to our community, and I know in
my heart, that he is trying his best to
start trouble with me and I feel his
comments to me were very "unbecom-
ing" and derogatory.

The violence implied in these statements is evident, and staying abreast of this
behavior is challenging. The language represents the "convict" way of doing
things. The peacemaking circles and the permanent party residents who serve
on them are important tools for intervention and change.

More serious violations (stealing, gambling, drinking, fighting) are Group
I violations and call for expulsion from the dorm. Clearly this is a non-
restorative response, but the chaplain and other inmate leaders think it is necessary given the realty of the prison environment. The honor dorm is a
cultural oasis of change within a highly retributive system. Its population is in
constant flux. If the dorm is overwhelmed with illegal behaviors, it could be
changed or abolished. Each inmate in the dorm is at a different place with respect to his character and desire to change. Dorm leaders do recognize it is
good to expand restorative practices when feasible. Discussion has taken place
about using a peacekeeping model to address Group I violations before the inmate returns to general population. Also, inmates expelled from the dorm can
reapply for residence after a six-month waiting period. This implies the inmate's behavior, not the inmate himself, is the problem.

CORRECTIONS OFFICER INVOLVEMENT
IN AND OUT OF THE HONOR DORM

Most conflicts and rule violations in the honor dorm do not involve corrections officers. "The police," as inmates call them, are alert for violations and
know they occur, but for the most part the honor dorm polices itself. If a corrections officer observes a violation or a conflict in the honor dorm, he or she
can intercede informally. In contrast, a formal intervention involves the choice
of a citation or a disciplinary action, which results in a due process hearing.

Citations and disciplinary actions require completion of paperwork. Corrections officers can refer a case to a peacemaking circle, but this is unusual because officers receive no training on restorative justice and circles.

I participated in a circle initiated by a female corrections officer who saw two honor dorm residents loitering in an unauthorized area. The officer thought the men would better understand the consequences of their behavior if she addressed it in a circle. She told me the honor dorm provides good opportunities to its residents and some men change after becoming dorm residents. During the circle the officer lectured the participants. She told them they risked losing a great opportunity to grow and change.

Using a restorative approach, inmate circle members asked questions to better understand the situation. As an invited participant, I asked the two men if they had a lot of free time on their hands. Perhaps they might want to enroll in one of the classes offered next semester. I queried both men about their relationship with their dorm mentors (Big Brothers) to better understand the kind of direction they are getting. Do they talk with their Big Brothers often? Do they get along? It was apparent that the residents and the corrections officer had a sincere desire to help the men improve their behavior in the future.

Conflicts in general population are often resolved according to the established pecking order with the ever-present undertone of violence. Bullies have their way in a prison environment. They push their weight around and intimidate the weaker men until someone bigger and more threatening comes along. When corrections officers get involved with conflicts and rule violations, they use the processes previously described—informal intervention or institutional write-ups (citation or disciplinary). A comparison between corrections-officer-initiated disciplinary actions in the general population with the honor dorm shows the dorm rarely needs formal officer intervention. The occurrence of citations and disciplinaries issued by the Alabama Department of Corrections in 2005 for the two environments is presented in figure 4.1. These data show corrections officer time is saved by the honor dorm arrangements. However, conflicts and rule infractions are not ignored in the honor dorm because a process for addressing them is in place. In 2005, seventy peacemaking circles were conducted in the honor dorm. In general population the frequent occurrence of serious violations makes it less likely that officers will become involved in nonviolent arguments and less visible conflicts.

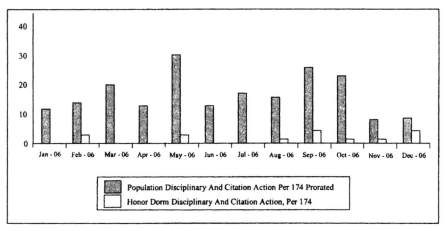

FIGURE 4.1.
Disciplinary and Citation (Combined) Comparison Chart for 2005

THE ELEMENTS OF A PEACEMAKING CIRCLE

In the honor dorm, the peacemaking circle is a *method* for practicing restorative justice. It is important to remember that restorative justice is a philosophy and a way of living. It is *not* a particular practice. It can be delivered in many ways. Likewise, peacemaking circles are not tied to the term "restorative justice." They were used by native peoples long before the movement began. However, as restorative justice programming evolved, it became evident that circles could enhance its practice. The following discussion on circle structure is informed by the work of Kay Pranis who was instrumental in bringing restorative programming to Minnesota in the 1980s.[2] Integrated with the description of circle structure are examples from the Holman experience.

Members sit in a circle with no table or other barrier. The circle shape suggests several things. First, it symbolizes the importance of community and the connection of individuals through community. Second, unlike the triangle, which implies hierarchy, all participants in the circle are at the same level and are seen as equals. This represents the importance of community participation and consensus decision-making. Third, a circle signifies safety—as in, "circling the wagons." Like a mother's womb, it is a secure place where you can be your "authentic self."[3] Authenticity encourages honesty, truth-telling, and taking responsibility. This is all necessary for effective conflict resolution. Circle members are free to be themselves and "tell it like it is," without judgment.

Finally, for some the circle is a symbol of healing. It represents the community coming together to repair harm that has been done.

Lest the circle become a formless free-for-all for venting emotions, with the most vocal and dominant voices taking precedence over others, there are best practices that provide structure and help circles achieve their goals. These practices or elements are used in any type of circle—whether it is for peace-making, sentencing, or simply discussing ideas. Peacemaking circles in the honor dorm have each of these elements and include:

1. Ceremony
2. Guidelines
3. A talking piece
4. Keeping/facilitation
5. Consensus decision-making[4]

A *ceremony* is used to begin and end the circle. Ceremonies are valuable be-cause they communicate the importance and special nature of the event, dis-tinguishing it from day-to-day routines having less consequence and significance.[5] In the drinking fountain incident, the keeper of the circle, a res-ident named Robert, called the circle to order and opened with a nondenom-inational prayer. This ceremony is fitting for a faith-based community. He subsequently asked circle members and participants to state a value important to them. For circles in the free world, stating values helps members get to know each other better and build trust. For the honor dorm, where the resi-dents are already familiar with one another, stating these values serves a cere-monial function and speaks to the higher purpose of the circle. It is a place of honor and represents all that is good about the honor dorm community. Ex-amples of values expressed by honor dorm circle members are education, in-tegrity, compassion, and respect. Altogether the ceremony reminds residents why they are present and the importance of the task at hand.

Guidelines are created by the entire circle, not just the facilitator, and re-sponsibility for implementing the guidelines lies with all the participants.[6] In the honor dorm, the guidelines are the same for all five permanently main-tained circles. Guidelines constitute a covenant governing circle behavior. All members agree to abide by them. Respectful conduct is one guideline for honor dorm circles. If a circle participant uses profanity or name-calling, circle members are expected to take responsibility to correct the situation. Another guideline is confidentiality. In the free world, participation in the circle is confidential. Given limited space in prison, others can see who is participating, but the circle discussion is confidential.

A *talking piece* is an object the circle uses to give each person an equal opportunity to speak. It is passed from person to person and only the individual holding the talking piece can talk. Holman circles use a feather. One Native American student told me that in her tribal community, the eagle feather represents rising above individual concerns and speaking to a higher power. The talking peace gives participants room to speak sincerely. It provides other participants the opportunity to listen carefully without formulating a premature response. It slows the pace of conversation and encourages circle members to be thoughtful and reflective. It also serves as an equalizer carrying the message that everyone has something to offer.[7]

Leading the opening ceremony, the *keeper* or *facilitator* of the circle makes the first move toward creating an atmosphere that is respectful and safe. He engages the members in a way that will encourage them to share responsibility for maintaining the circle. This can occur at any time during the process, but his role in the opening ceremony sets the tone. The keeper is not, however, responsible for finding solutions or for managing the group. He is not in charge.[8] The keeper summarizes the nature of the conflict at the beginning of the meeting, explains the guidelines and the use of the talking peace, denotes various stages of the meeting, and summarizes the agreement reached by circle members. In the honor dorm, the keeper also initiates the closing ceremony. At Holman, each circle has another position, a *secretary*. The keeper works with the symbolic material of the group while the secretary records the group's business. When alternative decision-making processes are used in a prison setting, detailed record-keeping is important for maintaining legitimacy, particularly when the practice is very different from the usual way of doing things.

Consensus decision-making means decisions made during the circle are agreed upon by all the participants. It implies that the members are willing to live with the decisions and support their implementation even though a particular individual may not agree with the decision 100 percent. Therefore, it requires serious listening and reflection before coming to a conclusion. It entails an attitude of open exploration rather than an attitude of winning or persuading, which is more common in courtroom proceedings. The more time that is allotted for the process, the more likely consensus can be achieved. If consensus does not happen within the time assigned, a follow-up meeting is scheduled or the group turns to a different form of decision-making. Consensus is more likely to occur if participants are committed to the process and the issue at hand is important to them.[9] Consensus decisions result in more effective and lasting agreements because the process gives power to everyone in the circle.[10] If the parties to the conflict agree to the outcome while in circle, compliance is more likely to occur later.

WHY IT WORKS

There is very little evaluation research on circle processes. Research on mediation practices is further along. Much of what we know about circles, both positive and negative, is anecdotal. However, most of us feel better using a practice grounded in a conceptual framework or a theory. This provides a rationale for the activity based on what we know (or think we know) about human and social behavior. The logic and experience of storytelling, the restorative philosophy, and affect theory help us understand the logic of circle processes.

Circles use *storytelling* rather than argument and debate to explore issues. Pranis explains that the experience of being connected promotes understanding, consensual decision-making, and healing.[11] Storytelling allows us to connect at a very basic instinctual and human level. If someone tries to persuade us through argument, our defenses and critical thinking come into play almost automatically. We become more concerned with how we see things and want to defend our own viewpoint. We want to label a behavior or a person "right" or "wrong." If someone is telling a story, we relax and openly appreciate how the other person experienced and understood a situation. Much as we read fiction to relax, appreciating the author's ability to provide insights into the book's characters, storytelling in the circle has the same effect. When Larry and Tom tell their story about the drinking fountain incident, there is no pressure to approve or disapprove of either account. Each has validity. This makes it easier for the parties to reach consensus.

Circle members can tell stories related to the problem at hand. This helps parties in conflict better understand the situation and take responsibility for what happened. In the drinking fountain case, Jim, a circle member, relates a story about misinterpreting the intentions of a fellow resident. He reminisces about the time he got angry with a guy in a Scrabble game. The man took a long time taking his turn and Jim thought the guy was purposely trying to irritate him. He also thought, "Maybe this guy is a bit slow in the head, and even though I enjoyed played Scrabble with him once before, this is the last time." Jim subsequently learned the other player was having a difficult time concentrating due to some medicine the clinic gave him for a migraine. Jim admits he completely misjudged the situation and felt pretty ashamed of himself at the time. Jim's willingness to share has a number of positive results. It shows he is not above the circle participants. It shows this is a community problem because Jim, a representative of the community, is willing to help resolve it. His contribution helps the participants feel comfortable working with their own conflict.

In chapter 2 we discussed *restorative justice*. The restorative approach when used in peacemaking circles suggests people are more likely to feel satisfied and make positive changes in their behavior when decisions are made *with* them rather than made *for* them. This is particularly important when rule infractions and disciplinary issues come before a circle. The restorative approach does not focus on the rule being broken. It focuses on the harm done by the behavior (rule-breaking). For example, when the circle considered the two inmates who loitered in an unauthorized area of the prison, its members expressed their concern about the "violators" following a slippery slope that could hurt them—a path that could eventually get them expelled from the honor dorm. The circle members also talked about how the men's actions affected the dorm community, possibly jeopardizing its status.

Donald Nathanson, a psychologist, became interested in explaining how circles and family group conferences work by applying *affect theory* to restorative practices in the 1990s.[12] Nathanson is a student of Sylvan Tomkins, who researched the psychology of affect in the early 1960s. An affect is an emotion or feeling. Observing children and adults, Tomkins identified nine affects and linked each to a typical response. For example, enjoyment/joy is a positive affect associated with smiling. Anger/rage is a negative affect and is associated with frowning, a clenched jaw, or a red face. There are two positive affects, six negative ones, and one labeled as neutral.

Applying affect theory to circles, Nathanson suggests human relationships are healthier when there is free expression of affect and when there is a structure that minimizes or transforms negative into positive affect. One negative affect particularly relevant to conflict and discipline is shame/humiliation. Shame/humiliation is uncomfortable, but it teaches us to look at harmful behavior and make appropriate changes. However, uncomfortable feelings are often avoided by withdrawing (isolation), attacking others (directing anger outwards), attacking oneself (depression), or avoidance (through drugs, alcohol, thrill-seeking).[13] Participatory and supportive circle processes address negative emotion like shame/humiliation in a healthy manner while holding a person accountable for harmful behavior. When supported by others, people are more likely to replace negative emotions with positive ones. This dynamic is produced through structured relational experiences such as circle processes.

Wachtel and McCold use affect theory to explain why restorative discipline works in schools.[14] Their ideas are presented in the social discipline window shown in figure 4.2 and can be applied to the honor dorm peacemaking circles as well. The window shows four approaches to maintain social norms and behavioral boundaries. Each approach has different combinations of control and support. The restorative domain combines both high control and high support and is characterized by doing things *with* people, rather than *to* them or *for* them. The honor dorm subscribes to this approach. Circles are authoritative because their decisions are binding. They are authoritative, not authoritarian, because decisions are made by consensus. Circles are not permissive. Inmates use write-ups and circles to hold each other to a higher standard of behavior than expected in general population. Circles are supportive because they focus on the harmful actions of the participant rather than labeling a rule violator as a bad person.[15] Community representatives offer their support to participants on behalf of the dorm. They treat participants respectfully and encourage them to take responsibility, change behavior, reconcile differences, and remedy harms. They are helpful and forgiving. Given the nature of circles, parties to a conflict and rule violators are more likely to leave with positive feelings about themselves, other parties to the conflict, and the community.

In prison settings, social discipline is practiced in ways suggested by the other three domains. The administration makes decisions for inmates (when to eat, when to sleep, how to dress, etc.). It does things to them when they break prison regulations. Punitive prison discipline promotes negative emotions and the acting out of shame in harmful ways. More often than not, prisons are neglectful because they tolerate immoral and unethical behavior.

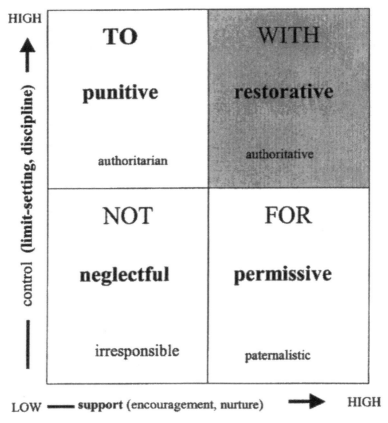

FIGURE 4.2.
Social Discipline Window.
Ted Wachtel, "SaferSanerSchools: Restoring Community Justice in a Disconnected World,"
International Institute for Restorative Practices, 1999. www.irp.org/library/safersaner-
schools/html (accessed 27 June 2008). Reprinted with permission.

Corrections officers think it is impossible or undesirable to enforce all of the rules or they believe it is permissible to hold inmates to a lower standard of behavior.[16]

BUT DOES IT REALLY WORK?

In 2006 I interviewed sixty-one honor dorm residents who participated in circles either as circle members, parties to a conflict, or both in the previous year (2005). It was not possible to interview participants who no longer live in the dorm. I asked inmates a series of open-ended questions to assess their perceptions of peacemaking circles. One of the questions asked, "Would you recommend the circle process to others in similar circumstances to yours?" Fifty-four of sixty-one residents said, "yes," they would, three said, " no," and four said, "it depended on the situation or the quality of the circle." The majority views circles as a legitimate and positive forum for conflict resolution in the honor dorm.

I also asked residents to identify what they like most and what they like least about peacemaking circles. More than one response is recorded when given. Table 4.1 shows twenty-eight of the responses fall in two categories—the opportunity to express feelings and the opportunity to talk about problems without threats, retaliation, or interruption. This suggests the storytelling approach is valued by many residents. The inmates also see circles as a peaceful way to resolve conflict (seventeen responses). Comments in other categories including the miscellaneous one are circles build better relationships, build respect, provide the opportunity to help people, encourage positive behavior, and promote honesty. Only six of the residents say there is nothing they like about circles.

Sixteen respondents found nothing they disliked about peacemaking circles (see table 4.2). Another fourteen responses point to lack of impartiality among circle members. Some (fourteen) imply circles could work better if their members and participants are better prepared, care more about participating, and are more honest during the proceedings.

Table 4.1.   Responses to Honor Dorm Questionnaire Item Administered to 2005 Circle Participants

What do you like most about peacemaking circles?	
Response category	# Responses*
A method to resolve conflict/solve problems	17
Opportunity to express feelings	14
Opportunity to talk about problems without threats, retaliation, interruptions	14
Nothing	6
Helps build better relationships	5
Miscellaneous responses	7
	63

N=61
*Multiple responses recorded when given

Table 4.2.   Responses to Honor Dorm Questionnaire
Item Administered to 2005 Circle Participants

What do you like least about peacemaking circles?	
Response category	# Responses*
Nothing	16
Lack of fairness	14
Lack of participation cooperation from circle members and participants	12
Too punishment oriented	10
They are too soft, should be more confrontational	3
Didn't agree with outcome	3
Miscellaneous other	5
	63

*Multiple responses recorded when given

Ten responses suggest circles are too punitive. Another three answers say circles are not punitive enough. Lack of agreement with the outcome, the time-consuming nature of the process, and lack of confidentiality are examples of miscellaneous comments. Only one response (miscellaneous category) shows fear of retaliation.

CHALLENGES

There are issues using circles in the honor dorm. First, circle participation is not voluntary. Unwilling participants may be less honest and more reluctant to openly share their stories. This is reflected in survey comments where some inmates complained their fellows were less than honest when they participated in a circle. However, given the potential for conflict and its escalation in prison, mandatory participation is understandable even when it makes the process less restorative. Some survey participants think alternative conflict resolution practices such as mediation should be available. Mediation involves only the two parties to the conflict plus a facilitator. However, the community-building feature of circles is less explicit in mediation. This does not rule out using restorative responses other than circles some time in the future.

Second, some residents think the honor dorm circles are unfair. Circle members are required to recuse themselves when there is a conflict of interest. In free world circles membership is more fluid. Circle members in the honor dorm must have permanent party status, volunteer for the task, and are on call each day of the week. They are drawn from a limited pool where everyone knows each other and has prior relationships. Perceptions of unfairness can be addressed if circles borrow from a commonly used practice in mediation. Mediation ground rules often include an agreement that if there is a perception of unfairness, parties to the conflict must stop the process. This is followed by a side bar where issues of fairness are addressed.

The limited number of people qualified as circle members can lead to burnout and the view that many do not participate fully. A few of the men indicated that some circles are better than others because the people in the good ones really like the work and take it seriously. It might be tempting to volunteer for circle membership over other dorm responsibilities that are seen as more time consuming. To address this perception, the department head for peacemaking circles could observe circle meetings on a periodic basis and provide input to its members. Short written evaluations by participants following the completion of a circle might provide helpful feedback, too.

The perception that circles are too punitive conflicts with the restorative philosophy. When I interviewed the men, it was clear that not all of them understand restorative justice when it applies to circles. A class on conflict resolution might help inmates understand the difference between restorative and retributive responses. Additional preparation of participants prior to the circle meeting could help residents know what to expect. The retributive nature of prisons and the judicial system makes it difficult for restorative justice to resonate. Sometimes, listening to the message of restorative justice is like trying to hear a harp against the backdrop of a heavy metal band.

REFLECTIONS

Peacemaking circles in the honor dorm bring conflicting parties together and treat the problem as a community issue. Learning new ways to solve problems, new ways to deal with old emotions, and new ways to relate to people are part of the circle process. Through storytelling inmates in circles learn to see things from other inmates' perspectives. Participants' stories range from individual understandings of what happened to similar incidents that occurred in the past. It is not as often that dorm circles meet to reconcile situations where one inmate is a clear victim and the other the offender. But when this happens, the same principles apply.

By promoting respect for all members in the circle and emphasizing that the circle is not a place for assigning blame but for making peace, the "playing field" is leveled and participants find a comfort level that enables them to relay their accounts of what happened. It is important for dorm residents to feel comfortable in the circle setting so they can talk in a way that helps to maintain a connection between themselves, the other parties to the conflict, and the rest of the community. Being able to see a situation from different viewpoints helps people come to terms with one another. Participating in the process builds community ties with the expectation that caring about community is a strong check on behavior.

This is a description of how restorative principles delivered through peacemaking circles work. Now let's review more detailed accounts written by some residents in the Holman Faith-Based Restorative Justice Honor Dorm to see what they think. These men are involved with circles in a positive way and are willing to reflect on what they mean to them.

Reflection 1

I am a member of a peacemaking circle and I can honestly say that if we didn't have peacemaking circles in the Honor Dorm, there would probably not be an Honor Dorm. Most of the circles I have participated in have always had a positive outcome. Residents that had to come to a peacemaking circle leave with good feelings toward each other, instead of holding onto feelings that could result in violence. The peacemaking circles provide an environment where problems can be addressed with fairness and justice. As a member of the peacemaking circle I have the opportunity to speak positive words into other resident's lives, in hopes of them taking those positive words and applying them to their lives. You can tell later if those words had their effect, and in most cases they do.

I have participated in peacemaking circles as both a member of the community and a party to a conflict. The time I had to call a person to a peacemaking circle over a conflict was to address some adversarial conversation that was addressed toward me. As to the outcome, I didn't actually receive the outcome that I expected, but just to have had the opportunity to confront those who were making the adversarial conversation was justice enough. As for me being called to a circle by another person, I feel that the person who did it only called me to the peacemaking circle to vent personal feelings, (which he did) however, when he started to vent his personal feelings and those feelings went beyond the rules of the peacemaking circle, the circle members quickly brought him back under the rules of the circle. Because of that process and rules that were there, the peacemaking circle provided an environment where I wouldn't be verbally abused.

Reflection 2

My experiences with the peacemaking circle process have been more good than bad; bad being the few times which are far and in between wherein an individual just simply refuses to cooperate, to open up, to be empathetic, if you will, or at the least allow someone else to empathize with them. You see, peacemaking circles have to do with relationships, and just like any healthy relationship it's all about giving and receiving. It brings to mind in this instance the relationships on a football field between a center, quarterback, and receiver in respect to their team as a whole. You see it's the center's responsibility to give the football at the right time to the quarterback and then he has to block for the quarterback or, in other words, make the allowance of space and time in a safe environment for the quarterback to do what he needs to do with the ball. It's the quarterback's responsibility to receive the ball. If he won't receive, the whole purpose of the team being on the field is defeated, but if he'll receive the ball he can then give a willing wide receiver the opportunity to make the team shine.

If the wide receiver is willing and able to receive what the quarterback is giving, if he'll then give it all he's got, the outcome is a touchdown. Sometimes you may have to try more than one time to get there, 1st, 2nd, 3rd, or even 4th down, but if everyone can pull together for the team. . . . This is the image I see when I think about peacemaking circles. I've seen people come into circles at odds with each other, leave the circle on the same team. You see the circle members working together as the center giving individuals the space, time, and safety they need to express themselves. Peacemaking circles give individuals the opportunity to be the quarterbacks of their own lives, by giving them a healthy way to deal with problems instead of them dealing with those problems in a way that takes from them the control and places that control in the hands of another. The circle also encourages the individual to use the benefits of working things out, or working along with others by way of understanding another, and allowing you to be understood. This is where the quarterback-wide receiver relationship comes in. Circles promote and create environments that cultivate trust. Before a quarterback will make a pass he has got to trust the receiver by developing an environment wherein individuals can come to understand each other. Circles lay the foundation for this kind of trust. Would I recommend the use of peacemaking circles as a form of conflict resolution? For sure, and that's a vote of personal experience.

Reflection 3

My experiences with peacemaking circles have made it possible for me to adopt different ways to approach conflicts in order to achieve resolution and growth. When a person is exposed to a setting, such as a peacemaking circle, wherein an issue that resulted in conflict is addressed, certain techniques that make up essential elements of the circle insure the possibility of establishing peace.

First off, when each member is required to state a core value that they treasure, this puts in the air things that strengthen the human fiber. There are also rules for how the circles must flow which extinguish the chances of the situation getting out of control. The talking piece that allows only the person in possession of it to speak insures one the right to talk uninterrupted and it also allows the members of the circle to view the conflict from different angles. The two opposing parties get a chance to hear the feelings and views of the person his conflict is with and vice versa. The members that make up the peacemaking circle are required to listen and, without bias, inject comments that don't attach a right or wrong label to either of the conflicting parties. The members attempt to dissect the varying comments in an effort to reach a means to reduce the issue at hand to an issue that can be surpassed without hate, violence, or division among people in the community. Introducing the effects that conflict has on the community is another tool that aids in establishing resolution.

I have seen better men made by way of the peacemaking circles. I have seen our community take on a cultural change as a result of peacemaking circles. People that had no effective coping and problem-solving skills were miraculously changed to people with very high conflict-resolution tactics through the use of peacemaking circles.

Reflection 4

Peacemaking circles help me to feel like I am an important part of the community, because it allows me to play a community role in solving problems. This gives me a sense of purpose in the community. One of the aspects of peacemaking circles that I especially like is the practice of storytelling. Storytelling allows different members of the circle to relate better to other people and to begin to see people with empathy. Also, relating to each other with stories is a nonthreatening way of illustrating a point of view. It helps to reinforce the bonds of connectedness that hold us together in community.

Reflection 5

Two residents were brought in before our peacemaking circle, they had a situation that arose when Bill, who at the time was acting as COD (coordinator on duty), confronted John about sitting on (leaning against) the computer table; instead of John replying "okay, good pull-up," he just flew off the handle into a rage of verbal abuse aimed directly at Bill. So at that point, Bill turned away and informed John he was being logged for a confrontation violation, which at the most was only going to be a half-point demerit, an eye-opener. But due to John's ongoing inability to develop people skills, his pride cost him a trip to a peacemaking circle to deal with this problem, also another write-up, which was upgraded to negative behavior. So we got together and circled up with our talking piece and began the circle. We allowed both men to tell their story, and through this process we were able to discover that John doesn't like to receive correction. He has a problem with being confronted, among other underlying, deep-rooted issues. The thing which stood out the most to me was that we as a peacemaking circle were able to say to John what he needed to be told about himself, and we did it with an entire consensus together in love, with respect and serious concern for John because he's getting out soon, and if he does not come to a place of developing his cognitive skills, and people skills, then he may end up coming back to prison or, worse, doing harm to himself or someone else.

What we as a peacemaking circle accomplished is unheard of in a maximum-security prison setting, but was made possible because of the culture change taking place here at Holman due to the establishment of a faith-based honor dorm built on the principles of restorative justice. Because of restorative justice, we are being taught how to address the special needs of prisoners and victims of crime, and how we can be able to stop victimizing each other. We are practicing on how to live again while incarcerated, then when the time comes for us to face our victims and/or their families, we will be equipped and educated in such a way that we will be able to begin to make things right and provide the means of proper restitution, not just monetarily, but relationally and socially as well.

NOTES

1. Annual Meeting of the Association for Conflict Resolution, Philadelphia, Pennsylvania, October 25–28, 2006.

2. Kay Pranis, *The Little Book of Circle Processes: A New/Old Approach to Peacemaking* (Intercourse, Pa.: Good Books, 2005).

3. Pranis, *Little Book of Circle Processes*, 11.

4. Pranis, *Little Book of Circle Processes*, 33.

5. Pranis, *Little Book of Circle Processes*, 33.

6. Pranis, *Little Book of Circle Processes*, 34–35.

7. Pranis, *Little Book of Circle Processes*, 35–36.

8. Pranis, *Little Book of Circle Processes*, 36–37.

9. Ron Claassen and Dalton Reimer, *Basic Institute in Conflict Management and Mediation* (Center for Peacemaking and Conflict Studies, Fresno Pacific University 1999), 41.

10. Pranis, *Little Book of Circle Processes*, 37–39.

11. Pranis, *Little Book of Circle Processes*, 39.

12. Donald L. Nathanson, *Shame and Pride: Affect, Sex, and the Birth of Self* (New York: W. W. Norton, 1992).

13. Donald Nathanson, *Shame and Pride*.

14. Ted Wachtel and Paul McCold, "Restorative Justice in Everyday Life," in *Restorative Justice and Civil Society*, ed. Heather Strang and John Braithwaite (Cambridge: Cambridge University Press, 2001), 114–29.

15. John Braithwaite, *Crime, Shame and Reintegration* (Cambridge: Cambridge University Press, 1989), 11–13.

16. Cyndi Banks, *Criminal Justice Ethics: Theory and Practice* (Thousand Oaks, Calif.: Sage, 2004), 137–45.

5

Cleaning up after Yourself

To empathize with someone is to vicariously experience the feelings of the other person. It is feeling their pain by imagining yourself in "their shoes" and viewing the trauma of crime through your victim's eyes.

—*Adapted from the W. C. Holman Faith-Based Restorative Justice Honor Dorm brochure*

Compared to retributive justice, restorative justice is a victim-centered philosophy. This means that the criminal justice system should first and foremost respond to the needs of the victim. But what does this really mean? To more fully appreciate this perspective, it is helpful to again contrast the two approaches to crime and justice.

Retributive justice says the state is the victim. Assume that Mary Jane is robbed and injured in Delaware. Her offender, Jack Brown, is apprehended and charged with the crime. When the case enters the court docket it reads *State of Delaware v. Brown*. Mary Jane's name is not listed because she is no longer the victim, at least officially speaking. If Jack is found guilty, Mary's injuries can be taken into account at sentencing as an aggravating circumstance, and she may even be awarded restitution for her doctor's bills. No doubt the prosecutor thinks he is acting on behalf of Mary Jane. He believes that Mary Jane will experience justice because Jack has been found guilty and sentenced to prison. Jack has received his just desserts, according to retributive justice, and the state, and Mary Jane should be satisfied with his punishment.

VICTIM NEEDS

Restorative justice questions this approach. First, Mary Jane is the real victim because she experiences the crime directly. There may be other victims as well, such as Mary Jane's husband, children, and parents because their lives are affected by Mary Jane's emotional response to the crime. Restorative justice places the harm experienced by Mary and these secondary victims front and center. Other movements, such as Victims' Rights, speak to these issues, too. Victims' rights organizations press for the legal and material needs of victims. For example, most states as well as the federal government now have laws giving victims the right to information about their cases as they proceed through the criminal justice system. They have also set up victim compensation funds, which are especially important for victims when offenders are not apprehended or cannot afford to pay the amount of restitution needed. Before victims' rights groups advocated for these changes in policy, the victim was largely ignored in the criminal justice system.

Restorative justice recognizes the importance of these legal and material needs but moves beyond them. Principally, the restorative philosophy argues that inflicting punishment on the offender does not restore the harm done to victims. It contends victims have needs that must be addressed before justice can be served. Along these lines, Howard Zehr identifies four categories of victim needs: information, truth-telling, empowerment, and restitution or vindication.[1]

Victims want answers to questions that are not available during a trial or in a plea agreement. Plea bargains involve private conversations. Even though the agreement is public record, the information the victim can glean from them is limited. Plea agreements are driven by the needs of the state and the offender, and occur in at least 95 percent of all criminal cases. The other 5 percent are tried in open court, but information is structured and filtered to meet the legal requirements of the system. The more serious the offense, the more likely a victim or the family has unanswered questions. The mother of a woman murdered in Texas wants to know what happened just before her daughter was shot. Did she suffer? What did she say, if anything? Only the offender can provide answers to these kinds of questions. In this case, the mother and her granddaughter meet the convicted killer. He tells them that her daughter's last words were, "I forgive you." This response provides relief and peace to the victims. The murder victim's mother turns to her grand-daughter and says with quiet pride, "See, that was your mama."[2]

In most states, victims do not have the opportunity to meet with offenders to get the information they need. In some, such as Texas, Ohio, and Vermont, victim-offender dialogue programs give victims this opportunity. The Vermont program describes why victims might want to participate in a victim-offender dialogue. The reasons include:

- To hear why the crime happened
- To tell the offender how it affected them and others
- To have questions answered
- To lessen the fear of a repeat crime and/or retribution
- To have the offender address the victim's needs
- To further their healing process[3]

Many victims might not want to meet with the offender. People heal in different ways. However, not to offer the choice is a serious failure in the criminal justice system. Research on victim-offender dialogue shows it is a very satisfactory experience for almost all victims who participate. A meta-analysis of thirteen victim-offender reconciliation programs in Canada found only one program where victims were more satisfied with the traditional justice system than the restorative approach.[4] Studies show that typically 80 to 90 percent of victims show satisfaction with victim-offender mediation, regardless of seriousness of the crime or different cultural settings.[5] Many of these studies are nonprison-based programs. However, in a prison program in Texas, all twenty victim-participants had powerful and positive experiences talking with their offenders.[6] Since victims self select for these kinds of programs, we cannot generalize this positive finding to what would happen if all victims met with their offenders.

A second victim need is truth-telling. An example is when victims tell offenders how the crime affected them, a benefit listed in the Vermont Victim-Dialogue Program. Chapter 4 discusses the therapeutic advantage of story telling. The opportunity for the victim to tell his or her story on their own terms, rather than within the constraints of a courtroom setting, is significant. Today, almost all states allow victims to enter a written or oral victim impact statement to the judge. The offenders never see the written impact statements. In open court, an option chosen by very few, the victim stands facing the judge with his or her back to the offender. The process gives the victim an opportunity to receive meaningful public acknowledgement of the crime's impact, but it does not allow direct communication between the victim and the offender.

A third need is empowerment.[7] Empowerment implies the ability of victims to control their lives after the crime experience has taken it away. Some victims feel empowered by buying a gun or a home alarm system. Others get involved in new projects they never dreamed about before they were victimized. Some victims are imprisoned by resentments against their offenders. While restorative justice does not demand or require forgiveness, in some cases an apology from the offender can help release the victim from the bondage of anger and bitterness.[8]

Another way to conceptualize victim needs is restitution or vindication.[9] When an offender is incarcerated monetary restitution is more difficult to obtain. However, a sincere apology can be offered as a form of symbolic restitution. In cases involving young offenders, victims sometimes see a promise to do better in the future, or taking steps to change through education, treatment, and vocational training to meet the need to see good come out of a bad. While retributive justice equates vindication with punishment, not all victims feel vindicated by this approach. They don't know what prison is really like for their offender. Has he or she every reflected on the harm they caused? If the offender is not given the opportunity to be accountable for what he did, can the victim truly experience vindication?

OFFENDER ACCOUNTABILITY

The notion of offender accountability brings us back to the honor dorm at Holman. The honor dorm operates within the constraints defined by Alabama statutes and the rules and regulations of the Alabama Department of Corrections. While Alabama statutes incorporate the concept of restorative justice, implementation is limited. Currently there is no provision for inmates to have contact with their victims, and indeed, contact is prohibited. Given these conditions, how can the honor dorm take a restorative approach?

First, from a restorative perspective:

Real accountability involves facing up to what one has done. It means encouraging offenders to understand the impact of their behavior—the harms they have done—and urging them to take steps to put things right as much as possible. This accountability, it is argued, is better for victims, better for society, and better for offenders.[10]

The honor dorm addresses this notion of accountability several ways: through opportunities to practice one's faith, through education, through exposure to surrogate victims, and through opportunities to be accountable to the honor dorm community.

All prisons are required to give offenders the opportunity to practice their religion. The faith-based honor dorm at Holman links faith with restorative practices in a mix designed to bring about personal growth and positive practical results. Most inmates understand that their faith provides lessons for personal growth and accountability. However, putting this faith into practice is more challenging. This is the case for most people, but even more so in a prison environment. Some inmates initially believe that accountability is a private matter between themselves and their higher power. Being sincerely sorry for what they did and expressing remorse in prayer is an example. Restorative education moves accountability into the community. However, it is difficult to imagine restorative justice working in the honor dorm without the moral framework supplied by spiritual teachings.

Chapter 6 addresses education in the honor dorm in some detail. For example, the required crime impact class is a basic orientation toward the effects of different types of crime on victims. The required courses, however, do not tackle the offender's personal relationship to his victim(s). To incorporate this component into honor dorm education, I created an empathy and accountability class in the summer of 2005. The class is elective but may become part of the core curriculum at a later date. It provides a more personal and intense experience, and therefore class size is limited. As the class grows in popularity, a larger number of students are accommodated by meeting together for general lecture topics and breaking into small groups with inmate facilitators who previously completed the course.

Inmates are encouraged to expand their capacity for acknowledging the harms they caused others by reading poignant victim accounts about surviving violent crime narrated to Howard Zehr in his book, *Transcending: Reflections of Crime Victims.*[11] Inmates are asked to identify victims they relate to and share the victim's stories with other inmates. They write essays on their readings. After reading victims' stories, one inmate wrote, "this is a life-changing book. Once you read this you will never look at crime the same. As an offender, I never thought of the lasting effects of crimes on victims. They really go through emotional roller coasters." Another inmate commented, "To use actual victims, their stories and their photos, was a combination punch that no one with an ounce of heart could duck."

Class members also write apology letters to their victims including a statement about what they did, what they were thinking at the time, and how their actions affected others. Although the letter is not mailed, it encourages offenders to share with another person (the teacher) exactly what they did adding to accountability in a more "public" way. Through subsequent exercises the men are encouraged to think about the kind of information their victims might want.

Accountability is a hazy term for many inmates. Guilt, shame, and the prison environment contribute to denial and minimization of their actions. One man in the class said it was very difficult for him to read victims' accounts of their physical and emotional suffering. Others find writing a series of victim-related letters challenging. To make the notion of accountability more clear and explicit, I break it down into several components.

- Owning up to what you did
- Addressing the resulting harms
- Encouraging empathy and responsibility
- Transforming shame[12]

In addition to spirituality and education, honor dorm residents who complete the empathy and accountability course are introduced to a victim impact panel. This consists of crime victims whose offenders are not incarcerated at Holman. Since Holman is a maximum-security prison, victims of serious crimes are invited to tell their stories. Some inmates avoid thinking about their victims by stereotyping them. Just as the public has exaggerated negative views about offenders, some prisoners associate victims with political groups who lobby for more punitive responses to crime. They see them as revenge seekers. This is one of the ways that offenders can "block" empathy. Victim impact panels use a storytelling process where offenders are not put on the defensive. This allows them to respond to the victim more openly and empathically. Even more importantly, it gives victims who wish to do so an opportunity to experience additional healing.

In May 2007, a rape victim and the father of a murder victim spoke to the men. Both individuals had time to reflect on their victimizations since they occurred many years ago. The rape victim said the experience helped her because as a victim advocate she approached her own victimization in a clinical and detached way. After more than thirty years, the panel helped her express pain and sorrow at a more personal level contributing to her strength and dignity. Subsequently she indicated a desire to return to the honor dorm, perhaps as a volunteer. Victims heal in different ways, and the restorative approach allows for one type of healing.

The father of the murder victim told his story in other settings prior to the prison visit. After talking in the honor dorm, he said, "Somehow it is always helpful to tell the story, although I don't know why." I asked him what he liked most about the experience. He replied, "The fact that many of the prisoners thanked us for coming." As we drove home he began singing a Peter, Paul, and Mary tune with a light and amusing verse about kids at a drive-in movie. For me his singing represented some easing of the burden of his painful loss. There was nothing that he did not like about the experience, according to a form he completed two weeks later.

How did the honor dorm residents respond? Their written evaluations of the event suggest it was a powerful learning experience. Their responses use the language of empathy. Asked what they liked most about the victim impact panel, inmates wrote things like:

- It let me see things through their eyes.
- The tones of a real voice that I could hear and feel hurt, pain, and strength in. The atmosphere born out of the stories they told will without a doubt remain with me forever. . . . I owe them another round of thanks.
- I felt it better enabled us to understand the victims' feelings, emotion, and pain. What they truly experienced as a victim of crime—especially violent crime. To realize how our own actions have affected and impacted so many other lives similarly—and to enable us to empathize with these victims in a way we never thought possible. I felt it has truly been an emotional and life-changing experience.

- The emotional impact. I had tears in my eyes. I don't think "like" is a good word in this question. I wanted to hear their stories and needed to, but I didn't "like" it.

Will this experience have an impact on the inmate's future behavior? To suggest so would be unrealistic. An inmate might be deeply moved hearing a victim's story in a controlled setting, but unable to appreciate its lesson at a later point in time. Still inmates did learn from this experience as evidenced by a sample of answers from the following question—was this experience helpful to you in any way? If so, please list how it was helpful.

- It made me, once again, reaffirm to myself that I will *never* be the cause of another victim. Help anyone who needs help in any way I can, whether they are a victim or a potential victim.
- It gets you to look at crime different and it makes you think about your crime and the feelings of your victim's family.
- Yes, I can see the pain that I caused people in the past.
- Yes, feeling their pain makes me not want to ever hurt anyone.
- It brought me closer in contact with the reality of what violent crimes do across the board. And from this point I know that in the future I would think twice to avoid causing a similar situation.
- It brought to the surface feelings that I need to experience and deal with as an offender.

Inmate healing and change is not a "one-shot deal." These sample comments show how victim impact panels contribute to a *process* that encourages empathy and responsibility. Personalizing crime makes it difficult for inmates to fall back on rationalizations and other psychological mechanisms used to avoid responsibility for the harm they caused. Similarly, victim healing is a process. One woman plans to participate in a victim impact panel in the honor dorm to better prepare her to meet her daughter's offender in another prison.

An evaluation of the Sycamore Tree Project by researchers at Sheffield Hallam University in England supports the value of victim storytelling for offender accountability.[13] The Sycamore Tree Project sponsored by Prison Fellowship tries to meet victim needs and increase victim awareness among offenders. Offenders complete a six-week course and trained facilitators bring surrogate victims and offenders together. Offenders, if they wish, can make symbolic restitution to those who they similarly victimized. Research analyzed 2,197 sets of questionnaires completed by inmates in the Sycamore Tree Project between 2002 and 2004. Pretest and post-test scores were compared to assess whether inmates are more aware of the impact of their crimes after participating in the program. The empathy scale measures cognitive (awareness) rather than emotional empathy. Findings show higher victim empathy after completing the program, although there was considerable variation in empathy gains across institutions. Data are currently not available on the relationship between empathy and behavior after release from prison.

While Holman honor dorm inmates cannot make direct amends to their victims at this point in time, many of them recognize they can make indirect amends by demonstrating responsibility in their day-to-day lives particularly in relationships with family members and the honor dorm community. A long-distance dad's program, available to inmates throughout the prison, encourages the development of parenting skills, particularly communication. It speaks to responsibilities that inmates have to their families and encourages them not to underestimate the role they can play in their children's lives, even behind bars. For most inmates, ties weaken the longer the men are in prison. Many relationships are destroyed before the men are sentenced. But for some the opportunity to communicate honestly and soberly with family members becomes a first-time reality in prison. The convict culture does honor family relationships. However, honor dorm opportunities give inmates the capacity to repair and strengthen these relationships in concrete ways.

When asked to describe the impact of their crimes, many inmates describe the harm they did to their own families. This recognition and subsequent actions to repair harm are part of the road to accountability. During a long-distance dad's graduation ceremony, one inmate sat at a table with his mother and daughter, meticulously cleaning his daughter's fingernails. When I commented that was a nice thing to do, he responded, "That's my job." Another inmate recently discovered his two daughters had been sexually molested by an uncle when they were younger. Interestingly, his daughters told their father about what happened before talking to anyone else in the free world. The honor dorm resident spent a great deal of time responding to his daughters, using a therapeutic approach based on what he learned in the honor dorm about the impact of child sexual abuse. He assured them they had no reason to blame themselves or feel shame, and they did the right thing even if their uncle gets into trouble. Finally, an inmate's sister asked him to write the eulogy for their mother who died of cancer. It was beautifully written from the heart and read word-for-word by the minister at the funeral service. In this case, even though this honor dorm resident had been behind bars for eighteen years, he assumed many of the responsibilities of the head of household during his mother's illness and death, including a clear-minded understanding of what to do each step of the way.

Last on the list, the circle process, described in chapter 4, gives men the opportunity to learn responsibility to the honor dorm community. They learn how an altercation that seems personal has implications for the entire dorm. Speaking honestly before a group of peers is a character-building process. Relationship-building activities such as circles, mentoring, and the big-brother program help self-absorbed inmates act their way into right thinking about their role in the community. Service opportunities discussed in chapter 7 also contribute to inmate responsibility. Inmates discover they can give something back to the community after years of taking from it.

MORE ON EMPATHY

After I told a family therapist friend about the prison empathy class, she responded, "Gosh, do you think this is something I could teach my clients? When I work with married couples, it would be so much easier if they had more empathy." Studying the role of empathy in social relationships is not new. Early theorists were interested in how people came to know the feelings of others so they could come to act compassionately. Darwin was one of the first serious writers to identify empathy as an important social process. Philosopher David Hume introduced the term in his book on moral development. Philosopher and economist Adam Smith claimed a crucial role for sympathy in moral motivation. And Freud thought empathy was the major way in which we understand other people, particularly those whose experiences and beliefs are different from our own.[14] In a present-day application, Birthways, a company that teaches teen pregnancy prevention, advertises "The Empathy Belly Pregnancy Simulator, a weighted garment that teaches people what it feels like to be pregnant by simulating over 20 symptoms and effects of pregnancy."[15] Many teachers use film and role-play as a strategy to help students better understand the perspective of others and the consequences of their actions.

Quite a bit of research is done on the role of empathy in offender change. Findings are mixed. Some studies, for example, find a relationship between empathy, offending, and recidivism. Studies of sex offenders show the relationship is not simple. Many sex offenders show empathy for people in general but not for their specific victims. Nor is empathy a simple concept to define and measure. Several stages of empathy are identified, including (1) recognition of another person's emotional state, (2) taking the perspective of the other person, (3) experiencing the same or similar emotion as the observed person, and (4) taking some action to ameliorate the other person's distress.[16] In the honor dorm course a formal definition of empathy is provided. However, inmates are also asked to present their own definition of empathy. They are encouraged to identify the things that block empathy. Many offenders are under the influence of alcohol and drugs when they commit their crimes. Though not a defense or excuse, the role that substance abuse plays in these events cannot be ignored. As one inmate says,

> I am not good at expressing myself with a big vocabulary. I'm more a street person, so my words remain small and simple after all these years. I pray God will forgive me for the people I've hurt. We never think about nothing when addicted to drugs, alcohol, or whatever, we only try to full fill our addiction.

From a restorative perspective empathy is a key factor in bringing about inmate accountability. Understanding the consequences of one's actions and their impact on victims is enhanced through the ability to empathize. Its demonstration by the offender can also contribute to victim healing. The bondage of resentment is more easily released when victims receive a sincere apology from their offender.[17] From the viewpoint of the moral prison, acknowledging the victim through empathic responses is simply the right thing to do. It is part of "cleaning up after yourself."

MORE ON SHAME

Shame can be an educational tool. A person who feels a moment of shame can learn much about himself or herself and others. Shame is normal and good if it is used constructively. As Sabini and Silver suggest, shame prevents "many of us doing things the world is better off without our doing.[18] Braithwaite elaborates on the role of community and shame in his book *Crime, Shame, and Reintegration* (1989).[19] He distinguishes between disintegrative shaming that labels and stigmatizes the offender causing future deterioration in behavior, and reintegrative shaming where community members hold offenders accountable for their actions, distinguish between the act and the person, and support the offender in behaviors that will return him or her to the community in good standing. Honor dorm peacemaking circles model reintegrative shaming.

On the other hand, Maxwell and Morris address the dangers of shaming. "In our view, [it] carries too many risks to be worth playing."[20] Many people associate shaming with hazing and its attendant humiliation. However, when practiced within a structure guided by restorative principles, such as peacemaking circles, there are built-in checks that can transform shame into accountability and feelings of shared responsibility and humanity. In the survey of circle participants, very few responses if any suggested an experience of disintegrative shaming. But peacemaking circles are based on behavior in the honor dorm community. How is shame from past experiences and behavior, including crime, addressed?

A small group of inmates explored shame in an honor dorm class. In addition to normal shame, we discussed shame deficiency and excessive shame.[21] Most people associate criminals with shame deficiency. A few character traits are lacking empathy, self-centeredness, and narcissism. Zehr notes that

> Contrary to popular belief, offenders often do feel guilt for what they have done. Yet a sense of guilt can be terribly threatening to one's sense of self-worth and self-identity. One study has concluded that offenders are characterized by tremendous fears and that their greatest fear is of the "zero-state," that is of personal worthlessness. Consequently, offenders utilize a variety of defensive techniques to avoid guilt and maintain their sense of self-worth.[22]

This seemed to be the consensus in class. Most offenders related more to the notion of excessive shame. Associated with excessive shame are negative self-descriptions using words such as such as fool, idiot, dummy, incompetent, weak, bad, and "a nothing."[23] While it is desirable for offenders to feel bad about what they did, feeling bad about who they are is not helpful. Rather than experiencing empathy and accountability, the shame-based person uses denial, withdrawal, arrogance, anger, and even exhibitionism to cope with such uncomfortable feelings. Therefore, transforming shame is important for encouraging accountability and promoting pro-social values.

Some researchers distinguish shame from guilt. Shame is a negative evaluation of the self and guilt is a negative evaluation of the act.[24] However, in a study of DUI cases, Harris found that these "moral emotions" were not so easily distinguished.[25] Shame/guilt was positively correlated with empathy and negatively related with anger/hostility. However, offenders who were ambivalent about what they did, experiencing unresolved shame, were more likely to feel anger and hostility toward other people connected to their case.[26] This underscores the importance of giving inmates the opportunity to own up to the harms they have done within a supportive environment.

A number of residents in the shame class teach the required honor dorm courses. They thought shame awareness needed to be shared with their fellows. As a result, they incorporated lessons from the shame class into the required courses and designated a "shame awareness week." They talked about where shame comes from, how it is experienced, how it can affect behavior, and how it can be processed in healthy ways.

Evaluations of the shame lessons were completed for five courses. Honor dorm residents were asked to rate the helpfulness of shame material to understanding themselves on a scale from one to ten with one being the least helpful and ten being the most helpful. One hundred sixty-four evaluations were completed with the possibility that an inmate might be attending more than one class. Ratings across the five classes ranged from 7.5 to 8.1.

Ratings on the 10-point scale for how the shame material helped individuals understand their fellows ranged from 7.4 to 8.5.

Many individuals gave the material high ratings and comments showed enthusiasm for the subject as well as evidence it was helpful. Several people want to continue the discussion of shame in greater depth. "We need a whole lot more of this kind of material introduced not only to this community, but [it] ought to be made available to every person incarcerated within these prison walls. How else can we ever consider change if we don't know something is really wrong about us and what we have done to ourselves and others." Another inmate comments, "It helps the most by looking at myself. Because I do not like to be in shame." Still another writes, "It helped me to understand some things about myself (feelings I would have and why) and to know that it just isn't me alone with these types of feelings." Another inmate recognizes for the first time that his own withdrawal is a response to shame. Only one inmate had a negative reaction to the material suggesting that shame is a "slave morality."

INMATE VICTIMIZATION

Sometimes appreciating the emotions and feelings of others can be enhanced by reflecting on times that we were hurt. In the empathy and accountability class we encourage this practice in an exercise where students are asked to think about a time when someone else treated them unfairly. The incident need not be a crime. Inmates pair up and are asked to share their reflections about how they felt after they were hurt, how they feel about it now, how the experience impacted their lives, and how the experience changed the way they looked at the world and themselves.[27] I listened to a man in one of the dyads describe how he was humiliated when he asked a young lady for a date at age thirteen. She refused, telling him he was stupid, ignorant, and uneducated. He shared that after the experience he treated women badly, although he is not a sex offender or a perpetrator of domestic violence. Subsequently when we discussed a crime victim story from the *Transcending* book, the same offender could not understand how a woman who had been abused as a child continued to seek out abusers later in life. The inmate is encouraged to make a connection with the long-lasting impact the young lady had on him when he was thirteen years old.

LETTER-WRITING EXERCISES

The most direct opportunity honor dorm residents have to make things right is apology letters written to their victims in the empathy and accountability class. Because of state law, these letters are not mailed. It is difficult for inmates to write the letters even though I am the only person who reads them. In the first class one of the inmates sealed his letter in an envelope with a note in large block letters, "DO NOT SHOW THIS TO ANYONE." The general nature of the letter failed to communicate what he did. Yet in the prisoner's mind, he wrote something so terrible he had to conceal it and pledge me to secrecy. Letter 1 shows an inmate who has the capacity to admit what he did. He demonstrates an understanding of the impact of his crime and a willingness to empathize with his victim.

Letter 1

To ——,

I don't know if you will ever read this letter, but I have to write it. I often wonder if you still think about that night 17 years ago when I did what I did to you. I remember from the trial and from what other people told me that you had a really hard time adjusting after I raped you. I was told that you required psychological counseling and that you quit your job. I look back at how I turned your life upside down and ask myself what kind of person would terrorize another person and degrade them the way I did you.

I tried for years to justify with some sick kind of reasoning that there was an explanation for the horrible act that I committed against you, but I finally gave up. I hate myself for what I did. It was a selfish and evil thing that I did to you and I have to live with that reality.

So, I deserve to be right where I'm at, in prison, and if I never get out then I know that I have nobody to blame but myself. But I've come to realize that there are things more important than getting out of prison, for instance this letter I'm writing. I need to tell you that I've tried really hard to feel at least some of the horrible fear and degradation that you felt that night I came into your bedroom and woke you up with my hand over your mouth and a knife to your throat.

I've read about the trauma that rape victims go through and I know I can never experience the intensity of it, but I have tried to imagine it. I have cried over the horrible realization of how I made you feel and experienced a shame so deep that I couldn't admit to another person what I did for years. I know that there is nothing I can do of my own power to make right the wrong that I created. So I am only doing what I can, even while realizing that it falls far short.

——, I am sorry. I hope that some how in the course of these last 17 years you have come to terms with what happened and that I am the only one with issues today. I hope you have found closure and don't even think about me except as a difficult time in your life that you got past and rarely give a thought to today. I pray that you have forgiven me for what I did even though I don't deserve it. I know the words "I forgive you" are words I've dreamed about for years. But they seem as unattainable as this life without parole that I'm serving. I don't know

what would be worse—to never get out of prison or to never receive forgiveness for what I did.

Please forgive me, ——! And please pray for me that God will help me to salvage something of this wretched life that I've lived. My shame will always be before me.

Now let's look at two additional letters that are somewhat less forthcoming.

Letter 2

Dear Mr. ——,

Over the years, some need in me has always wanted to get in touch with you, but I've been told it wasn't appropriate, nor would the state's attorney approve for me to let you know how sincerely sorry I am for putting you and your family through such an ordeal. I had no justification whatsoever for intruding into your home and causing such a scare.

You had the right to respond to a threat as you seen [sic] fit, yet fortunately, you chose to run out the door to seek help, and I do commend you for that, and I'm grateful and I thank God no one was harmed. Another person at another place might have acted a lot differently, and the result could have caused harm or ended a life. I believe God was watching out for both you and I on that night of November 29, 1991.

Before the trial, two-years later that I, and you, was compelled to attend, I conveyed to my attorney how remorseful I was, and that I would plead guilty, because I was, for as I've stated, I had no right or reason at all for being in your home. I was willing to accept any consequences, either punishment from the court, or compensate you in some form. I was even tempted to stand during the trial and let you know how sorry I was, and did not want us to be there.

Mr. ——, my problem was abusing alcohol (long story back to my Vietnam days), and that is the only times I've ever found myself in trouble, like on that night of November '91, or else our paths never would have crossed. I've tried to remember, yet vaguely I seem to recall a tall man that night, because on that January day of 1992 at my preliminary when I sat beside you on that hallway outside the courtroom, I still had no idea that you were my victim until we were seated in the courtroom. On that day when I found out you were a student of law, I told my attorney that I wanted to plead guilty, because I did not want a long drawn out course, or cause any more burden to you and your quest to become an attorney.

I've been concerned about you over the years and being here at Holman Prison since December 1994, I've heard of your firm down in Mobile. In fact I even rooted for you when your firm represented the University of Alabama's football program when the NCAA sanctioned them for some violations, but I lost how it turned out. Well, I hope.

Mr. ——, I could go on and on how much remorse I feel, but until I've been in your shoes, only then will I know whether or not to accept an apology, yet I pray and ask that you accept my humble apology or forgive me, and please know in your heart that you can be assured that for the rest of my life, there will be no more victims!!

Sincerely, ——

P.S. Mr. ——, I am praying that I do get a response, and I'm open for anything you might have to say.

Letter 3

Dear Victim,

I'm writing this letter hoping that it brings some closure and understanding to you. First, I would like you to know that you did nothing wrong. What happen [sic] was not your fault. I needed money and I went out to get it the only way I knew how. It was nothing personal.

All my life I've only known crime. I was raised by drug dealers. All I've ever known was 26 oz. is a kilo of coke, and 16 oz. in a pound of weed. I got my money when I was little by sacking up weed for my folks. That was my mom's side of the family. Now on my daddy's side was [sic] the robbers. I was brought up in the streets. So I never really knew what I was doing was harming people. It was my way of life.

So coming from a poor family in a poor project. That's all my family knowed [sic] and that [sic] what they taught me. I'm truly sorry that our paths crossed the way they did. If I ever get the chance to make this right I truly will.

Respectfully yours, ——

The second offender has a strong desire to connect with his victim and feels the need to do so for a long time. He does not say he broke into the man's home to rob him nor does he acknowledge the traumatic effects of his crime. Instead he minimizes the offense saying he intruded into the victim's home, caused "a scare," and put the victim through an "ordeal." There is no mention of a weapon. This shows how difficult it is for inmates to acknowledge the impact of their crimes. Letter 2 does show genuine remorse, a desire to take responsibility for harm done, and the beginnings of an empathic response. The offender wants to show he cares about the victim when he relates the story about the victim's law firm and its involvement with the University of Alabama football team. He also provides an interesting insight into the criminal justice system. His desire to admit guilt is trumped by a legal system that prescribes contesting it. More astounding is no provision to separate the victim and the offender before they entered the courtroom. Unbeknownst to victim and offender, they stood next to each other in the hallway before the proceedings began!

Both the second and third offenders studied victim needs in their restorative justice classes. One need is the victim's desire for information such as "why did this happen to me?" Victims often blame themselves, thinking, "If only I had done 'a,' 'b,' or 'c.' this wouldn't have happened." The offenders' references to their alcohol addiction and family background are not offered as an excuse, but as an explanation for conditions that influenced their behavior. In the third letter the inmate wants to assure the victim the crime was not his fault. However, he does not yet have the ability to directly state what he did. He talks instead about how their "paths crossed."

Letter 4 is a richer and more detailed account of the offender's thinking before he came to prison and after he learned about restorative justice. The letter addresses multiple victims.

Letter 4

Unless one knows the addictive effects of drugs on one's mind, you will not understand what happened to me that triggered my criminal ventures. This isn't an attempt to justify my wrongs, but only an attempt to explain what happened.

My drug use wasn't motivated by a craving for pleasure, but rather motivated by an effort to escape the fact that my life seemed to be going downhill. I began to feel tired of a life I couldn't turn around. Crazy as it may sound, I thought that increasing the speed of the downward trip would eventually end me and the trip . . . an indirect suicide attempt if there ever was one. To kick this off I went on a mass robbery spree to get money strictly for drugs. Being unarmed is how I convinced myself that no one could get hurt but me. I had no idea of the trauma I caused my direct victims, and indirect victims. I felt that I would soon get caught and possibly killed. I didn't. I felt [I] cared, but that was the drug-induced state of mind talking because after getting caught and the influence of drugs subsiding, I reflected on how I had created a graver situation.

Since all of this has happened a bunch of "what ifs" have haunted me. My feelings of guilt and shame have made me remorseful and my prayers have awakened in me a desire to be a better person. If nothing, I want to contribute to the atmosphere that surrounds me no matter where it's at (this side of the fence or the other side of the fence).

Along with my direct victims there are others who suffered from my actions. My son, ex-wife, mother, friends, neighbors. The children, possible spouses, neighbors, and friends of my victims have suffered also. This I never thought about until I began to think beyond myself and my person[al] problems. The traumas I have caused others I believe are impossible to list since traumas can last until reaching the grave.

Making things right I realize is easier said than done. The basic steps of admitting my wrong, realizing I must be accountable, and stepping out to help repair or attempt to repair the damage I've done must be done. I also feel I must change my thinking where it caused me to consider crazy things due to my personal problems. I must go forward with trying to salvage my life. Sift through the ashes of my life and retain all the good that wasn't destroyed. I must pour my energy into giving to the community wherein I reside. Above all, I believe I must pray and trust that God will guide me to what's best for myself and this world.

God bless us all who care and haven't realized how important it is to care.

Sincerely, ———

In letter 4, the writer directly acknowledges his crimes. Furthermore, he understands accountability. He shows awareness of the harm he caused but realizes given the circumstances, the best way to make amends is to change his thinking and behavior. He wants to contribute as much as he can to the honor dorm community, and he does. A master storyteller, this honor dorm resident is a respected teacher and models behavior for other inmates. He gently and compassionately approaches prisoners who have difficulty making the changes they need to live in the dorm. In one class, I asked each resident to share how they felt that day. This particular inmate proudly said, "I feel mature."

In the empathy and accountability course inmates are required to write three letters. The first is the letter of apology to the victim. In the second letter the offender places himself in the role of his victim, responds to the initial apology letter, and asks the offender (himself) questions. In the third letter the inmate answers his victim's letter.

Letters 5a through 5c are a complete set for this assignment.

Letter 5a

To the —— family,

Hello. This is —— and I'm not really sure how to begin this letter. I can never even come close to knowing the pain I've caused your family. And to say I'm sorry for what I've done, or to express any words of remorse, may sound hollow and cheap.

But I must say something and with all my heart I must ask your forgiveness. A forgiveness which I neither deserve or rarely expect you are able to give.

But of one I still must ask. Words are at a loss for me, for what can I say to someone who has lost so much.

And I pray that even this small effort will help you in some way.

And though I write this mainly with you in heart and mind, I would be dishonest if I were not to tell you that it is also partly for me. And I ask you to forgive me for that also. But I must live with the hurt I have caused your family. I have wept many nights for the pain I have caused. But I know I cannot and will not ever come close to the tears and grief your family have [sic] shed.

I am almost ashamed of mentioning myself in this letter but I want it to be as honest as possible.

I also want to say that if you have any questions whatsoever I will answer them with all honesty, hiding nothing.

And in closing I want to tell you that I pray for your family on a daily basis. I hope you can except [sic] that of me, but if not I understand and hope I haven't hurt you more by saying it.

May God be with you, ——

Letter 5b

Mr. ——,

To say I was shocked when I received your letter is an understatement. And at first I wasn't going to respond at all and even why I am at this time is a mystery to me.

You were correct in saying that you can't imagine the pain you caused me and my family, even after 25 years that pain is still fresh. It's a living thing that will most likely be with me till my last breath. And I HATE you for causing it. And I want you to endure as much pain as I have.

You ask for forgiveness in your letter, but I don't see that as a possibility. My Bible tells me I should but I don't really see it happening. I'm human not God.

But I think you are truly remorseful of what you did. That is most likely the only reason I'm writing this at all. And you should be remorseful for that evil act.

You said you would answer any of my questions. Well I have many, but can't bring myself to ask you yet. They hurt too much.

Even writing this little bit is very difficult. But the more I write the more I think I might want to meet you if to do nothing else but to spit in your face and allow you to see the pain you have caused.

Maybe some day I can do as you ask and forgive to some degree. But it will take God to do it, for I cannot.

Even though the inmate does not have his victim ask specific questions, in the reply letter he writes as though the victim asks for clarification about what happened.

Letter 5c

Hello ——,

I'm not really sure of myself here. I don't want to cause you more pain than I already have but you said you wanted to know.

I hope you don't feel I'm dodging here but I really don't remember much about that day. I remember pulling in the parking lot of the bank and picking —— up but after that point it's pretty much a blank. I was high on the drug PCP so I really wasn't thinking at all of what we were really doing. —— ran it down to me and I just said okay and it happened. It was as if I were in a bad dream. What I know of what happened mostly comes from my partner. We drove to where they were killed and he shot them. I didn't and probably couldn't have shot them, but I was there and I have and always will feel guilty of what happen [sic] and except [sic] the total blame of that day. The pain of what happened lives with me every day and I feel the pain and hurt for those I have hurt because of this. First of all for you and your family, but I also hurt many members in my family also. Many members in my family won't except [sic] that I was involved at all. Even though I've told them it was so.

The pain and hurt I've caused your family is almost more than I can compre-
hend. And I know you may not even want me to but I pray for you and your fam-
ily regularly.

I don't know what I can do if anything to ever right this wrong. All I can do that
I know of is pray for you. For it is God alone that can right this type of wrong or
heal this type of pain. I pray that God works this miracle for you and your family.

This letter shows the offender's awareness of the depth of his victim's pain and grief—it is so great that he humbly acknowledges there is nothing he can do by himself to make things right. He prays for the family regularly but concedes they might find this offensive. He hopes they don't, but he really doesn't know what else to do. How do you respond when you read this offender's letter to his victim? Is he on target given the circumstances of the case?

Most of the inmates are very hard on themselves when they write from their victim's perspective. One man's victim "responded," "Go to hell!" In a subsequent class I helped inmates formulate questions their victims might ask based on the apology letters. This helps sustain the "dialogue" between victim and offender and in most cases assists the offender in speaking more directly about his crime. This exercise is important because accountability means the inmate owns up to the exact nature of the crime and the harm it caused. For example, an inmate might want to say, "I had sex with her," rather than ac-knowledge what really happened, "I raped her."

Four of the five letters ask their victims for forgiveness. This may stem from some men's beliefs that a "sinner" must ask for such a thing. In a subsequent class on forgiveness we discussed whether asking for it places an undue bur-den on the victim. Many of the men think it does, or at least that such a re-quest is inappropriate for the initial apology letter. Still the frequency with which these letters beg forgiveness suggests its spiritual and psychological im-portance to the men. To explore this issue a little further, I asked volunteers from an empathy and accountability class in progress as well as members of a leadership group who previously completed the class to reflect on the follow-ing question—"Is forgiveness from your victim important to you? Why?" From a pool of twenty-one individuals I received thirteen written responses. Some believe that it is not important to receive forgiveness from their victims. For them, taking responsibility for their crimes occurs with or without victim forgiveness. One Muslim resident said his religion requires an offender to ask forgiveness from the victim. Others indicated that forgiveness would give them great personal comfort and that they would go to any lengths to get it. Still others thought that forgiveness was more important for the victim than for the offender because forgiveness will help the victim heal. Thus, forgiveness is important to these inmates for a variety of reasons. From a restorative perspective it is one of the ways that offenders as well as victims can facilitate reconciliation and healing.

NOTES

1. Howard Zehr, *The Little Book of Restorative Justice* (Intercourse, Pa.: Good Books, 2002), 14–15.

2. Lisa F. Jackson, "Meeting with a Killer," for *Court TV*, broadcast fall 2001.

3. Victim Services, Vermont Department of Corrections, Agency of Human Services, available at www.doc.state.vt.us/victim-services/vodp/vod-faq#difference (accessed 21 May 2007).

4. Jeff Latimer, Craig Dowden, and Danielle Muse, *The Effectiveness of Restorative Practice: A Meta-analysis* (Ottawa, Canada: Department of Justice, Research and Statistics Division Methodological Series, 2001).

5. Mark S. Umbreit, Betty Vos, Robert B. Coates, and Katherine Brown, *Facing Violence: The Path of Restorative Justice and Dialogue* (Monsey, N.Y.: Criminal Justice Press, 2003), 28.

6. Umbreit, Vos, Coates, and Brown, *Facing Violence*, 129.

7. Zehr, *The Little Book of Restorative Justice*, 15.

8. Howard Zehr, *Changing Lenses: A New Focus for Crime and Justice*, 3rd ed. (Scottsdale, Pa.: Herald Press, 2005), 47.

9. Zehr, *The Little Book of Restorative Justice*, 15.

10. Zehr, *The Little Book of Restorative Justice*, 16.

11. Howard Zehr, *Transcending: Reflections of Crime Victims* (Intercourse, Pa.: Good Books, 2001).

12. Adapted from Zehr, *The Little Book of Restorative Justice*, 17.

13. Simon Feasey, Patrick Williams, and Rebecca Clark, "An Evaluation of the Prison Fellowship Sycamore Tree Programme," Sheffield Hallman University 2005, available

at www.restorativejustice.org.uk/rj_&_the_CJS/pdf/Sycamore_tree_evaluation.pdf (accessed 7 May 2008).

14. W. L. Marshall, "Historic Foundations and Current Conceptualizations of Empathy," in *In Their Shoes: Examining the Issue of Empathy and Its Place in the Treatment of Offenders*, ed. Yolanda Fernandez (Oklahoma City: Woods N Barnes, 2002), 2–8.

15. Birthways Child Resource Center Inc., www.empathybelly.org/home.html (accessed 11 May 2008).

16. Liam Marshall, "Development of Empathy," in *In Their Shoes: Examining the Issue of Empathy and Its Place in the Treatment of Offenders*, ed. Yolanda Fernandez (Oklahoma City: Woods N Barnes, 2002), 36–52.

17. Zehr, *Transcending*, 45–49.

18. John Sabrina and Maury Silver, "In Defense of Shame: Shame in the Context of Guilt and Embarrassment," *Journal for Theory of Social Behavior* 27, no. 1 (March 1997): 12.

19. John Braithwaite, *Crime, Shame, and Reintegration* (Cambridge: Cambridge University Press, 1989), 84–89.

20. Gabrielle Maxwell and Allison Morris, "What Is the Place of Shame in Restorative Justice?" in *Critical Issues in Restorative Justice*, ed. Howard Zehr and Barb Toews (Monsey, N.Y.: Criminal Justice Press, 2004), 139.

21. Ronald Potter Efron and Patricia Potter Efron, *Understanding How Shame Affects Your Life* (San Francisco: Harper/Hazelden, 1989).

22. Zehr, *Changing Lenses*, 49.

23. Potter Efron and Potter Efron, *Understanding How Shame Affects Your Life*, 31–50.

24. Janice Lindsay-Hartz, "Contrasting Experiences of Shame and Guilt," *American Behavioral Scientist* 27, no. 6 (July 1984): 689–704.

25. Nathan Harris, "Reassessing the Dimensionality of Moral Emotions," *British Journal of Psychology* 94, no. 4 (November 2003): 457–73.

26. Nathan Harris, "Reassessing the Dimensionality of Moral Emotions," 470.

27. Barb Toews, *The Little Book of Restorative Justice for People in Prison: Rebuilding the Web of Relationships* (Intercourse, Pa.: Good Books, 2006), 47–48.

Learning the ABCs

The way to restore honor is by honoring one another, and the way we honor one another is through servanthood. Servanthood must be motivated by love—love for your community, love for God, or love for an honorable cause.

—An inmate instructor in the W. C. Holman Faith-Based Restorative Justice Honor Dorm

I ain't gonna kiss nobody's ass.

—An inmate student in the honor dorm

Education is central to honor dorm programming at Holman. But the role of education in prison reform is surprisingly controversial. Robert Martinson's "nothing works" treatise on the failures of rehabilitation programs discussed in chapter 1 contributes to this debate.[1] It concludes that educational programs, as well as many other efforts for inmate change, are largely unsuccessful. Another issue among unsympathetic citizens is those who commit crimes should be the last to receive educational subsidies. This principle of *less eligibility* was introduced in the first chapter. The Violent Crime Control Act of 1994/1995 eliminated Pell grant postsecondary opportunities for prisoners. This law presupposes that prisoners are the least deserving of educational benefits.

Professional educators were quick to respond with arguments for inmate schooling. While education is no panacea for social problems, research shows that adults without a high school degree or without postsecondary education are more likely to be incarcerated than adults with more education.[2] A national study on literacy sponsored by the Department of Education in 2003 compared inmate educational levels and literacy rates with those in 1992. (It is important to note that the prison population in 2003 was 50 percent higher than it was in the previous ten years.) While inmates in 2003 had higher average levels of education than those in the previous survey, 9 percent of them had never reached high school, and 28 percent never received a high school diploma or a GED (Graduate Equivalency Diploma).[3] Despite improvements between 1992 and 2003 on various measures of literacy, in the categories of prose, document, and quantitative literacy, the percentage of inmates with scores below the basic level in 2003 were 16 percent, 15 percent, and 39 percent, respectively.[4] Those in the below basic category can do only the most simple literacy tasks.[5] In 2003, those proficient in these categories of literacy were 3 percent, 3 percent, and 2 percent, respectively.[6] Sadly, the average literacy scores do not increase for inmates with increasing levels of education and are independent of their parents' educational attainment.[7]

The differences in educational attainment between a nonprison household sample and the inmate sample are significant for all categories of education.[8] For example, when the highest education level attained is high school graduation, the figure for the household sample is 26 percent high school graduate while the one for prisoners is 13 percent.[9] Fifty-one percent of the household sample has some postsecondary education, while the figure for inmates is 22 percent.[10] Prisoners have lower average literacy scores than households, with the greatest differences in quantitative literacy.[11] While national literacy study findings do not establish a causal relationship between education and crime, illiteracy and the failure to obtain a high school degree or a GED are risk factors for delinquency and other deviant behaviors.[12]

THE CASE FOR PRISON EDUCATION

Why should prisoners have educational opportunities? There are two lines of argument. One contends education is a necessary condition for rehabilitation. A second belief is education promotes safety and order in prison communities. The education-rehabilitation connection is not simple, and research findings are mixed. Barb Toews offers this explanation: "Individuals choose if and when they want to experience personal growth. It requires them to remove the cloak of offending and turn toward their inner, true self. For some, experiencing growth comes before accountability. For others, meaningful accountability triggers growth."[13]

From a restorative perspective, accountability is a key to offender change because it directly addresses one's criminal behavior and lifestyle. Taking responsibility for one's offenses can be the beginning of the change process motivating the offender to acquire the education and skills necessary to become a full community member.[14] On the other hand, the perspective that education offers an inmate may precede accountability but ultimately motivate the offender to choose it. When asked why they choose to move to the Holman honor dorm, several recently admitted inmates say it is the opportunity to better themselves, particularly through educational opportunities. When they first join the dorm, these inmates have no concept of the role of accountability in restorative recovery.

Another source of confusion about the relationship between postsecondary education and recidivism is research methodology.[15] It is difficult to establish a control group because most postsecondary programming is voluntary. When findings show a relationship between education and offender change, it may be that inmates who are less likely to recidivate are the same people who choose education. While these issues remain, Tewksbury and his colleagues cite thirteen studies completed in the 1990s that demonstrate a linkage between postsecondary education programming and lower recidivism rates.[16]

If education brings about offender change, how so? Some researchers argue postsecondary education contributes to the maturation of the offender.[17] Research on moral development suggests a primary role for education as the individual moves from a self-centered orientation to appreciation and understanding of a social view of morality.[18] The role of education in cognitive change, critical reflection, and transformative learning is cited by others.[19]

A second argument for prison education is its role in prisoner behavior. While a causal relationship is not established between postsecondary education and disciplinary problems, one study finds after postsecondary programming was eliminated from the Maryland Department of Corrections, within one year inmates on average spent four times as many days in disciplinary confinement.[20] Other studies show education promotes a peaceful environment.[21] From a management perspective, education programs provide an incentive for good behavior. A psychologist on the staff at Holman advocates more educational opportunities, including degree-earning programs, to give inmates hope, especially those with life-without-parole sentences. From a restorative perspective, education also enhances social interactions and promotes modeling of pro-social behavior.

Given the large percentage of inmates lacking a high school degree or its equivalent, it is important to include more basic education in prison programming. Moeller, Day, and Rivera interviewed inmates in Illinois and found they prefer reading and math be the focus of their education, although these inmates think the language arts, history, social science, and life skills should also be part of the curriculum.[22] The need to focus on very basic skills is highlighted by another group of reseachers who found 40 percent of adult and youthful offenders have learning disabilities compared with 11 percent of nonoffender adults.[23] In spite of these findings, most academic research focuses on postsecondary education, and it is difficult to locate studies on GED programming.

EDUCATION IN HOLMAN'S HONOR DORM

In Holman's honor dorm education falls into two categories. The first is basic education for residents lacking a GED or high school diploma; the second is community education including weekly required classes. The community education classes deal with honor dorm philosophy, life skills, crime impact on victims, and community.

The warden mandates GED enrollment for all honor dorm residents who have no high school degree. All honor dorm educational requirements, including GED preparation, support the restorative philosophy. This philosophy incorporates what Moeller, Day, and Rivera describe as "a basic human understanding that an education is a person's link to a better life."[24] From this perspective, restorative justice includes *all* parties impacted by the crime and supports making things right for *all* those affected. This means harm extends beyond the victim and the community. It means making things right for the offender, too. It calls for acquiring the skills necessary to live a full life in the community.[25] Community thus has two meanings at Holman—the community of the honor dorm and the hypothetical community where inmates hope to return or where they hope to contribute even if they remain incarcerated.

Addressing the need for basic education falls under the restorative practice of building offender capacities. Offender capacity includes the ability to grasp ideas, communicate, analyze situations, and cope with problems. Some offenders have no capacity to fill out a job application. Although all incarcerated people are classified by society as "at risk," those lacking a fundamental education are greatly "at risk," and have difficulty adjusting within the prison environment as well. Outbreaks of anger and rage are understandable given the nature of prison life, but they are also signs of the inability to solve problems peacefully. To reduce the risk of being sent to segregation for violent behavior, some inmates self-medicate by drinking prison-made whiskey or using other available drugs. But eventually this strategy fails. As their drug use increases, these same inmates become recognizable to prison officials. They are targeted for drug testing, fail the drug tests, and eventually return to the isolation of disciplinary segregation, beginning another cycle of rage.

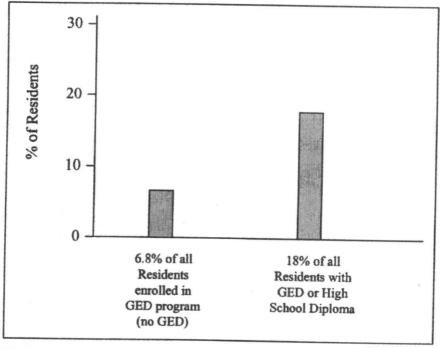

FIGURE 6.1.
Completed Two Years in the Faith-Based Honor Dorm.
Statistics provided by the Honor Dorm Database and Chaplaincy Programming

Low educational attainment is associated with the inability to succeed in the honor dorm community. Figure 6.1 compares data on GED completion with the ability to remain in the honor dorm for a two-year period. While some individuals voluntarily leave the dorm, most are terminated for rule violations. Between October 1999 and May 2004, 6.8 percent of entering honor dorm residents without the GED remained in the dorm after two years. For entering inmates with a GED or higher, 18 percent completed two years living in the dorm. Other studies on resident behavior in the honor dorm by education show similar results. Figure 6.2, for example, shows during the first semester of community education, a greater number of residents without the GED drop out of the dorm or are expelled from the dorm for behavioral problems. Other reports (figures 6.3 and 6.4) indicate residents without the GED incur dorm infractions at a higher rate than their more educated counterparts in their first and second semesters.

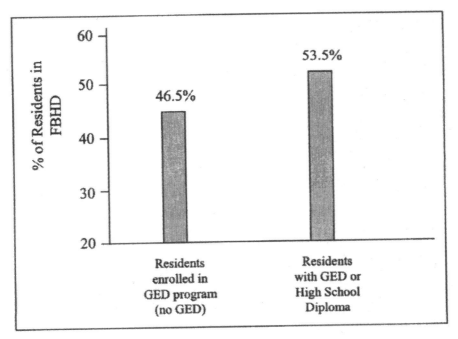

FIGURE 6.2.
First Semester.
Statistics provided by the Honor Dorm Database and Chaplaincy Programming

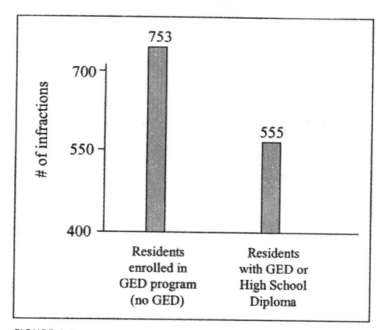

FIGURE 6.3.
First Semester.
Statistics provided by the Honor Dorm Database and Chaplaincy Programming

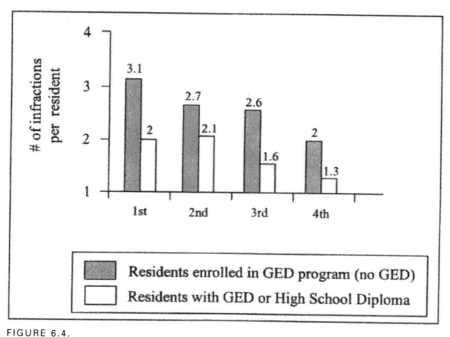

FIGURE 6.4.
Faith-Based Honor Dorm Semester Distribution.
Statistics provided by the Honor Dorm Database and Chaplaincy Programming

BASIC EDUCATION AT HOLMAN'S FAITH-BASED HONOR DORM

A requirement for entering and remaining in the honor dorm at Holman is an agreement to work toward a GED. This part of the application process involves a signed contractual agreement between the resident and the honor dorm community. Unless a resident produces a written certificate or diploma showing he has a GED or high school diploma, he is immediately enrolled in the dorm's basic education program. To remain in the honor dorm, he must demonstrate progress toward the GED.

The need for fundamental education is addressed by teaching offenders to read and write and by preparing offenders to take the GED. The local community college offers all Holman inmates assistance with training and testing for the GED. But as a result of funding cutbacks, these classes are very limited. For example, only inmates ready to take the GED examination are accepted into their program.

In 2006, the honor dorm had approximately 70 of 174 residents with no GED or high school diploma. The grade level for these seventy men ranges from kindergarten to the tenth grade with an average educational attainment of the fifth grade. The ages of these residents range from twenty years to seventy years old, with an average age of thirty-five. For many residents, if the honor dorm didn't require them to work toward their GED, they would not go there. Understandably, then, after being required to attend, many residents lack the motivation needed to apply their attention and time toward obtaining their GED. Of these seventy residents, only twenty are enrolled in the community college GED program. The remaining fifty residents are enrolled in the faith-based dorm study hall program.

The dorm study hall program for GED students passed through several phases since its inception in 2000. When the dorm was in a 114-bed dormitory, space was not available for a study hall. Inmates tried to use the dining hall for this function, but the former warden would not allow it without free world supervision. The program was at a standstill, until with the chaplain's help the local junior college began registering dorm residents in their GED classes that met in the institutional dining hall. There was room for approximately half of the available honor dorm students in the junior college GED class. The remaining students had to wait until the next registration period and hope they could register.

In the next phase, residents in the honor dorm taught classes under a junior college supervisor. When a resident passed a pre-GED test, he took the GED exam. Several honor dorm residents obtained their GED in this manner. But the program allowed students to meet only three nights a week. There was little support from the dorm with no space for desks and time set aside for concentrated study. A number of inmates have difficulty learning without this additional support. In December 2002, the dorm moved to a 174-bed facility, making space available for the needs of every resident without a GED. At this time, students not currently enrolled with the junior college GED program were required to attend a structured study hall in the dorm.

THE BASIC EDUCATION CURRICULUM

Providing a structured learning environment for forty to fifty people whose education levels range from a first grade to an eighth grade equivalency and also includes those who cannot read or write is a challenging task. The dorm education department created a literacy class to address the needs of residents without basic reading and writing. It is a self-contained, separate class from the rest of the study hall. It is important to instill self-esteem and self-confidence among members of this group. One way is to use reading material sufficiently basic for the students to understand, but with adult content. The dorm uses the *Laubach* reading series for teaching the literacy class. Since its inception, this class has an average of seven men. Honor dorm values make it wrong to leave these individuals behind, even though they are small in number, and it takes a great deal of time end effort to help them. They support the belief that everyone counts.

The remaining students follow two basic courses of study: math or language. The math curriculum is structured to pass the GED. It is designed to meet the student where he currently functions. The curriculum is separated into levels with the first working with "whole numbers" and the second studying "decimals." There are seven levels culminating with the most difficult one for most students—geometry. The language curriculum has a similar structure with each level consisting of several lessons. Until the student grasps the lesson he is studying, the next lesson is not attempted. After completing all six levels, the student learns how to write an essay and is prepared to take the language portion of the GED test. Every eight weeks students are tested to measure their progress in language and math. This gives them feedback about their development and teaches valuable test-taking skills. All of this work takes place within the framework of the study hall that meets seven days a week and uses tutors when necessary.

It is important to point out that honor dorm residents provide all of these services. The values of service and relationship-building are essential to delivering these programs. They are compatible with both the faith-based and restorative underpinnings of the dorm. Also evident is the value of building trust. Will the inmate who fails this week's lesson be the subject of gossip and ridicule in the hallways, or will he be supported, guided, and ultimately applauded by his fellow residents?

MENTORING

A report to the nation from the Commission on Children at Risk states, "In large measure, the cause of the crisis of American childhood is a lack of connectedness."[26] The commission speaks about two kinds of connectedness—close connections to other people, and deep connections with moral and spiritual meaning. A premise underlying the philosophy of restorative justice is that we are all connected through our membership in the community. Crime is a breach of these relationships. Breaches may also occur when honor dorm residents come in conflict with one another or fail to meet community responsibilities. The commission addresses where connections originate, concluding that they begin with groups of people organized around certain purposes such as families and voluntary associations. In recent decades groups that foster connections, particularly for children, have grown weaker.

Mentoring, referred to in chapter 3 as one of the basic elements of the honor dorm, provides relational investment in the community and promotes connectedness. The mentoring program at Holman is based on the idea that GED students ("at-risk" residents) are not only in need of an education, but also in need of guidance and encouragement through close relationships. Thus mentoring in the honor dorm exists not only to meet the needs of "at-risk" residents, but to augment community building as well.

The design of pairing mentors with mentees is not always ideal when it comes to a perfect match. The decision is made primarily on availability. However, it is yet another way of acting out a new way of thinking for the offender. By promoting mentoring relationships, the community is working to enhance accountability on a level that is less rule-centered and more focused on the attachments and obligations resulting from close interpersonal relationships.

GED students assigned to the study hall in the dorm enter into a written contract with the honor dorm community and receive a mentor. The mentor signs the contract along with the student. Mentors and mentees periodically evaluate each other by way of written evaluation forms distributed and maintained by the mentoring department manager. The department manager enters the evaluation results in a database located on a computer workstation in the dorm. Everyone associated with the mentoring program becomes part of a "web of relationships." Mentoring adds meaningful social context to the community and hopefully gives those involved a greater sense of meaning and purpose. Even though the mentoring program is primarily designed for "at-risk" residents, mentors learn valuable lessons of their own, including trust, patience, and caring.

The honor dorm addresses the issue of connections in a variety of ways including the GED mentoring program. The process of working toward the GED facilitates and prepares a resident for reentering society or for functioning within the honor dorm community. Yet simply requiring inmates to attend an institutional GED program is not addressing other factors putting these residents "at risk." Without addressing them, simply saying, "go to school and get a GED," is no different from their educational experiences prior to prison. Additional needs are addressed in the community education classes.

COMMUNITY EDUCATION AT HOLMAN'S FAITH-BASED HONOR DORM

Community education at Holman's faith-based honor dorm consists of the required weekly classes for all residents in the honor dorm. The required classes are integrated into the dorm's semester structure so that each semester a different set of class sessions are offered.

During a resident's first six months in the dorm, a twenty-eight-day orientation period and a five-month first semester period provides the structure for four cycle classes and the first semester curriculum. The cycle classes are taken during the twenty-eight-day orientation period and consist of classes (sessions) entitled: mentoring, introduction to restorative justice, empathy, and peacemaking circles. Each of these classes offers the new resident exposure to key concepts and practices of the dorm. The first semester curriculum is taught once a week and teaches the objectives and philosophy of the dorm. It introduces the restorative justice philosophy and values. A general objective is to answer the question, "What is Holman's faith-based restorative justice honor dorm?"

Table 6.1 shows a list of the twenty-six class sessions in the first semester. These classes meet resident needs in the critical transition period moving from general population to the honor dorm. This adjustment involves deeper changes than those implied by a change in physical location.

To illustrate first semester curriculum content, the session on "recognizing the need for help" focuses on interdependence. The general prison population fosters the belief "it's every man for himself" with an exaggerated emphasis on masculine independence and self-sufficiency. The session on "shedding our masks" looks at the need to conceal feelings in prison. It originates with the belief that other inmates take kindness for weakness. If inmates show kindness, others will take advantage. The reason for hiding the inmates' true character or intentions must be examined before residents are ready to shed their masks. Shedding masks is necessary for the success of the honor dorm culture. It is based on relationships, character, and honesty. Thus, true relationships

Table 6.1.   First Semester Curriculum

• Cycle Class 1 Mentoring Class	13. Repentance/Remorse
• Cycle Class 2 Introduction to Restorative Justice	14. Relationships Part I
	15. Givers vs. Takers
• Cycle Class 3 Empathy Class	16. Relationships Part II
• Cycle Class 4 Peacemaking Circles Class	17. Peacemakers vs. Conflict-Starters and Conflict Maintainers
1. Basic Philosophy of the Honor Dorm	18. Relationships Part III
2. Community Basic Objectives	19. Taking Advantage of Opportunities
3. Introduction to Restorative Justice	20. Restorative Justice Principles/Dynamics Part I
4. Confrontation Class	21. Understanding the Value of a Healthy Community and a Willingness to Be Responsible to It through Personal Investment
5. Paradigm Changes	
6. Recognizing the Need for Help	
7. Self-Betterment as an Individual Responsibility	
8. Shedding Our Masks	22. Restorative Justice Principles/Dynamics Part II
9. Blaming Society for Our Problems or Being a Part of Society's Solution for Solving Problems	23. Ethical Standards, Morals, and Integrity
	24. Values Clarification
10. Delaying Our Gratification	25. Boundaries of Behavior as Social Institutions
11. Accepting Responsibilities	26. Reinventing Our Lives
12. Spiritual Principles vs. Program Formulas	

cannot be built with masks on, true character cannot be built on top of a mask, and honesty cannot be disguised (first semester honor dorm class notes). A major goal is to move the inmates away from the convict mentality toward a more vulnerable and authentic self. The faith component of the dorm provides inmates with support for moving from one culture or worldview to another—a change sometimes accompanied by a great deal of anxiety and fear.

After a resident completes the first semester he begins the second semester curriculum and completes additional associated requirements such as a two-thousand-word essay. This curriculum focuses on life skills. It includes subjects such as anger, frustration, and awareness. Embodied in these twenty-six class sessions are lessons on coping and alternative ways to deal with conflict. The curriculum addresses the question, "How can I live and cope peaceably with my fellow residents in the dorm?" Coping skills are a large part of this curriculum along with raising the resident's awareness about situations and emotions causing stress and conflict. Table 6.2 shows a list of the twenty-six classes comprising the second semester curriculum. Some of the topics from first semester lessons are repeated so the resident better understands and internalizes the values underlying the honor dorm community.

After one year in the dorm a resident makes the transition from second to third semester. The third semester, crime impact, focuses on the effects of crime on victims and the community. This curriculum is divided into two parts, property crimes and personal injury crimes. A central component of the crime impact curriculum is the emphasis on offender empathy for the victim.

Table 6.2. Second Semester Curriculum

1. Awareness Affects Relationships	15. Relationship Building 1
2. Nurturance Affects Relationships	16. Relationship Building 2
3. Listening Skills	17. Frustrations and Discouragement 1
4. Character Building	18. Frustrations and Discouragement 2
5. Anger 1	19. Restorative Justice 1 (The victim)
6. Anger 2	20. Restorative Justice 2 (The offender)
7. Involvement and Consistency	21. Restorative Justice 3 (The
8. Mentoring 1	Community/The Engagement Process)
9. Mentoring 2	22. Looking beyond the Walls
10. Communication Skills	23. The Importance of Education
11. Integrity Part I	24. Convict Code vs. Honor Dorm Code
12. Integrity Part II	25. Gaining a Strong Sense of Community
13. Integrity Part III	26. Storytelling
14. Integrity Part IV	

This fits with the restorative notion that offenders are first and foremost accountable to their victims. Accountability comes in part through awareness of the harms they caused. Thus, even if the offender cannot meet the victim for a direct apology, he is cognizant of the effects of his behaviors on others. The third semester asks the question, "Who have I harmed and to what extent?" Table 6.3 shows a list of the twenty-six class sessions comprising the crime impact curriculum.

After completing six months in the third semester the resident moves into the fourth semester, called "community." The community curriculum educates residents about their environment, culture, and the concept of social change. Again, material introduced in previous lessons is repeated in a different context to encourage deeper understanding and change. The fourth semester asks, "Who am I in my community, and what is my role?" The courses for the fourth semester are listed in table 6.4.

In the community curriculum a pioneer theme is introduced illustrating how residents are moving into unchartered territory. It compares the honor

Table 6.3.   Third Semester Curriculum

1. Introduction to Crime Victimization/Trauma Part I
2. Introduction to Crime Victimization/Trauma Part II & Secondary Victimization
3. Introduction to Property Crimes
4. The Impact of Theft on Victims & the Community Part I
5. The Impact of Burglary on Victims & the Community Part I
6. The Impact of Burglary on Victims & the Community Part II
7. The Impact of Robbery on Victims & the Community Part I
8. The Impact of Robbery on Victims & the Community Part II
9. The Impact of Arson on Victims & the Community Part I
10. The Impact of Arson on Victims & the Community Part II
11. Introduction to Personal Injury Crimes
12. The Impact of Aggravated Assault on Victims & the Community Part I
13. The Impact of Aggravated Assault on Victims & the Community Part II
14. The Impact of DUI on Victims & the Community Part I
15. The Impact of DUI on Victims & the Community Part II
16. The Impact of Sexual Violence on Victims & the Community Part I
17. The Impact of Sexual Violence on Victims & the Community Part II
18. The Impact of Sexual Violence on Victims & the Community Part III
19. The Impact of Child Abuse on Victims & the Community Part I
20. The Impact of Child Abuse on Victims & the Community Part II
21. The Impact of Domestic Violence on Victims & the Community Part I
22. The Impact of Domestic Violence on Victims & the Community Part II
23. The Impact of Crime on Elderly Victims
24. The Impact of Homicide on Victims & the Community Part I
25. The Impact of Homicide on Victims & the Community Part II
26. The Impact of Homicide on Victims & the Community Part III

Table 6.4. Fourth Semester Curriculum

1. Culture (The Anthropological Perspective) Part I	12. The Characteristics of Community
	13. The Cheyenne Way
2. Culture (The Anthropological Perspective) Part II	14. The Pioneer Community Part I
	15. The Pioneer Community Part II
3. Culture (The Anthropological Perspective) Part III	16. The Pioneer Community Part III
	17. The Pioneer Community Part IV
4. The Postmodern Ethos	18. The Pioneer Community Part V
5. Culture (The Sociological Perspective) Part I	19. Three Themes of Participation in Community Part I
6. Culture (The Sociological Perspective) Part II	20. Three Themes of Participation in Community Part II
7. Culture (The Sociological Perspective) Part III	21. Three Themes of Participation in Community Part III
8. What Is Community?	22. Community & Forgiveness (Part I)
9. How Do Communities Define Themselves?	23. Community & Forgiveness (Part II)
	24. Community & Forgiveness (Part III)
10. What Does It Mean to Be a Part of a Community?	25. Community & Forgiveness (Part IV)
	26. Building a Totem-Pole
11. The Benefits of Community	

dorm with past pioneer communities where people depended on each other, were future oriented, and had a faith perspective. The pioneer analogy highlights obstacles and hardships associated with change as well as strategies for coping.

The first two years in the dorm take a resident through the four curricula and provide an educational foundation for entering the dorm's permanent resident status. At this time expectations are for the resident to move toward a more active role in the community. The concepts of education, assimilation, and self-actualization apply. The four-semester curriculum lays the foundation for assimilation into the honor dorm and in some cases it is a stepping-stone toward greater self-actualization. At this time another curriculum is available to inmates with permanent resident status. It is an optional curriculum residents can choose for continuing educational requirements. The restorative justice curriculum is a twenty-six-week in-depth study of restorative justice from its introductory basic principles to its various practices. Many of the restorative practices are used in the honor dorm. For example, residents that sit on the dorm peacemaking circles as their permanent resident assignments must enroll in the restorative justice curriculum in order to qualify for the peacemaking circle jobs. The restorative justice curriculum also prepares a resident for other educational opportunities available during his permanent

Table 6.5.   Restorative Principles Curriculum

1. Introduction	16. Community Justice: The Historical Alternative
2. The Victim	
3. The Offender	17. Community Justice: The Historical Alternative (the Retributive Option)
4. Common Themes for the Victim and the Offender (forgiveness)	18. Community Justice: The Historical Alternative (the Judicial Option)
5. The Issue of Power and Its Dynamics as It Relates to Victims and Offenders	19. Community Justice: The Historical Alternative (the Legal Revolution)
6. The Issue of Power Is at the Heart of the Offender Experience	20. Community Justice: The Historical Alternative (the Role of Common Law)
7. Continuing and Completing the Idea of Power	21. Community Justice: The Historical Alternative (State Justice Victorious)
8. The Mystification of Crime	22. Covenant Justice: The Biblical Alternative
9. Introduction to Retributive Justice	
10. Retributive Justice/The Basic Assumption, *Fixing Guilt*, That Shapes Our Response to Crime	23. Covenant Justice: The Biblical Alternative (*Shalom: A Unifying Vision*)
11. Retributive Justice/The Basic Assumption, *Just Desserts*, That Shapes Our Responses to Crime	24. Video: *Restorative Justice: For Victims, Communities, and Offenders* (Center for Justice and Mediation, School of Social Work at the University of Minnesota)
12. Retributive Justice/The Basic Assumption, *The Process*, That Shapes Our Responses to Crime	25. Video: *Justice Tree* (Mennonite Central Committee)
13. Justice as a Paradigm	26. Video: *Enough Is Enough* (Narrated by Howard Zehr)
14. Justice as a Paradigm/Applying the Paradigm	
15. Justice as a Paradigm/Changing the Face but Not the Content	

resident status. Table 6.5 shows a list of the twenty-six-week restorative justice curriculum modeled on Howard Zehr's well-known book, *Changing Lenses*.[27]

Another class available for inmates in permanent resident status started with an inmate discussion group. The chaplain organized the group to help offenders develop empathy for their victims and their fellows in the honor dorm community. The empathy group evolved into a class based on the book, *Transcending*, written by Howard Zehr.[28] The stories told in *Transcending* by victims of extreme violence are discussed among class members. The class is limited to approximately ten residents and usually consists of two groups of ten with time split between a free world teacher and facilitators for each weekly session. Additional class activities are writing mock letters to their victims. Then the residents put themselves in their victims' shoes as if they are the victim responding to the mock letters they originally wrote. The limited size of these empathy/transcending groups allows for more intimate sharing and expression of feelings than would normally occur in a larger class. This class helps build offender capacities for empathy and serves as a prerequisite for other restorative practices in the dorm such as victim impact panels. The importance of offender accountability is further addressed in chapter 6.

Other educational opportunities for inmates in permanent resident status include classes ranging from biblical history to courses in human development. Many of these classes are taught by free world volunteers. Examples include public speaking, prison history, rediscovering your masculinity, leadership, shame, Spanish, management skills, and long distance dads. This menu of courses gives residents continuing learning opportunities built on the core curriculum foundation.

EDUCATION STORIES

The resident heading the honor dorm's education department asked inmate volunteers to share their thoughts about the curriculum. These sharings are somewhat more formal than many entries in previous chapters because residents are responding to a writing requested specifically for this book. We begin with the reflections of two students who completed their GED in the honor dorm. These stories convey the obstacles residents overcome, with one inmate scoring below a third-grade level of education when he began his work. The stories also show the importance of relationships with other inmates for achieving this goal.

GED Story 1

As a resident here at Holman Correctional Facility, it was a time in my life where education was the last thing on my agenda. But, as I continued to meet individuals with an education that became real close friends of mine, I began to realize how important not having an education really was. It definitely frustrated me not having the ability to read, write, and do math. After all, I had individuals around me every day that would assist me in achieving this goal.

Therefore, I said to myself, I'm going to take advantage of this opportunity and get my GED. Although my grade average was 2.9 before I started, I wasn't going to be shameful to ask people for help. So, I chose mainly my friends —— ——, ——, and ——. These individuals were indeed willing to assist me in this long, hard journey of accomplishing my education. As a result, I began to work hard making an effort in every way to study books, tapes, and films. Within approximately three years, I accomplished my goal, obtaining my basic education.

Now, I have the privilege of sharing with others things I've learned by facilitating and teaching in a classroom setting.

GED Story 2

I achieved my GED in September 2001 while being a resident of our then-new Holman Faith-Based Honor Dorm. I was one of the first GED graduates out of our honor dorm GED program.

I will have to be honest and say, that if it had not been for the honor dorm's GED program I would probably never gotten my GED. I have always wanted to go back to school and get either my GED or high school education, but have always found some type of excuse to put it off. The honor dorm and the inmates at Holman encouraged me daily, which was some surprise to me, where you are in a prison system where inmates tend to low rate each other. The encouragement motivated me to work hard and study. I would really have to thank —— for working with me one on one, and no matter what he was doing, he would stop to answer any questions or help me solve a problem.

When I found that I had passed the GED test I had tears in my eyes, I had finally achieved something great. I had done something worthwhile for once in my life.

The next set of inmate reflections focuses on three of the four semester curricula, beginning with the introductory one. These stories convey an understanding of the link between course content and values and behaviors expected in the dorm. Self-improvement, responsibility, personal growth, interpersonal relationships, conflict resolution, crime impact, repairing harm, and forgiveness are themes addressed in these essays. For some inmates the curricula not only answer questions but raise many news ones. The inmate writing about crime impact clearly struggles with what he learned in his classes.

An Inmate Comments on First Semester Classes

The orientation set of classes is a valuable asset and tool to W. C. Holman Correctional Facility's Faith-Based Honor Dorm. The very first week, the basic philosophy of the honor dorm is expounded upon and explained. Then the inmate experiences a wide range of topics from confrontation class, paradigm changes, shedding our masks, and accepting responsibilities through restorative justice principles/dynamics.

Let there be no doubt about it; the orientation set of classes is important and vital for the new resident's smooth transition into the Faith-Based Honor Dorm. Things learned from week four's confrontation class is [sic] *expected to be used in the new resident's eventual confrontations with others. Week twenty-three's ethical standards, morals, and integrity will be vital for continued success as an honor dorm resident and eventually for a leadership position in the dorm. Mainly the orientation class guides the new residents into the new thinking and standard* [sic] *the Faith-Based Honor Dorm establishes.*

Life and Coping Skills

This is an invaluable class which teaches us all needed coping skills with which to function in our community and in all our relationships. I say this from the perspectives of both a student and a facilitator of this class. I feel the class serves as a weekly refresher or reminder that we can always improve our skills and upon our shortcomings.

An array of topics is discussed in this class. Since it is restorative justice–based, as are practically all of our classes, we do touch on restorative justice, crime victimization, the community at large, etc. What is constantly discussed are issues concerning anger, involvement, communication, and confrontation. We continually stress the importance of all relational issues, encouraging each other to build on and improve all our relationships in order to strengthen and establish a tighter-knit community that supports each other and at least relationally meets the needs of all members of the community.

Let us not overlook perhaps two of the topics we feel a need to constantly discuss: responsibility and accountability. This class has actually taught many people to be responsible and accountable perhaps for the first time in their lives. Naturally this is something we never have enough of. Human nature teaches us we can always develop better ways of being responsible and being accountable to our community.

Learning adequate and respectful ways of confronting peers is also an essential aspect of this class. Good confrontational skills are definitely a valuable asset to anyone in any community. Prior to taking this class, I had no idea of how many of us are totally lacking in this area.

Learning about conflict resolution is also priceless, as we know all communities have their share of problems, and this one is no exception. So we have a very real need to know proper ways to confront someone, to deal with conflicts as they arise, and hopefully be able to resolve our conflict peacefully.

We like to think our strengths as a community are the intrapersonal [sic] relationships we've established, but like all else, we need continual improvement in this area, too. So we hope to continue our goal and process of building new and better relationships with the aim of applying the knowledge and skills learned from the class to build a better community and a better tomorrow.

Crime Impact

The teaching of Crime Impact in the Honor Dorm has the mirroring effect of the pebble in the pond theory. Where you toss a pebble into a pond and watch the ripples that begin to encircle the point of impact in a forever widening circle. The pebble being the perpetrator, the pond is your victim, and the waves it creates are both victims' and perpetrators' family and friends. They all suffer from the fall out of this action.

This I realize is a very simple example of Crime Impact but the point is established, that all crimes great and small have a far-reaching effect on primary victims and secondary victims alike. No one escapes this circle. Not even you, who has nothing whatsoever to do with it. You suffer too.

The classes held in the honor dorm have the initial effect of what I term emotionalism. An example of this would be a church revival. You attend this revival, i.e., class, and the pastor, priest, preacher, whichever, lays a heavy dose of guilt or shame upon your mind and heart. Which in turn invokes a very strong emotional feeling of sorrow and remorsefulness. But needless to say those overwhelming feelings will soon disappear with time. The same holds true for these classes. At first you experience a great sorrow, and remorsefulness, toward your victim, as well as for your own family members, and friends. You see the harm and you feel the pain you've caused. Your mind races in a million directions all bearing the same wish to make things right.

How do you make things right?

Can you ever make things right?

Will there ever be peace and forgiveness?

Will the suffering ever end for those who've been harmed?

In some cases the answer is just plain No.

It will never go away!

But in others there is a point in life where the wounds have healed and forgiveness is real for everyone involved. . . .

Inmates must continue their education after completing the four-semester curriculum. Inmates consider their learning in two of these courses. In the first report a resident compares restorative justice with the current way of doing justice and speculates about the advantages of change. For the second essay a resident applies what he learned about shame in a very personal way. The shame concept gives him a way to interpret his past and present behavior as well as giving him a window on the future. His composition also shows a desire to share his insights with other members of the community.

Restorative Justice

I'm in the Restorative Justice class and what I have learned, I like. The concept of restorative justice seems so easy, hassle-free, and would cost a lot less than the criminal justice system of what we have in place now.

If we were under the restorative justice system, I believe the victim would feel more vindicated and at least come to a closure quicker if they were given more say-so.

The offender would most likely agree to the conditions of a victim layed [sic] out, rather than agree to a plea bargain with the state for prison time. All of this could be done in a cost-free way and short period of time.

The majority of crimes could be dealt with under the restorative justice system and it's hard to comprehend why it's not done. Could it be that a lot of "fingers" would not be able to go into the pie? Granted, there would be a lot of people out of work in the field of the criminal justice community, but economically the state or county would gain because they'd be able to funnel the funds to other agencies in helping people that need it.

A Class on Shame

When the class on shame was offered in the honor dorm, I didn't know what to expect. To my surprise grasping some knowledge about shame became one of the most rewarding experiences of my life. Before taking the shame class, I never would have attributed my past drug addiction, my failure to challenge myself, my belittlement of myself, or my belittlement of others to shame. Some of the material we had on shame termed it as the "master emotion." I concluded that the description was attached to shame because no one is immune to being affected by it. I discovered that there was good shame and bad shame. My good shame made me competitive in academics and sports, but my bad shame steered me in directions that caused me to be a drug addict, caused me to have low self-esteem, and caused me to embrace many other unfavorable modes of behavior from the classes. From the classes on shame I learned that a great deal of research had went [sic] into studying shame. Exposure to some of the things this research revealed caused me to not only better understand myself, but also better understand others and their behaviors. The classes had such an impact on me that I shared my findings on shame with all those around me. This subject matter I feel should be established as a curriculum of all levels of schooling. A lack of understanding when it comes to shame can be disastrous—school shootings, bullying, drug addiction, racism, and the list goes on. The bottom line is I am glad I participated in the curriculum on shame.

I personally asked an inmate to write the last essay. He is one of the younger dorm residents and shows a great deal of respect for education. I wondered why. He responded with a fairly lengthy writing contrasting education in his pre-prison life with how he sees it today. This inmate's family exposed him to the value of education at an early age, but as a teenager he was unwilling and unable to listen. Following his incarceration things changed. He obtained a GED and began a process he refers to as his edification.

My Edification

I was surprised when I was asked to write about my education and my history. Rather than amusing you about my being a high school drop-out, I would much rather enjoy telling of my edification. . . .

During my formal school years I would say that I was more of an okay student. Nothing spectacular and not straight As. I most often maintained a C and D average because of multiple suspensions. I was a mischievous youngster, always looking for a laugh. I didn't care if it was at my own expense or someone else's. I just wanted to have fun. For an example: I thought that it would be funny to pop firecrackers during class. This is where and when I learned the word pyrotechnic, because that was the word that the teacher used when he wrote me up.

My mother worked and still works for the school system. When I was young, I mean a baby, she was a substitute teacher. She taught me the three R's at home. I knew how to read instructions, count change, and write checks before I was ten years old. My mother taught me with practical application. I didn't have any qualms about writing and cashing checks for my allowance. My mother is the most dynamic woman that I know. She had two children and was divorced at a young age. She transcended government assistance and living in the projects to go to college and make a better life for herself and her children.

My father is a strong man. Back then he had a weakness for drugs and alcohol. He had always shown me love though. He taught me a lot of principles and spent a lot of time with me. As his relationship with my mother soured, his desire for the drugs and the alcohol grew stronger. Even though he and my mother separated, he still was very much a part of my life. He went to college, I don't think that he finished, but he did go.

My life coming up was average. I went to school with my friends from the projects and we all wanted to have fun. Most of us laughed and kidded our way right into the penitentiary. Coming from where I'm from, we glorified the hustler and the criminals because they had all the "stuff." So we imitated what they did. The way that they talked, walked, dressed, the cars that they drove, the music that they listened to, etc. We didn't even know that we acted and imitated our way into becoming a culture. I don't say that with pride.

During my years of acting, I fathered two children before I was sixteen. Didn't know what to do with them so I got deeper into "the game" to take care of them. I didn't see as much of them after that. The streets monopolized most of my time. I was still having fun. Living the life, or so I thought.

It's 1995 and I'm in the county jail at seventeen facing a capital murder conviction. I didn't have enough sense at the time to even understand that if convicted I could either die or die in prison. Some future, huh? I didn't know the gravity of what I had gotten myself into. I knew that I had maybe, a 70–30 percent chance of going to prison though. A lot of the guys from where I'm from, who'd been imitating and acting, were there with me also. We all acted our way right into a horrific situation.

I got convicted, sentenced to life without the possibility of parole, and sent to prison at the age of nineteen. I don't want to have fun anymore. A guy saw me, recognized that I wasn't trying to have fun anymore, and he pointed me in the right direction. He befriended me without the assumed/expected predatory type of basis you more often than not find in prison. He told me to read. To read anything that I can learn from and that I can learn from anything that I read. He told me, and I'll always remember it, to learn so that I will be a better person than I was when I came to prison. He explained that I was not to be angry with anyone other than myself for being here. For I was the one living in an ignorant state of existence. I was the one trying to be someone other than who I was. I placed myself in the justice system to be made the example of what not to do. I would be the deterrent for those who knew me and those who were leading the same lifestyle as I was leading. I would be the motivation for my own ascension out of the pits of ignorance. I needed all the motivation that I could get!

I began to study people whom I felt had led righteous lives. I didn't want to be them, per se, anymore, but to take some of their greatness and apply it to my own life. I have never been "slow," so I obtained a GED. Study and discipline became my thing. Jesus, Confucius, Muhammad, Malcolm X, Martin Luther King Jr., Ghandi, Marcus Garvey, Mother Theresa, and many, many more were my examples. Anyone who lived a righteous life and said great things. I studied the history of my people as much as could be found or ordered. I began to feel my pride and self-esteem shoot through the roof.

The prison opened an Honor Dorm, but at first I had to be convinced that it was not the prison inside a prison that everyone said it was. After a year or two, I got the word from a reliable source that the dorm was okay and was doing good things. I have not had a wild prison experience. I have been trying to combat arrested development with knowledge. It has worked well for me in some areas, but sadly I must confess that I enjoy watching South Park and eating cereal.

Keep in mind that what I'm about to say is how I think it happened, and not necessarily the way that my friend actually thought. The guy that taught the Restorative Justice classes was looking to incorporate some more guys into teaching of R.J. I attended the classes. I read the books. I am a social being. So, it was only sensible to add me to the team. Our R.J. classes are taught different from the other classes in the dorm. I knew that I was not to be a lecturer. A guy told me that I use the Socratic method of teaching. It seems very effective. In a nutshell, I simply learn all that I can so that I can teach it to others to try and effect a change in as many people as I can. Education is the only vaccine to combat the disease of ignorance.

Now my idea of fun is not the same as it used to be when I came to prison. I guess it can be called maturity. So whenever I speak about my education, I smile because it is not education at all to me. Everything that I've learned was used to turn me around, to correct me to set my feet on the path of mental, emotional, spiritual, and God willing, physical freedom. So, I choose to call it my edification. That is what my education did for me. It edified my thinking.

A WORK IN PROGRESS

Since the dorm began on October 18, 1999, its community educational structure has undergone a growth process. It went from a nonstandardized hodgepodge of classes taught by free world volunteers and a few inmate facilitators to the standardized four-semester structure that today guides a resident through his first two years in the dorm. When the dorm began, a great deal of emphasis was placed on simply structuring a person's life. Attending a class was just as important as learning anything because residents lived unstructured lives for so many years. Classes were more of a management tool at this time. The classes, however, did contain valuable lessons, and residents learned about the philosophy and objectives of what the honor dorm is all about.

Efforts were made to expand the number and variety of classes to provide a more diverse educational experience and to expose residents to restorative justice principles. The physical relocation of the dorm offered space for study halls and classes. This change was accompanied by standardizing the curricula and placing it into a semester structure. The orientation was included in a first semester curriculum, and the life skills classes were organized into the second semester curriculum. This rearrangement helped to redefine, clarify, and structure honor dorm education. After a six-month exposure to the objectives, philosophy, and "whys" of a new way of living, the second semester shows how to practice change through exposure to material on relationships and conflict resolution.

Subsequently the chaplain and a small group of inmate leaders decided to establish a third and fourth semester curriculum, but their content remained undetermined. During the spring of 2004 the chaplain asked some of the inmate teachers to review literature he received from a program in the Pennsylvania Correctional System. The program "Crime Impact" focuses on the effects of property and personal injury crimes on victims and the community. The program material complemented other projects in the dorm related to increasing inmate empathy. Therefore, using the Pennsylvania program as a model, the third semester curriculum was created.

By the spring of 2005, an effort began to complete the four-semester structure in the dorm culminating with a standardized class structure to guide a resident through his first two years in the dorm and prepare him for the role he would play as a permanent resident. Because of the influence of restorative principles and practices in the dorm, the chaplain decided to create a fourth semester curriculum focusing on the subject of community and incorporating ideas from the teachings of Dietrich Bonhoeffer[29] and Stanley Grentz.[30] With the help of a student from the University of West Florida, the first class outlines for the community curriculum were developed and taught in the dorm.

When the honor dorm began, one inmate with a B.S. degree taught most of the courses. Subsequently additional inmates were recruited to teach the core curriculum. The curriculum is sufficiently structured with outlines of lecture notes to enable resident teachers to cover the material uniformly but with their own personal teaching styles. Attempts continue to recruit free world teachers to offer classes. While the resident teachers do an excellent job, the inmates enjoy new faces, and an additional benefit of free world teachers is they assist with modeling behaviors conforming with honor dorm expectations. In the future the honor dorm leaders want to develop the capacity to offer residents postsecondary degrees. This will be a challenging effort because inmates are prohibited from using the Internet, and most education offered at a distance is delivered online.

Education in the honor dorm is essential for teaching inmates new ways of thinking and behaving. Most of the inmates respond positively to the core curriculum. They enter the honor dorm to improve themselves, and they understand education is essential to achieve their personal goals. New residents need to assimilate into a culture that contrasts markedly from the dominant one in general population. Without formal education, this assimilation would be difficult. Literacy training, GED preparation, and the core curriculum give inmates the capacity to live in a restorative community where accountability, honesty, interdependence, peaceful conflict resolution, and service are expected. The curriculum is not a science for success nor is it a hodgepodge of courses offered on an availability basis. It is highly structured and goal oriented. On the other hand, at this time it is not possible to formally evaluate specific benefits from the core curriculum, although comparisons between inmates with more education—a GED or higher—and those without show the former are more likely to succeed in the honor dorm environment. Other benefits are identified in the sampling of inmate reflections. Their writings show how educational opportunities provide something unique for each of them. In some cases inmates are learning their ABCs. In others they use their education to self-actualize and transcend the limits of the prison environment.

The restorative philosophy is central for giving inmate educational programming cohesion and meaning at Holman. It assumes the community and the inmate's place within the community are central to mature and responsible living. It values positive and supportive relationships as opposed to those based on self-interest alone. While the principles of restorative justice are not rocket science, they are difficult to apply in a prison environment. Education at Holman reinforces values and behaviors to heal the harm done by inmates to their victims, their families, and themselves.

NOTES

1. Robert Martinson, "What Works? Questions and Answers about Prison Reform," *Public Interest* 35, no. 4 (Spring 1974): 22–54.

2. Caroline W. Harlow, "Education and Correctional Populations," *Bureau of Justice Statistics Special Report* 2003, available at www.ojp.usdoj.gov/bjs/pub/pdf/ecp.pdf (accessed 10 May 2008).

3. Elizabeth Greenburg, Eric Dunleavy, and Mark Keitney, "Literacy Behind Bars: Results from the 2003 National Assessment of Adult Prison Literacy Survey," U.S. Department of Education. NCES 2007-473.

4. Greenburg, Dunleavy, and Keitney, "Literacy Behind Bars," 13.

5. Greenburg, Dunleavy, and Keitney, "Literacy Behind Bars," 14.

6. Greenburg, Dunleavy, and Keitney, "Literacy Behind Bars," 13.

7. Greenburg, Dunleavy, and Keitney, "Literacy Behind Bars," 26.

8. Greenburg, Dunleavy, and Keitney, "Literacy Behind Bars," 28.

9. Greenburg, Dunleavy, and Keitney, "Literacy Behind Bars," 28.

10. Greenburg, Dunleavy, and Keitney, "Literacy Behind Bars," 28.

11. Greenburg, Dunleavy, and Keitney, "Literacy Behind Bars," 29.

12. Kaniel Karpowitz and Max Renner, "Education as Crime Prevention: The Case for Reinstating Pell Grant Eligibility for the Incarcerated," Bard Prison Initiative, undated, available at www.bard.edu/bpi/pdfs/cirme_report.pdf (accessed 10 May 2008).

13. Barb Toews, *The Little Book of Restorative Justice for People in Prison: Rebuilding the Web of Relationships* (Intercourse, Pa.: Good Books, 2006), 48.

14. Toews, *Restorative Justice for People in Prison*, 49.

15. Richard Tewksbury, David John Erickson, and Jon Marc Taylor, "Opportunities Lost: The Consequences of Eliminating Pell Grant Eligibility for Correctional Education Students," in *Behind Bars: Readings on Prison Culture*, ed. Richard Tewksbury (Upper Saddle River, N.J.: Pearson/Prentice Hall, 2006), 317–28.

16. Tewksbury, Erickson, and Taylor, "Opportunities Lost," 319.

17. Tewksbury, Erickson, and Taylor, "Opportunities Lost," 319.

18. Lawrence Kohlberg, *Essays on Moral Development*, vol. 1, *The Philosophy of Moral Development* (San Francisco: Harper and Row, 1981).

19. Tewksbury, Erickson, and Taylor, "Opportunities Lost," 319.

20. Tewksbury, Erickson, and Taylor, "Opportunities Lost," 319.

21. Tewksbury, Erickson, and Taylor, "Opportunities Lost," 319.

22. Michelle Moeller, Scott L. Day, and Beverly D. Rivera, "'How Is Education Perceived on the Inside?' A Preliminary Study of Adult Males in a Correctional Setting," *Journal of Correctional Education* 59, no. 1 (March 2004): 40–59.

23. Richard W. Feller, Ruthanne Kastner, and Judith A. Whichard, "The Incidence of Scolepic Sensitivity Syndrome in Colorado Inmates," *Journal of Correctional Education* 51, no. 3 (September 2000): 294–99.

24. Moeller, Day, and Rivera," "How Is Education Perceived," 40–59.

25. Toews, *Restorative Justice for People in Prison*, 49.

26. "Hard-Wired to Connect: The New Scientific Case for Authoritative Communities," Executive Summary 2003, available at www.americanvalues .org/ExecSumm-print.pdf (accessed 11 May 2008).

27. Howard Zehr, *Changing Lenses: A New Focus for Crime and Justice*, 3rd ed. (Scottsdale, Pa.: Herald Press, 2005).

28. Howard Zehr, *Transcending: Reflections of Crime Victims* (Intercourse, Pa.: Good Books, 2001).

29. Dietrich Bonhoeffer, *Life Together: A Discussion of Christian Fellowship* (New York: Harper & Row, 1954).

30. Stanley J. Grentz, *Created for Community: Connecting Christian Belief with Christian Living*, 2nd ed. (Grand Rapids, Mich.: Bridge Point Books, 1998).

7

Working with Others

Faith without works is dead.

—*Based on James 2:15*

The first duty of a human being is to assume the right functional relationship to society—more briefly, to find your real job, and do it.

—Charlotte Perkins Gilman, *About.com: Women's History*

When a former corrections commissioner introduced honor dorms to the Alabama Department of Corrections in 1999, addressing staffing problems was the stated purpose. Honor dorms are managed with fewer security staff.[1] The honor dorm community's second goal is providing inmates opportunities for behavioral change. Since honor dorms are required to do more with less, honor dorm residents take primary responsibility for their operation.

Wardens and correctional staff typically take a dim view of inmate governance. Experiments with inmate self-rule were introduced as early as 1824 in the New York House of Refuge, a reformatory for juveniles. The reform functioned much like today's teen courts with rule violators judged and sentenced by their peers. Introduced by corrections superintendents, many early reforms did not survive after their founders left office.[2] In 1913 Thomas Mott Osborne established the Mutual Welfare League at New York State's Auburn Prison. The league proposed altering the concepts of penal confinement by creating a prison community whose members used democratic principles for solving problems. Supporters hoped inmate representatives would effectively channel the wishes of their fellow prisoners into sound policies and practices, at the same time making discipline easier for the warden and more effective for the inmates.[3] The consequences of reform in the New York system are not recorded, but a similar experiment introduced in Cheshire, Connecticut, in 1915 ended in failure after eight months. Inmates grew tired of widespread dishonesty and misrule and subsequently asked the administration to resume control of the prison.[4] Following this era inmate governance became primarily associated with disciplinary matters and evolved into the inmate trusty system. Prison administrators used it for keeping order and saving money. The court case *Gates v. Collier* brought an end to the trusty system in the early 1970s.[5]

Other models of inmate governance were introduced in the 1960s and 1970s.[6] Most wardens oppose these reforms, reasoning that inmates' criminal behavior makes them unfit for self-rule. Typically prison administrators mistrust inmates, thinking they will use their power for self-advancement. In the early 1960s Baker administered surveys to wardens at fifty-two prisons.[7] Among the forty-four respondents, only 13 percent experimented with inmate governance. One respondent briefly worked with inmate councils and responded negatively. "When a prisoner has adjusted enough to be able to advise how to run the prison, he doesn't belong here. He should be released."[8] A few institutional representatives had positive experiences with inmate councils, identifying two measures for success—prison administrators select trusted inmate members for leadership positions; and constitutions and bylaws specify the scope and function of inmate councils.

MANAGING HOLMAN'S HONOR DORM

Holman's honor dorm is best described as a self-managing community. The dorm exists separately from the rest of the institution, and its residents take no role advising the warden about prison operations. Assumptions about the rehabilitative function of self-management are not different from the beliefs of early prison reformers. An excerpt from the Mutual Welfare League's Constitution at Michigan State Prison says, "The objectives of this league shall be: by social intercourse to improve ourselves and to aid in the moral, intellectual, physical, and financial advancement of our fellowmen. To inculcate a higher appreciation of the value and sacred obligations of American citizenship."[9] These ideas are similar to the ones prescribed for the honor dorm community at Holman. But rather than teaching good citizenship through democratic participation, the honor dorm stresses moral development through spiritual, educational, and service opportunities.

There is no democratic decision-making body in the honor dorm. Three community managers selected by the chaplain meet with the Honor Community Administrative Review Committee (ARC) once per month. At one time community managers were called community representatives. Election of community representatives did not work because those elected acted on behalf of themselves, friends, and their constituents. Fearing the demise of the dorm, the chaplain returned to the appointment of trustworthy community representatives. Among some honor dorm residents, however, the expectation continued for democratic elections.

The chaplain firmly supports the bureaucratic management approach, and for clarification purposes the position of community representative changed to community manager.[10] Community managers must be in permanent resident status. They oversee the dorm, solve problems as they arise, and establish standard operating procedures as needed. They also serve as liaisons between the community and the administration as members of the ARC.

The ARC consists of the warden, chaplain, the honor dorm coordinator (chaplain's assistant), a captain, the classification supervisor, and a designated correctional officer. This committee oversees the continuing development of the dorm's standard operating procedures (SOPs), ensures that the SOPs are followed, and selects new honor dorm residents. The warden and the community managers meet with the ARC once per month. At this time community managers have the opportunity to make requests to the warden. However, the committee, as its name suggests, is in no way advisory to the prison administration. It is primarily an administrative arm for the warden conveying information on how the honor dorm works.

The honor dorm's internal SOPs further specify roles and responsibilities. A chain of command places community managers on top, followed by the senior coordinators, department heads, coordinators on duty, and crewmembers on duty. The command and control model is modified somewhat by more inclusive and participatory peacemaking circles described in chapter 4. The opportunity for ideas to move from the rank-and-file resident through the chain of command is limited. An innovative thinking group gives honor dorm residents a chance to discuss ideas for moving the honor dorm forward. All inmates are assigned to family circles as well, and these groups give residents an opportunity to express their feelings and learn from each other. Community meetings of the entire dorm are held but are informational in nature.

It would be easy to criticize the dorm's top-down structure. From a restorative perspective, is the honor dorm sufficiently inclusive and participative? Chapter 5 documents considerable efforts to involve all residents in basic and community education. Furthermore, all honor dorm residents must participate through their honor dorm jobs. The command and control approach is criticized by some residents as an overzealous need for control. However, through trial and error, others in the honor dorm community believe the present system works best to insure residents continue to enjoy opportunities for personal growth and responsibility denied to inmates in general population. Furthermore, experiments with democratic decision-making are not popular in prison communities.

DORM LEADERSHIP

Key leadership positions in the honor dorm belong to the community managers, senior coordinators, and department heads. Community managers are responsible for creating SOPs. I met with community members to develop an SOP on smoking. Smoking is not allowed in the honor dorm, although it is allowed outside of the dorm and in the recreation yard. In the evenings, some of the men smoke in the bathroom, especially late at night on cold winter evenings. Since a substantial number of residents find this behavior problematic, community managers held a meeting to discuss how to address the problem restoratively. The conversation moved between punitive approaches—demerit points and expulsion from the dorm after three strikes—to restorative ones involving education about the effects of secondary smoke or requiring violators to enroll in a nonsmoking course developed by one of the residents. The group adopted a rule providing education for first and second offenses, with various degrees of punishment if education fails. The ARC struck down the plan. The community managers also decided to give offenders the opportunity to meet with peacemaking circles.

Community managers are responsible for troubleshooting and making sure the community runs smoothly. It is important that the dorm administrator, in this case the chaplain, trusts community managers. Illegal operations or behaviors that violate honor dorm integrity need to be addressed quickly and effectively. In a prison environment where some officers and other inmates are hostile to the dorm, there is little room for error. Community managers are limited to a twelve-month term. The chaplain at Holman has high expectations for these appointed residents.

> Community managers are partners with the chaplain who work the daily praxis of the honor dorm vision. Good community managers are those who work well together as a team, using their talents, experiences, personalities, and relationships for the greater good of the honor dorm community. They work to help residents through conflict and to help residents disassociate arguments from personal self worth and honor. As exemplars community managers demonstrate a value of moral excellence in order to foster in others a desire for the same.[11]

Given the chaplain's expectations, his preference for personally selecting them is understandable.

Community managers appoint the senior coordinators (currently there are three). The senior coordinators are the eyes and ears of the honor dorm. They appoint coordinators on duty (subject to approval of the community managers) to help address daily problems in the dorm including rule infractions. Citations for rule infractions originate with the senior coordinators and coordinators on duty. The coordinators function as dorm monitors. There are behavioral guidelines governing confrontations with other inmates.

- Do not interrupt someone when they are talking.
- Do not argue with a resident. Say what you have to say without raising your voice and let that be sufficient.
- Do not use aggressive body language.
- Do not put the resident on the defensive.
- Have the attitude of trying to get problems or differences solved before they result in violations or infractions needing to be logged. Do not approach a problem with a made-up mind as to the nature of the problem. Differences are often mistaken as violations.[12]

Central to these guidelines is respect. Open-mindedness and problem solving approaches are valued over authoritarian decision-making. Coordinators are encouraged to discuss minor issues with residents rather than writing them up. Accountability is part of the process as well. Coordinators submit a statement of facts form describing the details of the alleged violation or infraction. They must make a note of the date and time of the infraction.[13] They also inform the resident about the write-up. In this case, due process procedures encourage respect. The inmate is not blindsided by the write-up and has the information he needs to address the problem. Since conflicts and many rule infractions are heard by peacemaking circles, a restorative rather than an adversary model is used. In the circle, fact-finding and the assignment of guilt are less important than understanding, problem-solving, and resolving conflict peacefully.

Do the senior coordinators and coordinators on duty manage restoratively? I interviewed one senior coordinator and nine coordinators on duty to find out. The senior coordinator served only three months on the job. He recognized the need for addressing the different personalities in the dorm rather than using a cookie-cutter approach. He said the job challenges him to do the right thing and, for this reason, it is fulfilling. He also said that without the senior coordinator position, the dorm would fold.

Coordinators on duty have between three months' and seven years' experience with the job. Four of nine coordinators described their jobs from a rule-enforcement perspective. One man says, "Someone has to enforce the rules." And another, "When you tell people they are wrong, they act like you're crazy." The remaining five used restorative language when describing their work. For example, "I need to deal with different personalities in the dorm and develop people skills to do this, for example, conflict resolution." A resident with seven years on the job says, "[They] need a push from me in my role to help people get on the right track to change." And one with only one week's experience observes, "[You] need to bring people to *awareness* [emphasis added] they are doing wrong. . . . You see others doing something wrong and you need to uplift them—not being a judging policeman." Most coordinators describe their jobs as challenging, interesting, or important. Only one man with six-and-a-half-months' experience thinks the work as routine.

JOBS AND THE CONCEPT OF SERVICE

The honor dorm uses a point system (merit/demerit) to gauge residents' eligibility to remain in the community or participate in special offerings such as family night dinners. Minimum point requirements are set for education and working honor community jobs. Points are allocated according to the residents' status in the semester structure. For example, residents in orientation receive two-and-a-half points for working their honor dorm community job while those in the fourth semester work more and receive fifteen points. Those with permanent resident status are assigned additional responsibilities such as participating in the Big Brother program or membership in peacemaking circles.

Points are recorded, calculated, and reviewed within specific time frames, and all information is entered in a computer database.

There are two broad job categories in the honor dorm. One category is managerial and consists of community representatives, coordinators, and department heads. The remaining posts are filled by crewmembers who work the various jobs in the community and report to department heads. Examples are service (cleaning), maintenance, laundry, education, audiovisual, library, tutoring, and information desk. Many residents have institutional jobs as well such as working in the tag plant or the metal fabrication shop. This work is paid, even though the wage is but a few cents an hour. In contrast, honor dorm community jobs are unpaid, and though required, are defined as community service.

Community service in the free world is typically voluntary. But in the private sector and the university system community service is strongly encouraged, so that in some cases it resembles a requirement. What does required community service mean in the honor dorm and how does it connect to restorative principles? Accountability first and foremost means taking full responsibility for one's crime, understanding its impacts or harms, and doing whatever possible and reasonable to make things right. But accountability also extends to the offenders' families and the community.[14] At Holman, the community is the honor dorm. Taking responsibility for an assigned, unpaid job and doing it to the best of one's ability is a first step toward community accountability. Second, service jobs promote values of interdependence, shared responsibility, productivity, and constructiveness.[15] Third, from the perspective of community reintegration, they serve a vocational function by teaching responsibility, time management, interpersonal skills, data entry, and maintenance skills among others. But how do those who fill community jobs see things?

I interviewed fifty-one residents in March 2008, to assess how they view their dorm community jobs. The senior coordinator signed up volunteers who perform a variety of tasks in the dorm. Fourteen have managerial jobs and thirty-seven are crewmembers. From a prepared list, I asked inmates to select a descriptor that *best* describes *how they see* their honor community job. Residents had four choices: a requirement, a service to the honor dorm community, a way to pass the time, and a way to improve skills. Of particular interest is whether residents see their jobs primarily as a requirement or as a service commitment. A corollary benefit is skill improvement. Finally, in a prison environment inmates may view their jobs as a way to structure their time.

Table 7.1 shows the questionnaire results. Forty of fifty-one residents (78.4 percent) see their job first and foremost as a service to the honor dorm community. Four residents think it as a way to improve their skills and only three each fall in the categories of a requirement or a way to pass the time. Fully 86 percent see their work in ways central to the honor dorm vision (service and skill development). Inmates with management responsibilities are more likely than crewmembers to describe their assignments as service (100 percent and 70 percent respectively).

To better understand residents' perceptions, I developed a list of seven adjectives describing work. These include routine, boring, challenging, interesting, fulfilling, stressful, and important. Which of these descriptors are inmates most likely to select? They most frequently choose the adjectives challenging,

Table 7.1. Residents' Descriptions of Their Honor Dorm Community Jobs

How do you see your honor dorm job?	N	%
Requirement	3	5.9
A service to the honor dorm	40	78.4
A way to pass the time	3	5.9
A way to improve my skills	4	7.8
Other*	1	2.0
Total	51	100.0

*One resident said none of these categories applied.

Table 7.2. Residents' Characterization of Their Honor Dorm Community Jobs

Which describes how you feel about your job?	N	%
Routine	3	5.9
Boring	6	11.8
Challenging	13	25.5
Interesting	5	9.8
Fulfilling	9	17.6
Stressful	4	7.8
Important	10	19.6
Other*	1	2.0
Total	51	100.0

*One resident said none of these categories applied.

important, and interesting (table 7.2). A coordinator on duty says his job is challenging. "I have to deal with many attitudes and perspectives. You need to learn to know people; the job changes as you get to know people better. You roam the dorm and talk to people . . . investigation and informal problem-solving." A classroom teacher (class facilitator) picks "challenging" because "the purpose is to touch people. You have to be creative and concerned in your heart to do it."

A crewmember in the audiovisual department works as a TV monitor. He coordinates the selection of television shows and movies for common viewing. Decision rules need to be developed and implemented. This crewmember sees his job as fulfilling because he "gets a chance to help the community by keeping down chaos." Another teacher thinks his job is fulfilling because he gets "a chance to help others get closer to their families." He gives the example of facilitating a relationship between a resident and his father living on death row at Holman. A member of the cleaning crew says his job is fulfilling because, "It gives me a purpose; I am doing something; it benefits me and everyone around me."

Almost 20 percent of the residents pick "important" as a job descriptor. The head of the learning experience department talks about his role in character development. A coordinator on duty sees his work with conflict resolution as important.

Another coordinator thinks his job is significant because, "Someone has to enforce the rules." A member of the cleaning crew remarks, "[it is] important to maintain cleanliness with so many people." And a crewmember with the community education department says with some pride, "[I] keep track of every class and put things in the computer. [It is a] record-keeping job. I like doing it. It gives me something to do, and I'm good at it. I make fewer mistakes."

Continuing with positive job characteristics, five men think their jobs are interesting. On the other hand, thirteen individuals see their jobs negatively, describing them as boring, stressful, or routine. Half of the residents choosing the term "boring" work on the information desk. They sit near the entrance to the dorm, and their responsibilities include monitoring individuals entering and leaving the dorm. The most important function is overseeing the sign in/sign out sheet. One desk monitor says the job entails too much idleness, and he would love to do something else. Another comments, "[It's a] useless job. . . . Impossible to keep track of people. It gives you no responsibility in reality."

After ten months on the job, a community manager describes his job as stressful. "It takes up a great deal of time, and it requires me to solve everybody's problems." He adds, "It's important—someone has to make the hard decisions. Blame is cast on you because of the difficulty in satisfying everyone." Stress is not limited to managerial jobs. A cleaning crew member says his job is stressful because he has to "pick up behind grown men." Another person doing the same job comments, "I don't like cleaning up after others in areas [where] it is their responsibility to clean up after themselves. [There is] no reason to leave hair and shaving cream on the sink." A library worker, a cleaning crewmember, and an audiovisual crewmember describe their jobs as routine. In addition to term limits for managerial positions, the SOPs stipulate a plan for crewmember rotation so individuals can experience different jobs.

THE VALUE OF SERVICE

The world's major faith traditions emphasize service. According to Muhammad Ali, "Service to others is the rent you pay for your room here on earth."[16] The Dalai Lama states "Our greatest duty and our main responsibility is to help others. But please, if you can't help them, would you please not hurt them?"[17] Christian writer Walter Brueggemann contrasts the individualism of capitalism with the relational covenant in the first and second commandments.[18] Love thy neighbor implies a service responsibility.

Research shows a relationship between religiosity and volunteering.[19] From a secular perspective Boss demonstrates a link between community service and levels of moral reasoning among a group of college students.[20] Among adolescents, community service has many developmental benefits including pro-social development and moral-political awareness.[21] Furthermore, changing from a self-centered place to an other-centered one yields emotional and psychological benefits. Twelve-step programs such as Alcoholics Anonymous and Narcotics Anonymous place service at the center of recovery.[22] A number of crime victims work with others to further their healing, even in some cases helping criminal offenders do better.[23] Research in psychoneuroimmunology, examines links between helping others and physical healing. Using a student sample, David McClelland and Carol Kirshnit measured an antibody that fights infection before and after his students viewed a film on Mother Teresa.[24] They found that simply watching a film on selfless service strengthened the immune response in the students. Although the service and its effects may vary, its association with moral, spiritual, and community development as well as healing is intriguing. Wilkinson found a relationship between community service work experience and lower recidivism rates among prisoners released from the Ohio Department of Corrections.[25]

While the survey of community jobholders at Holman does not directly address human development and healing, the language residents use for their work recognizes the importance of community and their relationship to it. "I'm helping the community doing things guys normally don't like to do." While another resident says, "I am doing something. It benefits me and everyone around me." These individuals hold routine unskilled jobs—ones that are neither interesting nor challenging from the perspective of most people.

An understanding of mutual responsibility emerges with statements such as, "Many hands is less work—everyone needs to do their part;" and "everyone needs to fulfill a role to maintain the dorm." Self-worth and personal power are evident as well. One inmate says, "There are different ways to clean up—the quick way and the right way," suggesting his efforts are among the best. And finally some residents demonstrate an awareness of relationships with others through their work: "[It] gives me an opportunity to relate to individuals in a way that is needed. . . . [I]t deals with personal growth, self betterment, maturity, responsibility"; and, "[It] enables me to talk to people more and helps me to be more empathetic and sympathetic." These excerpts portray inmates who through their community jobs are acting their way into different kinds of thinking—thinking that is less self-centered and more relational and community oriented.

ENFORCING RULES

Rule enforcement in prison is difficult for both correctional officers and inmates. Before entering the honor dorm inmates lived under the supervision of guards for many years. Correctional officers' authority is resented, but their role as rule enforcers is accepted.[26] Inmates mostly follow orders, even though they greatly outnumber their captors. What happens when inmates are given the responsibility to police themselves? Can they be fair? Is there such as thing as restorative enforcement?

Rule enforcement is a challenging part of working with others in the dorm. The convict code, "mind your own business," "do your own time," and "don't be a snitch," conflicts with inmate management and honor dorm community values. The honor dorm addresses these challenges through education (chapter 6) and by outlining roles and responsibilities in the honor dorm SOPs. Also, all residents agree to abide by the dorm's rules and regulations when they sign their Honor Community Contract.

The senior coordinator and coordinators on duty are responsible for securing compliance with honor dorm rules. But first and foremost, honor dorm SOPs direct them to conform with rules so others will follow their example. Any resident can log a violation using a statement of facts form. This can be problematic, particularly if he uses the process out of spite or retaliation. Filing a report with the intention to lash out is a violation of the honor dorm code. To prevent this problem the resident must obtain a statement of facts form from the coordinator on duty, who discusses the situation with the complainant, making sure a violation has occurred.

The coordinator on duty forwards the statement of facts forms to the senior coordinator. All violations are reviewed by a group of three managers and department heads with a community manager being at least one of the three. Once an alleged violation has been logged, only a community manager can void it. The selection of community managers is crucial because their impartiality could easily be questioned. After review, community managers assign demerit points and community service according to policies outlined in a merit/demerit system. Appeals are filed with the ARC.

In addition to due process, procedures for alleged rule violations prescribe respectful relationships. For example, confronters should refrain from using negative and threatening language or profanity. If a person is argumentative when confronted, the complainant should walk away and then log the alleged violation. These procedures were adopted over time as problems emerged.

Community peacemaking circles (chapter 4) are the most directly restorative component of the honor dorm community. Anyone can recommend a case for a peacemaking circle, although the request must proceed through the chain of command. Residents can recommend inmates with adjustment problems to peacemaking circles. Conflicts with no rule violation commonly go to circle as well. Among categories of rule violations, only those classified as Group II fall within the formal jurisdiction of peacemaking circles. Group II violations are not necessarily a violation of DOC rules, but are seen as detrimental to the honor dorm community. They are generally defined as negative behavior, undermining (or manipulation), insubordination, and adversarial conversation (defined as conversation that pits one resident against another). Civil libertarians might question Group II violations. In the free world these behaviors would be regulated, if at all, through informal social control. The rules are developed with the community in mind—that is they prohibit behaviors that could tear the fragile community fabric. Since peacemaking circles are used to address them, disciplinary procedures that normally pit the state against the individual do not come into play.

Behavior that violates DOC regulations is prohibited in the honor dorm. These violations are also handled by the three-member committee that reviews all infringements. This committee likewise issues recommendations for those who fail to perform their assigned community jobs. If a DOC violation occurs outside the honor dorm, it is addressed through the prison disciplinary procedures. To extend the restorative philosophy and secure more effective compliance there are cases where violations other than Group II's are referred to peacemaking circles.

There are two ways a resident can be dismissed from the honor dorm. One is to fall below the required points necessary to maintain residence. The other is to commit what is called a Group I violation or a cardinal rule. Examples of cardinal rules are violence or threats of violence, fighting, gambling, running stores, homosexual acts or public display of sexual acting out of any kind, pornography, drugs, stealing, or refusing to perform community service or other obligations for rule violations or those resulting from peacemaking circles. In addition, four Group II violations within the same semester can be considered a cardinal rule violation. After dorm procedures are followed, dismissals can be reviewed by the ARC. The chaplain envisions Group I violators appearing before peacemaking circles. This practice will help residents better understand the nature of the problem and give them an opportunity to understand and repair any harm to themselves, others, or the community. At this time most cardinal rule violators do not go to peacemaking circles.

COMMUNITY, SERVICE, AND THE INDIVIDUAL

Prisoners throughout the country attempt to give something back to the community. Some make toys for children at Christmas. Prison-based animal programs assist the visually and physically impaired.[27] Some inmates record books on tape for school children while those in lower-custody facilities partner with Habitat for Humanity building homes for low-income families.[28] It is not unusual to see small groups of men from local jails and state prisons maintaining streets and highways. Probably the best-known community service project was established by lifers at a maximum-security prison in Rahway, New Jersey. Popularly called "Scared Straight," the program introduced juveniles at risk to life behind bars.[29]

Unfortunately there is little progress at Holman for delivering free world community service. Inmates want to give something back. Many want to work with at-risk juveniles. A civilian supervisor from the metal shop shared his worries about his son's delinquent behavior with a resident lifer. He wanted some of the men in the honor dorm to talk with his son. Permission from the warden was granted, and the young man sat in a circle with a small group of inmates, listening to their stories. However, this was an isolated incident.

The Innovative Thinking Group wanted to sell doughnuts to the general population and give the profits to a local charity. The group met with the warden, he commended them for their initiative, and then cautioned that selling doughnuts might conflict with the canteen contract. He promised to bring the proposal to the legal department in Montgomery, the state capitol. Many months passed, but there was no word from the warden. Another proposal for children's books on tape died on the warden's desk.

Residents serve the dorm community in other ways besides their assigned jobs. One resident developed a nonsmoking program. Three inmates decided to resurrect the dorm newspaper, renaming it *The Paradigm News*. The title represents paradigm change from a retributive to a restorative justice model. Honor dorm residents partnered with inmates in general population for a Black History Month presentation. They showed the film *A Long Night's Journey into Day*, making comparisons between South Africa's apartheid and America's civil rights movement.[30] The honor dorm participants saw an opportunity to share restorative principles practiced in the Truth and Reconciliation Commission with other prisoners. The warden distributes a weekly newsletter to all Holman inmates. Dorm residents wanted to use a small column in the paper to share thoughts about peaceful conflict resolution. One entry appeared, but there was no encouragement for further participation.

It is human nature to be in conflict with the community. Individuals want independence and resist being restricted or suppressed by the majority. At the same time our identities, self-esteem, vitality, and reason for being are linked to community life. The plethora of rules, regulations, and standard operating procedures governing the honor dorm may appear oppressive. Alternatively they provide structure, making possible opportunities for transcending self-defeating behaviors and negative environmental influences. The rules are not developed in isolation, but instead evolved in response to community experience. Restorative language guides their implementation. Members of the honor dorm community—not correctional officers—bring rule violations to the residents' attention. A small group of people make the rules, but suggestions for their revision can be submitted in writing. Peacemaking circles encourage residents to take an active responsible role in problem-solving.

Before coming to the honor dorm, many residents did not have a community life. Some are former gang members. Many lived in disorganized communities. Because of alcohol and drug addiction many led isolated lives. When student volunteers visit the dorm, the men are impressed. Growing up they did not see young people working for social purposes. In her work on developing compassionate communities through the power of care-giving relationships, Tyson observes, "for the many people who are not raised in the embrace of genuine care-giving love or whose families, despite their efforts to care for the children are devastated by war or disaster, the nature of the communities in which they then reside makes all the difference for their development."[31]

In its design, the honor dorm tries to connect its residents with the community through education, service, and other relationship-building activities. New ways of relating to community are strongly encouraged through required community jobs. Some residents have little interest in their work and receive small satisfaction from it. Still, the majority of those sampled see their work in relationship to the community and find satisfaction in it. Those with management positions and those sitting on peacemaking circles are encouraged to show sympathy and compassion for others.

In an ideal world, decision-making in the honor dorm would be more participative, rule-breaking would have no retributive content, and service would be voluntary. But compared to past attempts to change prison culture, the honor dorm enjoys considerable longevity. Restorative practitioner Ron Claassen understands the need for back-up when participants reject restorative approaches.[32] In the free world, the criminal justice system functions this way. In the prison, demerits and in some cases expulsion from the dorm exist for this purpose.

Community service and honor dorm governance continues to evolve, and the future will reveal more about the dorm's restorative potential. The honor dorm philosophy recognizes that offenders will be challenged to take responsibility for their lives when released.[33] Hopefully their transition will be more successful if inmates assume responsibilities before they return to the community.

NOTES

1. "Standard Operating Procedures," Holman Correctional Facility, Faith-Based Restorative Justice Honor Community, November 15, 2004, unpublished, 2.

2. J. E. Baker, "Inmate Self-Government," *The Journal of Criminal Law, Criminology, and Police Science* 55, no. 1 (March 1964): 39–47.

3. Baker, "Inmate Self-Government," 41.

4. Baker, "Inmate Self-Government," 42.

5. *Gates v. Coller*, 349 F. Supp. 881, 896 (ND Miss. 1972).

6. John J. DiIulio Jr., *Governing Prisons: A Comparative Study of Correctional Management* (New York: Free Press, 1987).

7. Baker, "Inmate Self-Government," 43.

8. Baker, "Inmate Self-Government," 44.

9. Harold M. Helfman, "Antecedents of Thomas Mott Osborne's 'Mutual Welfare League' in Michigan," *Journal of Criminal Law and Criminology* 40, no. 5 (January–February 1950): 598.

10. Cheryl Swanson, Grantt Culliver, and Chris Summers, "Creating a Faith-Based Restorative Justice Community in a Maximum-Security Prison," *Corrections Today* 69, no. 3 (June 2007): 62–63.

11. Chris Summers, chaplain, W. C. Holman Correctional Facility, personal communication, March 15, 2008.

12. "Standard Operating Procedures," 10.

13. "Standard Operating Procedures," 10.

14. Barb Toews, *The Little Book of Restorative Justice for People in Prison: Rebuilding the Web of Relationships* (Intercourse, Pa.: Good Books, 2006), 50–59.

15. Toews, *Restorative Justice for People in Prison*, 76.

16. Muhammad Ali, Daily Celebrations, www.dailycelebdrations.com/service.htm (accessed 3 March 2008).

17. Dali Lama, Daily Celebrations, www.dailycelebdrations.com/service.htm (accessed 3 March 2008).

18. Walter Brueggemann, "Covenant as a Subversive Paradigm," available at www.religion-online.org/showarticle.asp?title=1727 (accessed 11 May 2008).

19. Jerry Z. Park and Christian Smith, "Too Much Has Been Given . . . : Religious Capital and Community Volunteerism among Churchgoing Protestants," *Journal of the Scientific Study of Religion* 39, no. 3 (September 2000): 272–86.

20. Judith A. Boss, "The Anatomy of Moral Intelligence," *Educational Theory* 44, no. 4 (December 1994): 399–416.

21. James Youness and Miranda Yates, *Community and Social Responsibility in Youth* (Chicago: University of Chicago Press, 1997).

22. *Alcoholics Anonymous*, 4th ed. (New York: Alcoholics Anonymous World Services, Inc., 2001), 89–103.

23. Howard Zehr, *Transcending: Reflections of Crime Victims* (Intercourse, Pa.: Good Books, 2001).

24. David C. McClelland and Carol Kirshnit, "The Effect of Motivational Arousal through Films on Immunoglobutin A," *Psychology and Health* 2, no. 1 (1998): 31–52.

25. Reginald A. Wilkinson, "The Impact of Community Service Work on Ohio State Prisoners: A Restorative Justice Perspective and Overview," *Corrections Management Quarterly*, available at www.drc.state.oh.us/web/Articles/article63.htm (accessed 3 March 2008).

26. Cyndi Banks, *Criminal Justice Ethics: Theory and Practice* (Thousand Oaks, Calif.: Sage, 2004), 139–40.

27. Gennifer Furst, "Prison-Based Animal Programs: A National Survey," *The Prison Journal* 86, no. 4 (December 2006): 407–30.

28. Community Service, Ohio Department of Rehabilitation and Correction, www.drc.state.oh.us/web/commserv.htm (accessed 3 March 2008).

29. Juvenile Awareness Program, www.wild-side.com/scaredstraight.html (accessed 11 May 2008).

30. *A Long Night's Journey into Day*, directed by Francis Reid and Deborah Hoffmann, 2001.

31. Katherine Tyson, "Developing Compassionate Communities through the Power of Caregiving Relationships," *Journal of Religion and Spirituality in Social Work* 24, no. 1/2 (April 2005): 31–32.

32. Ron Claassen, "An Introduction to Discipline that Restores," Center for Peacemaking and Conflict Studies, Fresno Pacific University, available at disciplinethatrestores.org/IntroDTR.pdf (accessed 11 March 2008).

33. Hans Toch, "Inmate Involvement in Prison Governance," *Federal Probation* 59, no. 2 (June 1995): 34–39.

8

Getting to the Next Grade

Is rehabilitation restorative? No. Is restorative justice rehabilitative?
Sometimes.

—Gordon Bazemore and Dee Bell, *Critical Issues in Restorative Justice*

Record numbers of Americans are behind bars, and nearly 650,000 former inmates arrive at our communities' doorsteps each year.[1] At least 95 percent of
prisoners get released at some time.[2] How will these new arrivals fit into our
communities? Given recidivism rates as high as 67 percent, many people are
struggling to find answers on how to reduce them. The honor dorm experience at Holman does not have sufficient time or research to determine the relationship between its restorative approach and recidivism. However, there is
some evidence that an investment in these kinds of programs may have a positive impact on reducing crime relapse.

As a senior researcher for the RAND Corporation in the 1980s, Joan Petersilia and her colleagues warned that a substantial number of felony probationers committed serious crimes in Los Angeles County. Given their crimes
and criminal histories, she found it virtually impossible to distinguish between those sent to prison and those sentenced to probation.[3] Widely dissem-
inated, Petersilia's research supported new sentencing structures for better
community protection. Although not her intention, these findings supported
the "get tough" sentencing policies of the time. In *When Prisoners Come Home,*

Petersilia follows up with this observation: "We spent the last decade debating who should go to prison, for how long, and how we might pay for it, and we paid virtually no attention to how we would cope with prisoners after they left prison."[4] Indeed, the Bureau of Justice Statistics estimates that 50 percent of those released from prison will be in trouble with the law within three years of their release.[5] Once tolerated, this revolving door has become too consequential to ignore. As a result, reentry is at the top of the agenda among policymakers in national government.

The Department of Justice Office of Justice Programs (OJP) has a web page on reentry. Described as "the use of programs targeted at promoting the effective reintegration of offenders back to communities upon release from prison or jail," the OJP outlines a comprehensive strategy for meeting the needs of ex-offenders, including drug and alcohol abuse, housing, job training, education, and work.[6] During the 1980s and 1990s serious high-risk offenders got long prison terms in high-security institutions with little if any rehabilitative programming. Some spent most of their time in isolation, depending on how well they adjusted to prison life. Rehabilitative efforts focused on lower-risk inmates with relatively short prison terms. So today many high-risk offenders will be returning to society with little if any preparation.

Faced with significant numbers of newly released prisoners, including those convicted of serious crimes, the Bush administration created a Prison Reentry Initiative. Designed as a cooperative effort among several federal agencies, it funds state reentry programs. In addition, Bureau of Justice Assistance grants are awarded to state departments of corrections for developing prerelease services for prisoners transitioning back home.[7] In April 2008, President Bush also signed the Second Chance Act that creates an interagency council on reentry, provides additional funding for state programs, and authorizes direct grants to nonprofit organizations for mentoring and other services for returning adult and juvenile offenders. Some nonprofit organizations, such as the Kellogg Foundation, have a strong interest in prison reentry, particularly in developing opportunities for small business ownership.[8] Along these lines, the Association for Enterprise Opportunity, a trade association for nonprofits making small business loans, plans training for its membership on the subject of micro-enterprise opportunities for newly released prisoners. These significant programs suggest a departure from a legacy of neglect. But given economic downturns and budget shortfalls, will these programs be adequately funded? And if so, will they work?

REHABILITATION VERSUS REINTEGRATION

The language of offender programming is often confusing. From a restorative approach it is important to distinguish between treatment or rehabilitation and reintegration. Bazemore and Dooley compare the two models in figures 8.1 and 8.2.[9] The treatment model sees the offender as a client with deficiencies needing fixing, which might include how the offender thinks. Cognitive restructuring therapy can effectively address errors in thinking contributing to violence and other antisocial behaviors. In addition to treatment, rehabilitation programs attend to offenders' needs such as education and job training. A process for coordinating services offered in the community such as housing, employment, and counseling creates a comprehensive reentry program for offenders.

John McKnight, a critic of the traditional medical (allopathic) approach to treatment, says: "Its radical position grows from the unique belief that the malady is *in* the person and the cure is achieved by professional intrusion *into* that person. In that understanding the allopathic faith stands isolated in therapeutic history as it ignores both the world around the person and the person as healers."[10] Providing an alternative viewpoint, McKnight comments:

> In contrast, nearly all other regenerative ideas comprehend an inextricable relationship between the person and the social and physical world in which he or she resides, and an immutable force in the person's own will to heal. So it is that most time-tested healing rites convene community, draw power from the earth, and call on the spirit of the afflicted.[11]

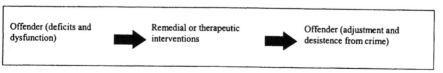

FIGURE 8.1.

Treatment/Remedial Model.
Gordon Bazemore and Michael Dooley, "Restorative Justice and the Offender: The Challenge of Reintegration," in *Restorative Justice and Community: Repairing Harm and Transforming Communities,* ed. Gordon Bazemore and Maria Schiff (Cincinnati, Ohio: Anderson, 2001), 115. Reprinted with permission. Copyright © 2001 by Matthew Bender & Company, Inc., a member of the LexisNexis Group. All rights reserved.

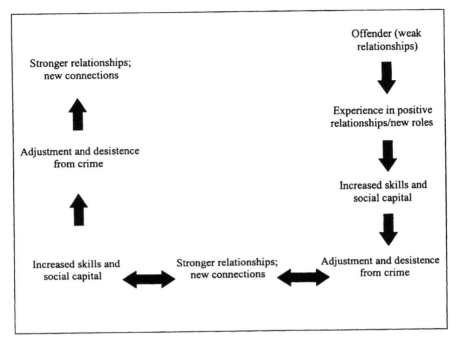

FIGURE 8.2.
Restorative/Relational Model.
Gordon Bazemore and Michael Dooley, "Restorative Justice and the Offender: The Challenge of Reintegration," in *Restorative Justice and Community: Repairing Harm and Transforming Communities*, ed. Gordon Bazemore and Maria Schiff (Cincinnati, Ohio: Anderson, 2001), 115. Reprinted with permission. Copyright © 2001 by Matthew Bender & Company, Inc., a member of the LexisNexis Group. All rights reserved.

McKnight's observation speaks to the philosophy underlying the restorative/ relational model in figure 8.2. It *assumes* the offender's desire or willingness to take responsibility as a precondition for change. It *recognizes* the importance of relationships and community connections for offenders' healing and transformation. Typically prior to incarceration, the offenders' pro-social relationships are already weak. They become further isolated in prison. Not surprisingly, the newly released prisoner has little if any social capital.

Developing networks of social support through school, work, church, and private associations is something many of us do over a lifetime. While these social networks are sometimes intentionally developed, they are a routine part of human life. They serve as a basis for skill development, knowledge, experience, and social support.

They also provide informal social controls.[12] We are less inclined to lie, steal, cheat, hurt, or maim when in addition to our conscience, we are habituated to caring what our neighbors, friends, and families, think about us. We have investments, commitments, and attachments that moderate impulses to misbehave. It is difficult to imagine a world without these relationships and supports and the kind of thinking they engender, but this is how the world of the convict and the newly released prisoner actually is. Restorative practitioners are not opposed to the traditional treatment and rehabilitative approaches, but the restorative approach focuses on repairing social relationships. Offender healing and change may result from this normative theory. One's thinking changes after behaving in new ways in relationship with others.

As a precursor to restorative practices, psychologist Robert Eglash developed the concept of creative restitution in the 1950s.[13] Working with adult and juvenile offenders, Eglash found the treatment system lacked both effectiveness and humanity. At the time Elgash also worked with destitute alcoholics and attended several Alcoholics Anonymous (AA) meetings. He was impressed with the warmth and caring of the AA fellowship. Two steps in the twelve-step program captured his attention so profoundly that it changed his perceptions on offender reparation: Step nine requires making direct amends to all those harmed except when doing so would injure them or others; step twelve suggests continuing to work with other alcoholics.

These principles gave birth to creative restitution—restitution that could include a monetary settlement but goes further in spirit and practice whereby "an offender, under appropriate supervision, is helped to find some way to make amends to those he has hurt by his offense and 'to walk a second mile' by helping other offenders."[14] Congruent with the principles of the restorative/relational model, restitution is something that is done with others. By helping others, the offender begins developing a capacity to contribute to society rather than taking from or depending on it. This approach replaces service dependency with active, caring relationships.[15]

The field of intrapsychic humanism finds a place for care-giving relationships in the development of self-regulating behavior.[16] Emmy Werner compared resilient children of alcoholics with those with severe developmental problems by age eighteen.[17] She found that resiliency is supported by internal competencies (strengths) the child can draw on *as well as* external levels of support from their care-giving environment. Her research points to bidirectional effects, whereby children with traits engaging to caregivers, such as being affectionate, are more likely to receive attention from their caregivers. This two-way relationship points to what some observers find objectionable in the unidirectional rehabilitative model (figure 8.1) that renders the offender a receptacle who passively receives help. His or her strengths and contributions remain unrecognized and unacknowledged.

In a restorative/relational model Bill, a newly released offender, initially receives support for food and clothing from his church (figure 8.2). His friends in the faith community discover he is a good singer who developed his voice in the prison choir. He joins the church choir, which sorely needs another tenor, and meets Joe, who owns a landscape company. Joe wants an additional worker during the summer months and offers Bill a job. Bill eventually builds his own lawn business, receiving a micro-enterprise loan from a local nonprofit. He hires Tom, recently released from prison. Bill not only provides work for Tom, but also listens, shares his experiences, and provides emotional support. These supports help Tom with the stresses and strains transitioning to society. In this process Bill builds social capital. His relationships are caring, responsive, flexible, interdependent, dynamic, and voluntary. His quality of life does not depend on getting one-size-fits-all services from a large bureaucracy. He can make contributions to the community. Others appreciate his involvement. The process continues and extends itself, reflecting the natural relational nature of healthy interdependent communities.[18]

While these principles are helpful guidelines, the real world of offender reintegration entails numerous challenges. Do communities have the willingness and the capacity to work with ex-felons? The "Not in My Back Yard (NIMBY)" reaction to former prisoners is real, particularly for sex offenders.[19] Large numbers of Americans, including ex-felons, lack affordable housing and work opportunities during economic downturns. Furthermore, many inner-city communities are permanently damaged by powerful social and economic forces such as deindustrialization, de facto segregation, and out-migration to the suburbs.[20] Mapping technologies show a disproportionate number of former prisoners return to these communities where family, schools, voluntary associations, and other support structures are weak.[21]

Even in healthy communities where Americans generously volunteer their time and money, a "culture of excessive individualism" prevails, giving Americans less of a social safety net than countries with a strong communitarian bent.[22] In America "even compassion is 'bounded' by the culture of individualism. Compassionate behavior is managed by being segmented into limited roles (e.g., a few hours of volunteer work). If pursued so extensively that it interferes with a person's self-interest, such behavior is regarded as an unhealthy obsession."[23] Substantial numbers of Americans do not think they can count on family, friends, neighbors, or the government for assistance should they become ill, implying that in America the need for support exceeds its availability.[24]

A RESTORATIVE LOOK AT COMMUNITY

Every community has a stake in the crime problem, particularly crime desistance among the 650,000 men and women released from prison each year. Community members may debate their level of accountability and responsibility for crime, but few people would argue against education, mentoring, employment opportunities, recreational opportunities, and strong families for inoculating against it. For restorative justice the emphasis on community stems from its core values of inclusion, participation, accountability and responsibility, interdependence, healing, and problem-solving. Peacemaking circles, community reparative boards, and family group conferences are restorative practices that address crime within a web of relationships that more closely approximate the community than a courtroom setting.

The most controversial argument for community involvement stems from the movement's spiritual roots. Inherent in spirituality, as opposed to religiosity, is the reverence for life accompanied by a sense of the connectedness of all people to something bigger than themselves.[25] This human bond includes all members of society as at once victims and sinners, implying the need for compassion, mutual responsibility, and forgiveness. This approach is at odds with the "us versus them" mentality defining the retributive adversary model.[26] It also conflicts with the propensity to isolate and shame the offender after completion of his or her sentence. If we are one another's keepers, as community members we share responsibility for mending conditions that contribute to crime and for helping victims and offenders overcome their difficulties. For the offender, "making things right allows [him or her] to restore a relationship to the universe, God, or the creator."[27] Feelings of isolation give way to feelings of connection, experienced as a source of support.

This need for support gets dramatized in John Irwin's *The Felon*, written over three decades ago.[28] After interviewing ex-convicts, he reported a lack of meaning and sense of belonging, particularly after the "pink cloud" of freedom wears off. In prison men fantasize about their freedom, but the reality is far different. While prison has its negatives, the men Irwin interviewed felt isolated. The world was a cold place, friendships were hard to make, and former inmates felt they did not fit in. These perceptions have little to do with the need for services or the stigma of being an ex-offender.

Abraham Maslow's hierarchy of needs (figure 8.3) illustrates the importance of meeting various levels of need.[29] According to this model, after bio-

FIGURE 8.3.
Maslow's Hierarchy of Needs.
This figure is based on Elton Reeves's description of the different levels of need. Elton Reeves, *The Dynamics of Behavior* (American Management Association, 1970), 33–41.

logical, physiological, and security requirements are satisfied, people seek be-
longingness. A sense of belonging is met through family, friendships, work relationships, and community responsibilities. The restorative approach
recognizes these needs and seeks to reconnect victims and offenders with their
respective communities in meaningful and satisfying ways.

Often community is defined as a geographical place, but some restorative
practitioners define it in terms of an "event" or as a "community of care," that
is, those who care about the event or care about people affected by the event.[30]
This is the case when restorative practices such as circles and conferences address harms caused by conflict, misbehavior, or crime. When possible, it is desirable for ex-prisoners to reconnect with their geographical communities.
This assumes those who care about the offender live there. But just as new
families are created for orphans, communities of care can be created for those
whose former neighborhoods encourage crime or are otherwise nonsupport-
ive environments.

Reintegration means "re-entry into community life as a whole, contributing productive person. This means more than being tolerant of the person's
presence; it means acceptance of the person as a member. It requires action on
the community's part."[31] At the most basic level it requires provision of services (figure 8.3). In Alabama, prisoners are released with ten dollars of "gate
money." Inmates typically earn well below minimum wage in prison indus-
tries, and these monies are quickly spent for stamps, canteen items, and in
some cases restitution.[32] Initially, then, social welfare assistance is a priority.
Second, it is desirable to assign a support worker to assist with services and offer understanding and emotional support.[33] Offenders released on parole typically work with a parole officer. However, for those offenders at the end of
their sentences, this kind of structure and support is unavailable. Finally, offenders can be encouraged to form support networks including families,
friends, voluntary associations, and faith communities.

Community support is more difficult to obtain in highly individualized
and urbanized societies.[34] Furthermore, for some offenders, friends and family members are part of the problem. For individuals lacking "natural" support groups, it is necessary to build them.[35] Circles of Accountability and
Support (COSA) were established in 1994 in Ontario, Canada, to help sex offenders adjust to the community and to prevent re-victimization. Since then,
these programs have expanded throughout Canada and in some locations in

the United States.[36] Each COSA consists of four or five trained volunteers who meet with the ex-offender to provide physical, emotional, and spiritual support. In a 2005 Canadian evaluation of COSA ex-offenders, 90 percent say they could not have adjusted as well without COSA, and two-thirds say without it there is a strong possibility they would have committed another crime.[37] In the same study, a public opinion survey shows 68 percent feel more comfortable with a sexual offender in the community knowing he belongs to a circle. Finally, COSA participants have significantly lower recidivism rates than those in a control group.

Support groups created specifically for offenders leaving prison may be helpful. However, by creating a subculture, these groups may fail to reintegrate ex-offenders into the larger community.[38] Support groups such as Alcoholics Anonymous and Narcotics Anonymous provide friendship and support and are particularly relevant given the high percentage of drug and alcohol abuse among prisoners. Finally, federal and state governments are tapping faith communities for assistance with reintegration efforts.

Alabama's Governor Riley is impressed with the faith community's flexibility and effectiveness working with disaster victims. In May 2008, he invited eight thousand churches to a reentry summit to receive information about ex-convicts' needs and about what faith communities can do to help the ten thousand former inmates released in Alabama each year. The goal is to match each offender with a church. While many churches participate in prison ministries, working with prisoners in the community is a different venture. More cynical church members may question the government's motive. Is it simply trying to shift the financial burden to churches? Creating a level of comfort among members of faith communities is particularly challenging. What are they getting into? What should they do and how should they do it? Is it safe? How much time will it take? What is the benefit for them? When is it time to let go of offenders who seem unresponsive and unwilling to help themselves?[39] While inmates are well received in some churches, many may not open their doors to inmates.[40] Furthermore, the needs of non-Christian, agnostic, and atheist offenders need to be addressed.

COMPREHENSIVE REINTEGRATION PROGRAMS

In May 2004, the minister of corrections in New Zealand challenged his country to world leadership in reintegration. New Zealand's Department of Corrections makes a distinction between rehabilitation, which includes activities directed toward the offender, and reintegration, which relates to social and environmental obstacles to a nonoffending lifestyle.[41] The country's reintegration plan is a work in progress. A reentry partnership model recognizes the need for law enforcement, corrections, and the community to share resources, support, and responsibility for released prisoners. The importance of coordinating reentry activities is also addressed. Five regional reintegration team leaders and sixteen reintegration caseworkers have been added to the New Zealand Prison Service.[42] This continuum of care approach acknowledges the need to begin reentry programming prior to release with continued support after leaving prison.

The reintegration caseworkers are assigned to prisons and work with the inmate, the family, parole officers, and community agencies toward achieving reintegration goals. The prison service is moving away from halfway houses because they are not easily accepted by communities, and unless tightly monitored, are difficult places for modeling pro-social behaviors.[43] New Zealand plans to develop a comprehensive approach offering practical support (housing and job training), treatment addressing offender attitudes and behaviors, and "emotional relationship-based holistic support."[44] Yet Kim Workman, national director of Prison Fellowship in New Zealand, says offender reintegration operates in a theoretical vacuum.[45]

This seems to be the case worldwide where prisoners are released with only some guidance and supervision by their parole officers. Those who are released at the end of their sentences are on their own. Workman says,

> the traditional literature of aftercare remains devoid of broader policy visions that place the offender in the context of community and give specific consideration to the role of neighborhood organizations, local socialising institutions, or citizen supporters in the reintegration process. Though some aftercare reintegration discourse has recently begun to attend to the *human capital* issues of employment and education, with few exceptions the field has failed to address how community-produced *social capital* can be an important intervening factor aimed at increasing the likelihood of offender transition to conventional life.[46]

Workman suggests the restorative approach helps focus on the underpinnings of a more comprehensive approach to aftercare.

With this in mind, Operation Jericho was developed by Prison Ministries in New Zealand to address the need for social capital.[47] The program connects former prisoners with receptive churches who then provide social and spiritual support. While the components of a reintegrative model have yet to be specified and tested for their effectiveness on behavior, some empirical studies show a relationship between social support and crime.[48] The mental health literature documents a relationship between community support and recovery.[49] Furthermore, within the rehabilitative model, caring supportive relationships between therapist and offender correlate with treatment success.[50]

The institutional component of reentry is important as well. This includes building offender assets prior to release so that community interventions are more effective.[51] Socialization into community roles can begin in prison through community service, education, and victim offender programming. It is important to provide inmates with guidance on relationships and to help them maintain relationships with their families.[52] A British review of prison release strategies and recidivism suggests that prisoners who have developed good coping strategies for everyday situations are more likely to succeed in the community.[53] According to the British study practical responses focusing solely on social service provision are less effective than those *also* concentrating on offender responsibility.

AN EMERGING PROGRAM

Alabama is responding to the reentry movement. Faced with at high recidivism rate and a prison system at 200 percent over capacity, Governor Bob Riley hired a private contractor to develop a strategic plan for prisoner release in Alabama.[54] While Alabamians may prefer to lock the door and throw away the key, large numbers of offenders are returning to prison at an average cost of thirty-seven dollars per day. The Alabama Department of Corrections (ADOC) Mission Statement reads, "to confine manage and provide *rehabilitative services* [emphasis added] for convicted felons in a safe, secure, and humane environment, utilizing professionals who are committed to public safety *and to the positive re-entry of offenders into society* [emphasis added]."[55] Rehabilitation and reentry had not received high priority in Alabama in the past.

As in most states, offenders in Alabama face serious obstacles after returning to society.[56] When Eddie got out of prison, he had difficulty getting a driver's license. The Alabama Department of Public Safety required two forms of identification. Acceptable forms of identification included old drivers licenses, voting identification cards, and birth certificates. A prisoner identification card was not an approved document. Eddie made four visits to get the paperwork for his driver's license. It took him two years to obtain it. He couldn't get a job or a check cashed without the license. He said, "I might as well go back to prison." He eventually broke the law and returned to the penitentiary.[57] In 2008, the Alabama Department of Public Safety agreed to use the prisoner identification card for documentation.

Mickey left the penitentiary on Christmas Eve of 2006. He planned to live in a halfway house but did not have enough money for rent. He instead entered a work release facility in Mobile. His release papers ordered him to Montgomery on December 26 for a hearing with a judge and his parole officer. No arrangements were made to transfer the case from Montgomery, where Mickey's case originated, to Mobile, so Mickey bought a round-trip bus ticket to Montgomery. After arriving, he discovered that the hearing had been cancelled for the holidays. It was rescheduled for December 28. Mickey had no money to purchase another bus ticket. Meanwhile he borrowed $2,200 from a friend in New Orleans because he did not have a job, and had also met a woman with whom he returned to drugs. He was arrested and sent to the Mobile County Jail. As one observer notices, "The system seems designed for prisoners to return."[58]

Danny had consensual sex with a fifteen-year-old woman who became pregnant and pressed charges against him. She withdrew her complaint, but the system moved forward without her. Danny is now twenty-two and remains in jail. He is classified as a sex offender and does not have the money to obtain an approved address. He wants to get a job, pay child support, and marry the mother of his child. Yet, he cannot be released because he lacks family support as well as the required $1,000 to establish a residence.[59] Such laws and government regulations that hinder reintegration should be reviewed and rescinded when possible. Otherwise, as one prison chaplain noted, we are operating in Biblical times, when lepers were isolated in colonies. Today, these colonies often take the shape of homeless camps under bridges.[60]

To prepare for its reintegration effort, Alabama is developing a marketing and education plan involving the courts, corrections personnel, businesses, local nonprofits, and faith communities. The governor established the Alabama Community Partnership for Recovery and Reentry (CPR) to engage community groups with reintegration and to develop an information clear-inghouse for those leaving courts and correctional facilities.[61] He envisions the program as a grassroots approach. Community sponsors and families can register with CPR as partners. CPR will provide training to participants and maintain informational websites at the county level.

The ADOC corrections commissioner appointed a reentry coordinator to work with institutional and community representatives on a discharge plan. After soliciting feedback from DOC representatives and external sources, sev-eral matters came to the forefront: including addiction and recovery; job, ca-reer, and financial skills; faith, social, and character-building skills; health, education, screenings, and referrals; family reintegration skills; and law en-forcement issues.[62] As of this writing there is no decision about when prere-lease programs should be initiated for those leaving the system. A prerelease center at Limestone Prison plans to implement a program that begins 120 days prior to release.[63]

THE FAITH-BASED RESTORATIVE
JUSTICE HONOR DORM AND REINTEGRATION

It is difficult to predict which inmates will desist from crime. Parole failure and recidivism get more attention than the success stories.[64] Those who study rein-tegration efforts agree that successful outcomes are more likely when substan-tial institutional efforts prepare inmates for reentry.[65] In addition, input from inmates is important for building these programs. Interviews with prisoners show many have difficulty requesting help.[66] Some of the problem stems from convicts' distrust of law enforcement, service providers, and supervision agen-cies. For example, when an honor dorm resident shared a problem with me, I suggested meeting with the prison psychologist. He rejected the idea. He said if released, he will work with a psychologist who is not part of "the system."

Many inmates sincerely want to become productive community mem-bers.[67] But their ideal image of their community role does not match their ca-pacity to form solid pro-social identities. One study finds, "Offenders may lack both the personal resources and social relationships necessary to sustain an identity as a law-abiding citizen, as well as a realistic understanding of what the roles themselves will entail. We believe that trying on the roles of produc-tive citizen, responsible citizen and active citizen provides, at a minimum, an imaginative rehearsal for their assumption upon release."[68]

The honor dorm at Holman does not explicitly prepare inmates for release. But it does integrate inmates from general population into a subculture more closely approximating the pro-social values in the free world community. The faith-based component of the dorm emphasizes character-building. Spiritual and religious beliefs have meaning in Maslow's framework as well. Self actualization, the higher needs of human beings, are met for many through the "transcendent and the sacred."[69] The honor dorm could be described as a growth community as inmates progress though various levels of transformation.[70]

The honor dorm's restorative component encourages offender accountability. This includes accountability for harm done to victims, the community, one's family, and oneself. Repairing harm involves making direct amends when possible. In practice it requires making a positive contribution to the honor dorm community through education, work, service, and relationship building. The restorative philosophy promotes offender accountability because it is the right thing to do. When offender transformation and change occur as a result, rehabilitative goals are realized. The emphasis on community can be considered a rehearsal for community roles in the free world.

Examples from honor dorm programming illustrate its relevance to rehabilitative and reintegration goals. A review of Britain's resettlement programs concludes that offender responsibility is important for reducing recidivism rates.[71] Honor dorm work and education requirements enhance responsibility. Restorative programming is particularly helpful for understanding and owning up to the consequences of one's actions.

A 2003/2004 review of reintegration initiatives in New Zealand found its programs do not provide offenders with sufficient guidance prior to release for building pro-social relationships.[72] Holman honor dorm peacemaking circles, mentoring programs, and teaching opportunities are designed to further respect, care, and mutual responsibility. Some inmates try on formal leadership roles, while others learn to share informally. Service work means producing something for the community, not simply benefiting from a more comfortable environment. The emphasis on relationship-building is supported by recent findings showing a link between social and emotional learning and student success.[73] Central to this type of learning is managing emotions and resolving conflict peacefully. For example, in the CSF Buxmont schools for special needs students, social and emotional learning is effectively developed through restorative practices.[74]

Those working with reintegration programs are keenly aware of the offenders' need to develop the capacity for accountability and productivity in the community well before they leave the institution. Workman notes "offenders need some minimal level of skill, or *human capital* to develop and maintain strong, positive relationships. They need assets that allow them to take advantage of the 'connectedness' that can be experienced through good relationships with employers, teachers, friends, fellow church members, etc."[75] For many offenders building social capital requires more than giving them a list of available services when they leave prison. It likely requires a longer socialization period than 120 days in a prerelease facility, although further research will tell us more.

Inmates often experience difficulty negotiating the educational and behavioral requirements of the honor dorm (see table 8.1). Nearly half (45 percent) get expelled for rule violations, which amounts to an average of twenty-nine inmates per year. Rule violations include fighting, threats of violence, public masturbation/sexually acting out, possession of contraband, dirty urines, exceeding number of citations allowed, removal by DOC officials, failure to meet points/dorm requirements, and refusal to do dorm or community service work. Another 15 percent leave on their own volition. Thus three-fifths of its residents did not function well in the honor dorm community. The data suggest the honor dorm screens those with difficulty conforming to pro-social behaviors and values. But several inmates expelled for fighting or using drugs reapplied to the honor dorm after meeting the minimum requirement of six months of discipline-free behavior and have since become model honor dorm residents.

Thirty-one percent of those entering the honor dorm were transferred to other institutions for a variety of reasons. In some cases, an inmate's behavior qualifies him for transfer to a less secure institution closer to home. In other cases, inmates with good prison records seek transfers to less secure facilities with special programming to enhance their possibility for early release. Given these circumstances, and the fact that a substantial number of honor dorm residents have life sentences, only twenty-five inmates have reached the end of their sentence or were paroled since the honor dorm was established in 1999. Follow-up data for these men are currently unavailable. Interviews with them would provide useful information about their perceptions on the impact of the honor dorm experience on post-release behavior.

Table 8.1. Reasons for Noncompletion of First Two Years (Permanent Resident Status) between October 1999 and April 2008.

Reason	N	%
Transferred	180	31.4
Left on own volition	88	15.3
End of sentence/paroled	25	4.4
Requested lock-up	6	1.0
Deceased	1	0.0
Expelled	261	45.5
Misc.	13	2.6
Total	574	100.2*

*Total does not equal 100 percent due to rounding
Source: Statistics provided by Honor Dorm Database and Chaplaincy Programming.

Of 843 inmate candidate possibilities since the honor dorm opened, 176 or 20.9 percent completed the first two years in the honor dorm, achieving permanent resident status. Adjusting for ninety inmates currently in the dorm who have not completed two years, the successful completion rate is 23.4 percent.

Table 8.2 shows the completion numbers for subsequent semesters after reaching permanent residency. Very few inmates who achieve permanent residency leave for rule violations. For each subsequent semester, the majority of residents who leave are transferred to other institutions. Attrition due to rule violations is between three and four inmates each year. While tentative, these data suggest a model for pro-social conditioning that may be useful for future pre-entry programming.

In a guide to restorative justice in prison Edgar and Newell state, "Motivating the person who has offended to behave more sociably is the key issue for the criminal justice system."[76] Hopefully prison communities can prepare inmates for new roles before they return to society. This preparation involves more than providing inmates with phone numbers to call for support after leaving the penitentiary. It may require longer socialization periods than those typically provided in prerelease programs.

Creating a "sanctuary" in prison where inmates can feel safe and model healthy coping relationships is a beginning.[77] In the case of prison, inmates not only need to learn ways of behaving never learned in the free world, they must also unlearn the negative coping behaviors typical of prison life. Chris Summers, chaplain at Holman Prison, observes:

Table 8.2.   Completion Numbers after Reaching Permanent Residency between October 1999 and April 2008.

Of 843 inmate candidate possibilities, 176 completed the first two years in the honor dorm.

Of 176 residents that have finished the first two years the following list shows how many of these residents have completed successive years as permanent residents:

First Year	135		135/165 (81.8%)
Currently in first year		11	
Transferred		19	
Parole		2	
EOS		3	
Left of own volition		2	
Dirty urine		2	
Failed to meet pt req.		1	
Citation		1	
Second Year	108		108/154 (70.1%)
Currently in second year		12	
Transferred		9	
Paroled		1	
EOS		1	
Refused to do comm. service		1	
Deceased		1	
Failed to meet pt req.		1	
Didn't meet GED obligations		1	
Third Year	76		76/136 (55.9%)
Currently in third year		18	
Transferred		6	
Released on probation (split sentence)		1	
Left of own volition		1	
Requested to go to segregation		1	
Fighting		1	
Dirty urine		1	
Drinking alcohol		1	
Citation		1	
Not attending req. class		1	
Fourth Year	38		38/108 (35.2%)
Currently in fourth year		28	
Transferred		2	
EOS		1	
Outgated to court		1	
Left of his own volition		1	
Deceased		1	
Citation		1	
Fighting		2	
Fifth Year	32		32/105 (30.5%)
Currently in fifth year		3	
Fighting		2	
Drinking alcohol		1	
Sixth Year	21		21/97 (21.6%)
Currently in semester		8	
Transferred		1	
Paroled		2	

Source: All Statistics provided by Honor Dorm Database and Chaplaincy Programming.

As a result of inmates spending numerous years in a carceral society (i.e. either the forced submission to the custodial management systems of government and the survival maneuvering in the real world of the convict system) and then re-entering into a very different society, that is, the "free world," teaching and applying "normal" communal foundations is directly linked to the success of inmates' reintegration into our communities. The reintegration process should be the transformation of the inmate's criminal thought into productive citizenry who contribute to society's well being. In simple critical terms, however, reintegration of this type will not take place unless we strongly realize and effectively work with the damage our punitive prisons have produced.[78]

Chaplain Summers identifies a second layer of socialization that compounds the challenges of introducing ex-convicts into community life. The concept of separate, safe places or sanctuaries within prisons, where inmates can begin to experience different ways of thinking and acting has appeal. If reintegration programs do not recognize the multiple layers of negative socialization experienced by inmates and use reentry programs only as a quick fix to alleviate prison costs and overcrowding, attempts to end the prison-to-society-to-prison cycle are likely to fail.

In spite of considerable research on the subject, it is difficult to predict who will win and who will lose from the current focus on reentry programs. After observing the progress of inmates in the honor dorm, it is clear there is no one-size-fits-all program.

Residents in the honor dorm progress each at a different pace. Some fail miserably before they are ready to try again. Time spent in the honor dorm at Holman reduces behaviors that serve as proxies for law violations and other deviant behavior. While this process does not quickly move large numbers of individuals from institutions back to the street, it has the potential to provide a foundation for sound decisions that will not disappoint the public and the inmate.

NOTES

1. "Reentry," Office of Justice Programs, U.S. Department of Justice, available at www.reentry.gov/ (accessed 2 April 2008).

2. Timothy Hughes and Doris James Wilson, "Reentry Trends in the United States," Bureau of Justice Statistics, U.S. Department of Justice, ojp.usdoj.gov/bjs/reentry/reentry.htm (accessed 2 April 2008).

3. Joan Petersilia, Susan Turner, James Kahan, and Joyce Peterson, *Granting Felons Probation: Public Risks and Alternatives*, R-3186-NIJ (Santa Monica, Calif.: The Rand Corporation, 1985).

4. Joan Petersilia, *When Prisoners Come Home* (Oxford: Oxford University Press, 2003), 14.

5. "Reentry," Office of Justice Programs.

6. "Reentry," Office of Justice Programs.

7. "Reentry," Office of Justice Programs.

8. Nicole Lindahl with Debbie A. Mukamal, *Venturing Beyond the Gates: Facilitating Successful Reentry with Entrepreneurship* (New York: Prisoner Reentry Institute John Jay College of Criminal Justice, 2007).

9. Gordon Bazemore and Michael Dooley, "Restorative Justice and the Offender: The Challenge of Reintegration," in *Restorative Community Justice: Repairing Harm and Transforming Communities*, ed. Gordon Bazemore and Maria Schiff (Cincinnati, Ohio: Anderson Publishing, 2001), 115.

10. John McKnight, *The Careless Society: Community and its Counterparts* (New York: Basic Books, 1995), 137.

11. John McKnight, *The Careless Society*, 137.

12. Travis Hirschi, *Causes of Delinquency* (Berkeley: University of California Press, 1969).

13. Laura Mirsky, "Albert Eglash and Creative Restitution: A Precursor to Restorative Practices," *Restorative Practices E Forum* 2003, available at www.iirp.org/libarary/eglash.html (accessed 24 March 2008).

14. Mirsky, "Albert Eglash," 1.

15. McKnight, *The Careless Society*, 122–23.

16. Katherine Tyson, "Developing Compassionate Communities though the Power of Caregiving Relationships," *Journal of Religion and Spirituality in Social Work* 24, no. 1/2 (April 2005): 31–32.

17. Emily Werner, "Resilient Offspring of Alcoholics: A Longitudinal Study from Birth to 18," *Journal of Studies on Alcohol* 47, no. 1 (1986): 34–40.

18. McKnight, *The Careless Society*, 136–37.

19. Kim Workman, "Prisoner Reintegration: Toward a Model of Community Fellowship," available at www.rethinking.org.nz/images/pdf/2006%20Conference/19%20Kim%20Workman.pdf (accessed 24 March 2008).

20. Francis T. Cullen, "Social Support as an Organizing Concept for Criminology: Presidential Address to the Academy of Criminal Justice Sciences," *Justice Quarterly* 11, no. 4 (December 1994): 527–59.

21. "The Reentry Mapping Network," Urban Institute, available at www.urban.org/projects/reentry-mapping/index.cfm (accessed 12 May 2008).

22. Cullen, "Social Support," 532. Also see John Braithwaite, *Crime, Shame and Reintegration* (Oxford: Oxford University Press, 1989), 84–89.

23. Robert Wuthnow, *Acts of Compassion: Caring for Others and Helping Ourselves* (Princeton: Princeton University Press, 1991), 121–20.

24. Robert Wuthnow, *Acts of Compassion*, 11.

25. Kimberly Bender and Marilyn Armour, "The Spiritual Components of Restorative Justice," *Victim and Offenders* 2, no. 3 (July 2007): 251–67.

26. Bender and Armour, "Spiritual Components," 257.

27. Bender and Armour, "Spiritual Components," 259.

28. John Irwin, *The Felon* (Englewood Cliffs, N.J.: Prentice Hall, 1970), 107–19.

29. Abraham Maslow, "A Theory of Human Motivation," *Psychological Review* 50, no. 4 (1943): 370–96.

30. Paul McCold and Benjamin Wachtel, "Community Is Not a Place: A New Look at Community Justice Initiatives," in *Repairing Communities through Restorative Justice*, ed. John G. Perry (Lanham, Md.: American Correctional Association, 2002), 39–53.

31. Daniel W. Van Ness and Karen Heetderks Strong, *Restoring Justice: An Introduction to Restorative Justice*, 3rd ed. (Cincinnati, Ohio: Anderson/Lexis Nexis, 2006), 102.

32. Stephen C. Richards and Richard S. Jones, "Beating the Perpetual Incarceration Machine: Overcoming Structural Impediments to Re-entry," in *After Crime and Punishment: Pathways to Offender Reintegration*, ed. Shadd Maruna and Russ Immarigeon (Devon, U.K.: Willan Publishing, 2004), 201–32.

33. Van Ness and Strong, *Restoring Justice*, 96.

34. Braithwaite, *Crime, Shame, and Reintegration*, 168–74.

35. Van Ness and Strong, *Restoring Justice*, 105–7.

36. "Circles of Support and Accountability," Center for Peacemaking and Conflict Studies, Fresno Pacific University, available at peace.fresno.edu/cosa/ (accessed 12 May 2008).

37. "Circles of Support and Accountability: An Evaluation of the Pilot Project in South-Central Ontario," Correctional Services of Canada 2005, available at www.csc-scc.gc.ca/text/rsch/resports/r168/r168_e.pdf (accessed 12 May 2008).

38. Van Ness and Strong, *Restoring Justice*, 107.

39. Interview with Vickie Locke, Locke Group, consultant to Governor Riley, Alabama Community Partnership for Recovery and Reentry, April 15, 2008.

40. Omar M. McRoberts, "Religion, Reform, Community: Examining the Idea of Church-Based Prisoner Reentry," Urban Institute, Reentry Roundtable 2002, available at www.urban.org/uploaded pdf/410802_Religion.pdf (accessed 12 May 2008).

41. Workman, "Prisoner Reintegration," 141–42.

42. Phil McCarthy, "Prisoner Reintegration: Looking Forward," New Zealand Department of Corrections 2006, available at www.corrections.govt.nz/public/news/prison-fellowship-conference/phil-mccarthy-speech.html (accessed 24 March 2008).

43. McCarthy, "Prisoner Reintegration."

44. McCarthy, "Prisoner Reintegration."

45. Workman, "Prisoner Reintegration."

46. Workman, "Prisoner Reintegration," 146.

47. Workman, "Prisoner Reintegration."

48. Cullen, "Social Support."

49. Cullen, "Social Support."

50. Paul Gendreau, "The Principles of Effective Intervention with Offenders," in *Choosing Corrections Options That Work: Defining the Demand and Evaluating the Supply*, ed. Alan T. Harland (Thousand Oaks, Calif.: Sage, 1996), 117–30.

51. Workman, "Prisoner Reintegration."

52. McCarthy, "Prisoner Reintegration."

53. Mike Maguire and Peter Raynor, "How Resettlement of Prisoners Promotes Desistance from Crime. Or Does It?" *Criminology and Criminal Justice* 6, no. 1 (February 2006): 19–38.

54. Interview with Vickie Locke.

55. "Reentry Update," Alabama Department of Corrections, April 2008.

56. Richard and Jones, "Beating the Perpetual Incarceration Machine," 201–32.

57. Interview with Chaplain Bill Founds, Mobile Work Release Center, Alabama Department of Corrections, April 14, 2008.

58. Interview with Chaplain Bill Founds.

59. Interview with Chaplain Bill Founds.

60. Interview with Chaplain Bill Founds.

61. Interview with Vickie Locke.

62. "Reentry Update," Alabama Department of Corrections, March 2008.

63. "Reentry Update," Alabama Department of Corrections, March 2008.

64. Richards and Jones, "Beating the Perpetual Incarceration Machine," 226.

65. David M. Altschuler and Troy L. Armstrong, "Intensive Aftercare for High-Risk Juveniles: Policies and Procedures," Office of Juvenile Justice and Delinquency Prevention, U.S. Department of Justice 1994, available at www.ncjrs.gov/pdffiles/juvpp.pdf (accessed 13 May 2008). See also Christopher Uggen, Jeff Manza, and Angela Behrens, "'Less than the Average Citizen': Stigma, Role Transition, and the Civic Reintegration of Convicted Felons," in *After Crime and Punishment: Pathways to Offender Reintegration*, ed. Shadd Maruna and Russ Immarigeon (Devon, U.K.: Willan Publishing, 2004), 261–93.

66. Faye S. Taxman, Douglas Young, and James M. Byrne, "With Eyes Wide Open: Formalizing Community and Social Control Intervention in Offender Reintegration Programmes," in *After Crime and Punishment: Pathways to Offender Reintegration*, ed. Shadd Maruna and Russ Immarigeon (Devon, U.K.: Willan Publishing, 2004), 233–60.

67. Uggen, Manza, and Behren, "Less than the Average Citizen," 265.

68. Uggen, Manza, and Behren, "Less than the Average Citizen," 265.

69. S. Muhammad and M. J. Tehrani, "Prison as a Growth Community: A Prison Reform Project in Iran," *The Journal of Humanistic Psychology* 37, no. 1 (Winter 1997): 98.

70. Muhammad and Tehrani, "Prison as a Growth Community," 92–100

71. McGuire and Raynor, "Resettlement of Prisoners," 19–28.

72. McCarthy, "Prisoner Reintegration."

73. Laura Mirsky, "New Research Shows that Social and Emotional Learning Improves Academic Achievement," *Restorative Justice E-Forum* 2008, available at www.safersanerschools.org/library/caselstudy.html (accessed 13 May 2008).

74. Paul McCold, "Evaluation of a Restorative Milieu: Replication and Extension of 2001–2003 Discharges" (paper presented at the annual meeting of the American Society of Criminology, Nashville, Tenn., Nov. 13–16), 1–6.

75. Workman, "Prisoner Reintegration," 147.

76. Kimmett Edgar and Tim Newell, *Restorative Justice in Prisons: A Guide to Making It Happen* (Winchester, U.K.: Waterside Press, 2006), 109.

77. Barb Toews, *The Little Book of Restorative Justice for People in Prison: Rebuilding the Web of Relationships* (Intercourse, Pa.: Good Books, 2006), 82.

78. Personal communication with Chaplain Chris Summers, W. C. Holman Correctional Institution, Atmore, Alabama, April 4, 2008.

9

How Guardians See It

In many respects, guards may be the most influential employees within correctional facilities simply by virtue of their numbers and high degree of interpersonal contacts with inmates on a daily basis.

—Mark Pogrebin and Burton Atkins, *The Challenge of Crime in a Free Society*

Since Alabama faith-based honor dorms are established by order of a former corrections commissioner, they can be changed or abolished if their support is undermined. Given the importance of correctional officers with respect to their role, numbers, and ability to collectively influence administrative decision-making, it is important to understand how corrections officers at Holman view the faith-based restorative justice honor dorm.

While restorative justice is not the same as rehabilitation, the honor dorm stands within the rehabilitative tradition of corrections. Popular stereotypes of officers place them at odds with organizational change and the rehabilitative ideal. The inherent conflict between treatment and custodial roles is frequently mentioned in the corrections literature.[1] But the true picture of correctional officers' attitudes and orientations is more complex. Research on correctional officer attitudes toward inmates in a "get tough" era found that a majority of correctional officers in local facilities show strong support for rehabilitative programs.[2] In this context, guards do not necessarily have an intrinsic appreciation for rehabilitation, but see it more as an inmate

management strategy.[3] Interestingly, officers who take a human services perspective tend to be older and have more seniority than their colleagues.[4]

Typically, any prison struggles with the conflict between offering offenders
opportunities to change and the function of maintaining order and security.
In the officer's mind, these functions are not necessarily at odds. For example,
she might think when enforcing rules she is helping the inmate learn discipline. On the other hand, distinct prototypes of staff-inmate relationships exist and are relevant to understanding the support we might expect an honor
dorm environment to receive. Sarah Ben-David and her colleagues offer a
classification of staff-inmate relationships empirically verified at a prison in
Israel.[5] This typology includes all staff members including corrections officers, guards, therapists, and nurses.

- The "punitive" type abstains as much as possible from communication with
  inmates, maintains authoritative status by ordering and demanding submission and obedience, and stereotypes all inmates—regardless of physical
  or mental status—as "bad" or "mean."
- The "custodial" type relates to inmates as "kept" people and views guards'
  tasks as one of keeping the ward and the inmates clean. Inmates are expected to obey orders, and communication is limited to talk and role requirements.
- The "patronage" type is protective, generally an authoritative figure who
  grants assistance, protection, and guidance to inmates perceived as weak
  and who answers inmates' instrumental needs and requests. Inmates are expected to cooperate with guidance efforts but not to "obey" or "submit."
- The "therapist" type views inmates as patients—or as suffering from illness—and views his or her role as one of advising or guiding willing cooperative patients. Interaction is limited to professional, therapeutic
  interactions, and relationships are controlled by ethical and professional
  considerations.
- The "integrative" or "personal" type has an egalitarian orientation and is
  flexible, adaptable, and readily available for interaction. Inmates are perceived as people with status equal almost to that of the staff. Mode of interaction varies with need and circumstance and may be punitive, therapeutic,
  or custodial.

Correctional officers in the Israeli prison are almost evenly distributed across four of the five prototypes, with no officers falling in the integrative category. Therapists are found in each category but most favor integrative and therapeutic approaches. The findings also suggest that correctional officers supporting rehabilitative activities do not wish to participate in them.[6] Other than the interaction necessary for rule enforcement, these officers prefer to maintain social distance from inmates because of distrust and fear of manipulation. Correctional training reinforces this attitude warning officers about the dangers of close or friendly relationships. Prison design even reinforces the mandated inmate-officer relational barrier. A raised platform where the officer on duty is stationed is located in the center of the Holman honor dorm. This architecture exemplifies the avoidance of officer-inmate interaction in the dorm. A sign warns inmates not to step into the area where officers observe the inmates. From the elevated platform officers distribute the mail, but there is little individual interaction.

Mary Ann Farkas constructed a typology of corrections officers based on their orientation toward rule enforcement, feelings of mutual obligations toward fellow workers, orientation toward negotiation or exchange with inmates, and their desire to incorporate a human service approach into their work.[7] Based on interviews with officers in two Midwestern prisons she found 43 percent are "rule enforcers" and 14 percent are "hardliners." Twenty-two percent were "people workers" and 14 percent "synthesized" roles. Eight percent were loners—preferring to work by themselves in towers or perimeter patrol. Each type was associated with certain officer characteristics. For example, rule enforcers were younger, had less seniority, and tended to work late afternoon or evening shifts.

THE GUARDIANS AT HOLMAN

These studies show officer orientations toward inmates are not necessarily the hostile ones portrayed by the entertainment media. Some officers are "people workers" and others shift roles from custodial to service orientation depending on the situation. Others have a negative view of inmates and prefer to maintain as much distance between them as possible. The honor dorm at Holman evolved with these considerations in mind. First, it is housed in a maximum-security prison where order, safety, and custodial functions predominate. Second, the honor dorm cannot function without rules and regulations. In various ways, general population inmates differ from honor dorm inmates. The greatest difference is demonstrated in the participatory rule enforcement required of all honor dorm inmates. This participatory model generates an expectation of fewer violations resulting from a sense of greater accountability and inmate ownership of the structured community environment. Third, the chaplain and some honor dorm inmate leaders are aware of the need to mediate between restorative goals and practices in the honor dorm and the custodial nature of the institution. The chaplain promotes the honor dorm, but also shows deference to prevailing values and attitudes in the environment, weighing honor dorm priorities and initiatives against perceptions of those in custodial roles. A captain was concerned about inmates who participated in peacemaking circles and were not accountable for resulting verbal agreements. In this case, the circles were an alternative to traditional DOC disciplinary action. After a period of time, correctional officers discovered some inmates denied their involvement in a previous DOC violation. The captain's remedy was to require a written agreement signed by participating inmates. Honor dorm residents must now sign all circle agreements, which become a matter of record.

The chaplain addresses the political realities of running an honor dorm in a high custody facility through mediating behaviors. He takes care to thank correctional officers for opening gates, taking extra time to search volunteers, and escorting volunteers to and from the honor dorm. When a volunteer donated an office chair to the dorm, the chaplain wisely chose to place the chair in the officer's station. Extra food brought to honor dorm residents by their relatives on family night is donated to the correctional officers. Some honor dorm residents do reports and PowerPoint presentations for the administration. There is an awareness of the fragile position of the dorm in a maximum-security prison. For example, when I interviewed correctional officers at Holman, a number of them were concerned about housing life-without-parole inmates in a detached dorm situated close to the fence. They view the honor dorm primarily as a security risk rather than a place where meaningful change can take place in the lives of inmates. Another example of conflicting culture is the honor dorm library, which offers inmates opportunities to learn and grow. From a custodial perspective, it is a place where contraband can be hidden, making it much harder to secure the area.

Some officers are cynical about the honor dorm and think the behaviors of honor dorm residents are no different from those in general population. The honor dorm population is in a state of flux, with some residents leaving at their end of sentence, others being removed for disciplinary reasons, and new members entering when vacancies occur. Inmates who are not socialized into the honor dorm culture or who remain on the fringes of the community provide officers with good reason to take a law enforcement approach to the dorm. These inmates continue a deviant lifestyle and choose the honor dorm to advance their own comfort.

One of the most emotionally painful disconnects between the honor dorm culture and the custodial one occurred when the warden invited the Alabama DOC Correctional Emergency Response Team (CERT) to search the prison for contraband in the early morning hours of a hot summer day in July 2006. The search was motivated by reports of more than usual amounts of marijuana in the facility. The unannounced search included the honor dorm. Residents were sleeping when the team arrived. CERT members ordered the residents to lie face down on their beds while officers went through residents' personal belongings. CERT dogs jumped on prisoners' beds sniffing for drugs. Personal items were confiscated including a knee brace issued by the infirmary to one of the residents. Usually, when searches are conducted, residents sit on their beds. The order to lie face down was a punitive and humiliating experience. Inmates were then ordered to stand outside in their underwear for almost two hours until the search was completed. The dorm's emphasis on respect and honor deteriorated quickly. It was a stark example of the difficulty of maintaining a positive environment in a punitive custodial setting. One resident tried to put a bright face on the situation saying it taught him how powerless a crime victim feels when attacked. However, the major lesson learned is the prison staff has total power over the inmate, and any gains in inmate autonomy and responsibility can be taken away at any time.

HOW HOLMAN CORRECTIONAL OFFICERS SEE THINGS

In early November 2006, I interviewed an availability sample of sixty-three corrections officers and their supervisors, about two-thirds of the officers who work at the prison. The survey included open- and close-ended questions to determine what officers like and dislike about the honor dorm, what their major concerns are when assigned to the dorm, and the extent to which officers think the dorm contributes to the overall functioning of the institution. Officers working all three shifts responded over a two-day time period and participation was voluntary. Eight officers declined to answer the questions. Some officers on the first and third shifts are assigned to the honor dorm and others are not. When I interviewed officers on the second shift, I was escorted by a sergeant who decided not to introduce me to the officers who have no experience with the honor dorm. Perceptions of both groups are important because those who have not worked in the dorm do formulate opinions about it. Furthermore, inmates from the honor dorm interact with officers when they travel to other parts of the prison for exercise, visiting, eating, and attending religious services.

On a scale from one to ten with one being least helpful and ten being most helpful, I asked officers to rank the honor dorm according to how well it contributes to the smooth functioning of the prison. Some officers see the faith-based dorm as fairly isolated from the rest of the population. From their perspective, work with the men in general population, segregation, or death row is not affected whether the honor dorm exists or not. Corrections officers give the honor dorm an average ranking of 7.9 for advancing the operations of the prison. The average rating given to the honor dorm did not differ substantially by race or gender. These findings correspond with other prison surveys where corrections officers' attitudes are not clearly differentiated by race or sex.[8] Years of service show the greatest difference in rankings. Using the midpoint of 15.5 years of service, officers with less time with the department of corrections give the honor dorm a 7.2 average ranking while those with more than 15.5 years of service provide an 8.8 ranking. Substantial differences are also found between the first (morning), second (afternoon), and third (evening) shifts with rankings of 7.9, 6.9, and 8.6 respectively. Officers on the second shift who see the honor dorm as less helpful have the lowest average seniority among the three shifts.

Officers with supervisory responsibilities are more likely to appreciate the contribution of the honor dorm to prison operations. Some want to see the honor dorm concept expanded to other units. Others think it gives them greater flexibility when making assignments. They don't need to worry about female officers, cadets, or those with less experience when they are assigned to the dorm. One lieutenant with twenty-four-and-a-half years experience as a correctional officer notes efficiency improvements. "We can without reservation house 174 people with minimum staff. It houses double that for other dorms where we have more problems." One sergeant with twenty-two years in corrections work observes, "Inmates are better behaved [in the honor dorm] and they cooperate with staff better. They live among themselves better and govern themselves. It will make it easier for them to get back into society." This officer ranks the honor dorm with a score of ten and says he would assign a score of fifteen if he could. Sixty-four percent of supervisory officers give the honor dorm a rating of eight or higher for its contributions to prison life. A captain assigned to segregation and death row—with little direct experience with the dorm—says it is considered to be an aid to corrections staff because its inmates have an incentive to abide by the rules and regulations. When the warden leads prison tours, he describes the honor dorm as "one of our successes."

I asked corrections officers what they like least and what they like most about the honor dorm. Table 9.1 shows role ambiguity and role conflict is the biggest issue for officers. To illustrate, an officer on the first shift comments, "Some (not all) lose track that they are incarcerated. This affects [the corrections officers'] authority and [leads to] insubordination." Another remarks, "Some have too much power, and it goes to their heads. They think they are officers." One lieutenant on the first shift observes, "The inmate population seem to think line officers' authority is less than or outweighed by their [the honor dorm's] punishment or conflict resolution systems."

Since officers with more seniority give the dorm higher rankings, it is possible they are more comfortable with their roles and less threatened with status concerns voiced from those with fewer years in corrections. One officer

Table 9.1.   Distribution of Responses* on What Officers Like Least about the Faith-Based Honor Dorm.

Item	Number of Responses
Role conflict and issues related to rule enforcement	21
Need better screening device for qualifying inmates	14
No concerns	12
Security; too many LWOP's**	9
Misc. other (available on request)	8
Don't know	5

N=63
*Multiple responses are recorded.
**Life without parole

with six years experience complains, "We cater to them [honor dorm residents] too much. Inmates who hold office think they can tell officers what to do. There is not enough supervision. They get away with too much. They are pampered." As indicated earlier, attitudinal research on corrections officers shows that seniority is associated with positive attitudes toward rehabilitation and other corrections reforms.

Officers who complain about inmate governance do not see it so much as a source of stress but more as a threat to their status in the prison community. They are also concerned with prison leaders who are too harsh on their fellows, inmates who resent being disciplined by other inmates, and the possibility that inmate leaders will be less fair than corrections officers in disciplinary matters. Interviews with the officers suggest their opinions about fairness are influenced by complaints from other inmates, some who have been removed from the dorm for rule infractions. In some respects the officers' concerns are well founded. Honor dorm residents report it is difficult to train inmate coordinators to be fair and firm as opposed to the two extremes of laissez-faire and harsh rule enforcement. As they phrase it, "we are a work in progress." Ironically, the appeals to higher standards of conduct in the honor dorm and the use of inmates to assist with rule enforcement contribute to a better work environment for the officers.

Table 9.1 shows two additional officer concerns—the need for better screening of honor dorm residents and the number of its residents who are sentenced to life without parole. The latter concern stems from the location of the honor dorm close to the perimeter fence. When the dorm first opened, screening was more rigorous, taking into account the inmate's lifestyle and the common knowledge of the inmate's character. A committee oversaw this process. Eventually the warden decided in the interest of fairness, more inmates should have access to the dorm. Requirements for candidacy to enter the dorm was reduced to a numeric formula. The formula for general population inmates to enter the honor dorm is to lead a discipline-free life for six months and to live in population for a minimum of ninety days. This approach does not take into account correctional officers' knowledge and honor dorm residents' experience with the intentions and behaviors of those who want to be admitted. This includes the psychological problems that make honor dorm living difficult for some men.

While the new formula potentially adds greater fairness, its problems are shown by a recent violent conflict in the honor dorm. An individual considered psychologically unstable and known for past difficulties with inmate relationships was admitted into the dorm because he met the basic criteria. One day at three in the morning, several inmates heard him laughing hysterically in the bathroom. Soon after the outburst, he attacked a sleeping inmate with a prison-made knife. The inmate victim survived, but under the new rules the safety and security of the honor dorm suffered a setback.

The second concern is the belief that inmates with life without parole sentences are a security threat. This perception has intuitive appeal. According to this scenario, if an inmate has no hope, why not prepare a breakout, even though it is risky? Most of the lifers I work with in the dorm do have hope. They hope for changes in the law or a reduction in sentence. Some of the men find meaning serving as role models and investing their time with inmates who have parole dates. Furthermore, these men have adjusted well to prison and have demonstrated maturity, responsibility, and accountability at levels often not realized among younger prisoners with shorter sentences. The Alabama Department of Corrections has a web site informing the public about prison escapes. An examination of the sight reveals none of the escapes are from Holman, and most are made by men and women who serve shorter sentences in less secure institutions.[9]

What do correctional officers like most about the honor dorm? Table 9.2 shows they like the rehabilitative potential of the honor dorm, using phrases such as "opportunity for inmate change," "promotes responsibility," and

Table 9.2. Distribution of Responses* on What Officers
Like Most about the Faith-Based Honor Dorm

Item	Number of Responses
Programming: opportunity for inmate change, promotes responsibility, provides purpose	23
Inmate conduct: cooperation, respect, fewer rule violations	14
Self-governance, dorm runs itself	13
Atmosphere: clean, quiet, orderly	10
Efficiency/staffing	3
Physical layout/security	3
Don't know; little or no experience with honor dorm	7

Number of respondents (N)=63
*Multiple responses are recorded

"provides a sense of purpose." This finding supports previous studies documenting a subgroup of officers who are oriented to inmate change. Three additional categories—inmate conduct (cooperation, respect, fewer rule violations), self-governance, and a clean, quiet, and orderly atmosphere are responses expected from officers who assume a custodial role. When officers are assigned to the dorm it requires little supervision on their part. One female officer said, "The other guys [in the honor dorm] help us more than our own co-workers."

Officers' concerns when they work in the honor dorm contrast with the ones they have when assigned to dorms occupied by the general population (tables 9.3 and 9.4). Some officers say when they work in the honor dorm they need to guard against getting too relaxed. They speak of the difficulty remembering routine security and safety measures and treating the honor dorm as they would other dorms in the prison. Some officers repeat issues about the possibility of lifers escaping. Thirteen officers were unable to identify a specific problem or concern when assigned to the faith-based dorm.

Officers have similar worries about security issues when assigned to dorms for the general population. However, they are more likely to identify specific problems such as fighting, alcohol and drug use, gambling, sexual activities, weapons, and violations of the dress code. One officer says, "You have to tell them everything, like little kids. There is no structure." Another officer notes how stressful these dorms are: "Everyone is making demands." A female officer comments, "You have everything to worry about." With few activities to occupy inmates and no incentives for inmates to take responsibility for themselves, officers working in these dorms experience more responsibility, more threats to their safety, and more stress.

**Table 9.3. Distribution of Responses* on Officers'
Greatest Concerns When Assigned to the Faith-Based Honor Dorm.**

Item	Number of Responses
Routine security and safety concerns	17
No concerns	13
Not applicable (not assigned to dorm)	13
Potential for escapes	11
Other misc. (available on request)	9
Getting too relaxed	4

N=63
*Multiple responses are recorded.

Table 9.4.   Distribution of Responses* on Officers' Greatest Concerns When Assigned to the Dorms Other Than the Faith-Based Honor Dorm

Item	Number of Responses
Safety/security issues	20
Fights	15
Not applicable (not assigned to dorm)	15
Other rule violations (alcohol, drugs, sex-related, gambling)	14
Other misc. (available on request)	6
No concerns	2

N=63
*Multiple responses are recorded.

RESTORATIVE JUSTICE FOR CORRECTIONS OFFICERS

Kay Pranis, an independent trainer and facilitator for peacemaking circles, uses restorative justice to improve staff relationships in prison. At a national restorative justice conference she described a workplace deeply in conflict at Moose Lake Correctional Institution in rural Minnesota.[10] A group of midline and frontline staff at Moose Lake invited Pranis and her colleagues to discuss the possibility of introducing restorative practices to inmates. After discussing the possibilities the staff insightfully asked, "How can we do restorative justice when we treat each other like we do?"

Talking with corrections officers at Moose Lake, Pranis discovered they spoke the language of victimization not from inmates but from the prison culture. Staff experience two types of victimization: (1) from the way they treat each other and (2) from the structure. Corrections officers are taught in the Department of Corrections training academy not to trust inmates or even other guards. One Moose Lake corrections officer commented, "The more we didn't care about them [inmates], the more we didn't care about each other." Pranis saw an unbelievable amount of pain, anger, and frustration. People in their twenties were counting the days until retirement. They hated their jobs and felt trapped.

In her initial work Pranis identified one officer who expressed a great deal of anger about the administration's response when he tried to take leave time. She discovered that this single experience represented deeper and broader feelings about how the organization treats the officers. The officers at Moose Lake felt dehumanized by the organization's rigid hierarchical structure. She also discovered a culture of fear. Correctional officers fear making mistakes, doing the wrong thing with inmates, and being blamed or set up by each other. She noticed many of the correctional officers fear losing their jobs—a feeling not grounded in reality, since state employees enjoy substantial job security. Pranis explains that when individuals feel helpless, their analysis of power is off kilter.

Pranis and her colleagues worked with the employees at Moose Lake emphasizing a different set of values—inclusion, respect, shared leadership, and continuous learning. Today, every prison in Minnesota is working on restorative processes to address staff conflict. The work at Moose Lake began in 2002. Correctional officers realized circumstances could be different for them. Before the work began in earnest a corrections officer told Pranis, "You still have your innocence. I lost mine a long time ago." After using peacemaking circles, the officer said, "I was wrong. You can get your innocence back."

It is difficult to determine whether corrections officers at Holman fit Pranis's description of the walking wounded. Warden Culliver's newsletter, which is distributed weekly to the staff, gives a mixed picture. On the one hand, Thanksgiving and Christmas are celebrated in the visiting yard with potluck dinners and lovely decorations. On occasion the warden has special lunches for the staff—usually hot dogs and hamburgers—and serves the officers himself. After two officers died in an automobile accident in 2007, the warden arranged a special Christmas lunch for family survivors and made provisions for gifts for the deceased officers' children.

On the other hand, the nature of corrections work, particularly the detailed rules and regulations whose enforcement the warden considers crucial for achieving his goals, creates stress for corrections officers. Each week the warden points out a number of rules and regulations that officers, from his perspective, are not enforcing with sufficient rigor. Examples from the month of August 2007 include:

> We must be consistent in our enforcement of the rules. The more consistent we are, the less problems we'll have from one staff member to another.[11] We are continuing to lose too many disciplinaries and it is taking too long to get incident reports signed and back in. We must do better at this. Inmates who received disciplinaries and they are not held in a timely fashion or are lost because of due process violations, will be released back to population.[12]

The warnings and reproaches apply to all manner of operations in the facility.

> One thing we found coming from the kitchen was an excessive amount of grease. We have three grease traps before the grease gets to the drains, and all were full. We have to do a better job at getting the grease in the container behind the kitchen.[13]

Speaking to false alarms in a particular zone of the perimeter fence, the warden warns,

> Birds really seem to like this area between 2:30 and 6:00 p.m. We must guard against being complacent with the numbers of alarms that are going off in this area. This is one of our most vulnerable areas, and we cannot get to the point that we take it all for granted that it is birds or the wind.[14]

And on another matter of security

> While conducting progress review in segregation on [sic] today and [sic] inmate ask [sic] about a transfer and then stated he heard there would be a transfer on next week. I thought this was interesting as we had to cancel a transfer for the past Wednesday. It was obvious to me that staff members had been speaking too much in the wrong place. We should be mindful of what we say in the presence of our inmate population. It is a security breach for inmates to know when they are being transferred from the facility.[15]

These are samples of rule-oriented communications between the warden and the staff during a one-month period. The newsletters also contain a number of "atta boys" and other expressions of concern and appreciation for staff members. Nevertheless, when I read the newsletters and place myself in a correctional officer's shoes, I can't help but think, "When will I get caught making a mistake and will I get fired?" Fear was expressed on several occasions while being searched before entering the institution. When I bring educational items with me, officers worry whether admitting the material will violate one of the rules. One officer said half teasing, half concerned, "You're going to get me fired." This particular officer has only three years remaining before retirement. Thinking about rule enforcement as a source of pressure, I asked a corrections officer if his work at Holman was stressful. He responded, "Yes, sometimes it is." I followed up with, "Which causes you more stress, the inmates or the administration?" Without hesitation he responded, "The administration."

Providing birthday or sympathy cards in the honor dorm is against volunteer rules prohibiting volunteers from giving cards or items to particular inmates. Volunteers view these cards as an intentional practice to normalize human relationships in a hostile environment. This "card" rule frustrates those who want to provide greater support to the residents. It is disturbing when a student inmate's wife of twenty-five years is dying of cancer and providing an inspirational card is against the rules. The chaplain's role is more ambiguous. He is charged with providing comfort to prisoners. This role is not always easy for the chaplain, especially when his volunteers make further suggestions to humanize the environment. He frequently expresses the fear of being fired or losing the honor dorm altogether. This is after working twenty-seven years with the Alabama Department of Corrections. A more striking example of the fear-based culture occurred when the warden tried to locate the source of a large amount of marijuana smuggled into the institution. The chaplain usually keeps his van unlocked in the parking lot. This is in the institution's parking lot where there is twenty-four-hour surveillance. During this time, he said he was locking the van for fear of someone (officers, cadets, or support employees) planting contraband in his vehicle and subsequently being fired and charged with possession of drugs. This is a not uncommon example of fear-based thinking influencing the perceptions and behaviors of prison employees on a daily basis.

A PERSPECTIVE ON CORRECTIONS OFFICERS AND THE ORGANIZATION

Attempts to incorporate correctional officers into a culture of reform began with the rehabilitation movement in the 1950s. When rehabilitation approaches were abandoned for more punitive ones, prison reformers thought the fruits of affirmative action—the recruitment of more minorities and women into the corrections field—would buffer the public's tough-on-crime attitude. Research shows the political climate does not have a significant impact on correctional officers' orientations toward punishment or treatment.[16] However, the expectation that minority and female officers would be more receptive to prison reform than their white male counterparts is misplaced.

While there are some differences in attitudes toward prison work by gender and race, according to a number of studies these characteristics are mediated by job satisfaction and organizational variables.[17] Corrections officers' attitudes and values are the result of an interplay between officer characteristics on the one hand, and prison organization and culture on the other.[18]

Holman's organizational culture fits the "bureaucratic control model" described in Deliulio's *Governing Prisons*.[19] The warden's leadership is tough, and firm, but compassionate. There is a strong emphasis on enforcing the norms and values of a "civilized, noncriminal society" such as cleanliness, neatness (including the dress of officers and inmates), being punctual, and working hard. Warden Culliver's management style contrasts with his predecessor who had a reputation among inmates and officers for silent toleration of inmate rule violations (drugs, alcohol, and relatively open homosexual behavior). This approach was a form of inmate control as long as inmates did not resort to violence among themselves or with the staff.

The majority of line officers do not understand what the "culture" of restorative justice is. They have a greater conceptual understanding of a faith-based honor dorm, which makes sense given the origin of the honor dorms in the Alabama Department of Corrections. Officers with the rank of lieutenant and higher clearly understand the nature of restorative programming, particularly the peacemaking circles. Yet, Holman also illustrates an inmate change-oriented program must primarily fit into the confinement purpose. In her review of the implementation of social policy in prison, Chih Lin observes that rehabilitation programs must conform to the control function if they are not to be "abandoned or marginalized."[20]

For prison officials, a major component of keeping prison order is establishing and maintaining routines. To the extent that programming challenges the normal interpretation of routines, it is likely to be opposed. Honor dorm agendas, programs, classes, and meetings are constantly interrupted by the priority of daily prison routines. These include "the count," mail call, pill call, sick call, classification interviews, religious services, trade school, industry, meal time, and more. All of the interruptions are necessary but at times are used to diminish the importance of honor dorm values, daily objectives, and overall goals. Many attempts to build relationships and humanize the prison environment take second place to the way security is done or various perceptions of how the honor dorm agenda compromises security. One prison researcher remarks, "Because keeping order is such a central aim within prisons, its demands can crowd out any functions that programs might have."[21]

While a number of Holman's officers appreciate the rehabilitative potential of the honor dorm and its management advantages, others are antagonistic. But the tensions between organizational structure and culture and restorative programming appear more relevant than individual officer attitudes. However, the attitudes of officers remain important to the extent that the organizational culture is expressed through them. In this regard, the officer core at Holman is generally supportive of the honor dorm because it helps them perform the task of maintaining order and security. Their attitudes do vary with respect to how much the honor dorm contributes to the smooth functioning of the institution, with supervisory officers having the greatest appreciation for its role.

BACK TO THE FUTURE

How might correctional officers at Holman be involved with restorative justice in the future? When interviewed, a number of the ranking officers said they were highly skeptical about the honor dorm when it was first introduced. They now state they are pleasantly surprised how well it works. A captain and an assistant warden want to see the honor dorm approach extended to other dorms in the institution. However, the capacity to expand the honor dorm and to give correctional officers a more active role in the restorative process is limited at this point in time.

Many correctional officers like the opportunities the Alabama Department of Corrections provides for good pay, job security, and liberal fringe benefits. These men and women are not particularly ambitious or motivated to learn new things. They sometimes function as a team or family, pulling together when the need arises, but most initiatives to enhance professionalism or to change the prison culture stem from the warden or the chaplain. There is also a clear demarcation between the professional and caring staff (psychologists, classification officers, the chaplain) and the zookeeper mentality of many correctional officers. Certain line officers enjoy the challenge of "mixing it up" with high-spirited and recalcitrant inmates. For them, loud commands and living on the edge is more interesting than reasoned and peaceful problem-solving.

Officers who are ambitious seek overtime work or second jobs. Some earn as much as $60,000 a year doing this. Some officers abuse the overtime opportunities, calling in sick and then collecting extra pay doing "overtime." Others fall prey to the temptation to make extra money smuggling drugs into the prison. Thus officer retention becomes a second concern in the challenge to maintain staffing levels in the facility.

It is difficult to recruit correctional officers in the small town, rural environment of southwest Alabama. While well-paying jobs are not plentiful, individuals with higher education levels and professional ideals are more likely to leave the area. Home to a large Indian reservation, the Creek tribe is expanding its small casino into a large hotel-casino-spa complex, creating additional job recruitment competition for the Alabama DOC. In addition, there are other correctional job opportunities including a medium-security prison one mile from Holman. Officers who do not choose to interact with inmates with a restorative approach can vote with their feet and accept alternative employment.

On a day-to-day basis the officers struggle with multiple tasks in an overcrowded and understaffed prison. The social distance between prisoners and inmates helps officers survive psychologically.[22] The needs and the demands of prisoners are endless. Officers and inmates alike wear a mask to hide any glimpse of their feelings—fear, caring, concern, or vulnerability. Some inmates say they can see who the officers really are. They look closely for signs of humanity. Some reach out only to be rebuffed by the officer whose career and survival is based on control, stigmatizing inmates as untrustworthy, and relegating inmates to a passive role.[23] Others receive small acts of kindness— a sandwich from the vending machine in the visiting area, a plate of turkey and dressing from the office Christmas party, an inquiry about whether an injury received on the basketball court is healing.

The officers hide their emotions so well that I have misinterpreted their character. Based on my observations, one captain is barely human. Many of the inmate leaders, however, see him as a straight-up guy who shows them consideration in a number of ways. When I learned this about the officer, I began to interact with him more—primarily through facial gestures or an occasional joke or warm exchange. He always responds positively, but is quick to replace the mask.

Educating prisoners about restorative justice values involves a great amount of time and commitment. As long as the faith-based restorative justice honor dorm operates as a parallel system where officers are marginally involved in its operation and perform their traditional custodial functions in the remainder of the prison, the system seems to work. Glimpses of officer interest for participation in restorative practices are rarely seen, and for those officers who are interested, it would be difficult to assign them full time to the honor dorm because of staffing constraints. Given the interview results, it is possible to identify a corps group of officers who show a willingness to work more directly with restorative programming. But until there is a greater change in the culture of the prison, participating officers would find themselves facing greater role conflicts including isolation from other correctional officers.

A restorative visioning effort for correctional officers includes training in the values and practices of restorative justice at the state level, career paths for those who choose this approach to corrections, and ample support. Officer support would include attention to the special needs of corrections officers who select restorative work. It would be a mistake to assume that correctional officers will have an affinity for restorative justice or that it will necessarily improve their job environment, at least in the short run. Integrating restorative justice principles with correctional work is one of the greatest challenges facing prison reform.

NOTES

1. Donald Cressey, "Contradictory Directives in Complex Organizations: The Case of Prison," *Administrative Science Quarterly* 4, no. 1 (June 1959): 1–19; John R. Hepburn and Celesta Albonetti, "Role Conflict in Correctional Institutions," *Criminology* 17, no. 4 (February 1980): 445–59.

2. Mary Ann Farkas, "Correctional Officer Attitudes toward Inmates and Working with Images in a 'Get Tough' Era," *Journal of Criminal Justice* 27, no. 6 (November–December 1999): 459–506.

3. Farkas, "Correctional Officer Attitudes," 503.

4. Farkas, "Correctional Officer Attitudes," 502.

5. Sarah Ben-David, Peter Sifen, and David Cohen, "Fearful Custodial or Fearless Personal Relations: Prison Guards' Fear as a Factor Shaping Staff-Inmate Relation

Prototype," *International Journal of Offender Therapy and Comparative Criminology* 40, no. 2 (June 1996): 96

6. Ben-David, Sifen, and Cohen, "Fearful Custodial," 100–102.

7. Mary Ann Farkas, "A Typology of Correctional Officers," *International Journal of Offender Therapy and Comparative Criminology* 44, no. 4 (August 2000): 431–39.

8. Farkas, "Correctional Officer Attitudes," 503–4.

9. ADOC Escapes, Alabama Department of Corrections, www.doc.state.al.us/escape.asp (accessed 14 May 2008).

10. Kay Pranis, "Healing and Accountability in the Criminal Justice System as a Workplace: Applying Restorative Justice Processes" (presentation at the National Conference on Restorative Justice, Kerrville, Texas, June 24–June 27, 2007).

11. Grantt Culliver, *The Key*, W. C. Holman Correctional Facility, Atmore, Alabama, August 3, 2007, 2.

12. Culliver, *The Key*, 2.

13. Culliver, *The Key*, 1.

14. Culliver, *The Key*, 1.

15. Culliver, *The Key*, 2.

16. Farkas, "Correctional Officer Attitudes," 501–5.

17. Eric G. Lambert, Nancy Lynne Hogan, and Shannon M. Barton, "Satisfied Correctional Staff: A Review of the Literature on the Correlates of Correctional Staff Job Satisfaction," *Criminal Justice and Behavior* 29, no. 2 (April 2002): 115–43; Dana M. Britton, "Perceptions of the Work Environment among Corrections Officers: Do Race and Sex Matter?" *Criminology* 35, no. 1 (February 1997): 85–105; Mary K. Stohr, Nicholas P. Lovrich, and Marcia J. Wood, "Service versus Security Concerns in Contemporary Jails: Testing General Differences in Training Topic Assessments," *Journal of Criminal Justice* 24, no. 5 (1996): 437–48; Eric G. Lambert, Nancy L. Hogan, and David N. Baker, "Gender Similarities and Differences in Correctional Staff Work Attitudes and Perceptions of the Work Environment," *Western Criminology Review* 8, no. 1 (April 2007): 16–31.

18. Nancy C. Jurik, "Individual and Organizational Determinants of Correctional Officer Attitudes toward Inmates," *Criminology* 23, no. 3 (August 1985): 523–40.

19. John DiIulio, *Governing Prisons* (New York: Basic Books, 1987).

20. Ann Chih Lin, *Reform in the Making: The Implementation of Social Policy in Prison* (Princeton, N.J.: Princeton University Press, 2000; Oxford: Oxford University Press, 2000), 31.

21. Chih Lin, *Reform in the Making*, 31.

22. Kimmett Edgar and Tim Newell, *Restorative Justice in Prisons: A Guide to Making It Happen* (Winchester, U.K.: Waterside Press, 2006).

23. Edgar and Newell, *Restorative Justice in Prisons*, 57.

10

What's Next

Replacing prison with restorative physical, relational, and emotional spaces may seem unlikely. It assumes that society embraces restorative values. This begs the question, then, of how to create a restorative society. I believe such a society begins with the individual. When a person acts restoratively, including in prison, it influences others.

—Barb Toews, *The Little Book of Restorative Justice for People in Prison: Rebuilding the Web of Relationships*

Prisons are places where inmates sit and wait. They wait for a better life, without any knowledge or preparation for how to achieve it. Some pass the time developing their bodies. Others exercise their minds reading everything they can. Music and painting are also a source of solace. Inmates live in an inner world where the learning and maturity that develops through relationships with others passes them by. Some dull the pain and loneliness with alcohol and drugs, further retarding the maturation process. The former warden who told an honor dorm resident, "We'll keep you here until you get old," finds his statement supported by research showing inmates do eventually "age out" of crime. But is warehousing large numbers of young men and women until they get old the best we can do? And what should happen with men who committed their crimes at a very young age, who now show reform tendencies, but face a sentence of life without parole?

Retribution and just desserts are deeply embedded in our psyches. Restorative justice poses a challenge, asking, "Is this the only way to do it?" We won't know until the public in general and victims in particular have greater exposure to restorative values. Currently, many of our assumptions about crime and punishment go unchallenged. But restorative approaches are gaining recognition. Today, there are few college textbooks on crime and punishment that do not include restorative justice as a legitimate alternative approach. A number of European countries, particularly Britain and its former colonies Canada, New Zealand, and Australia, are moving faster in restorative directions than the United States. Meanwhile, the popularity of faith-based initiatives in the United States suggests the potential for an infusion of restorative values in prisons.

TRANSFORMATIONS

In 1999 former Alabama Corrections Commissioner Mike Haley had an opportunity to initiate faith-based honor dorms in Alabama due to prison overcrowding. His major concern though was what happens when inmates get out and what happens to those in prison for a very long time.[1] He wanted people who serve time to come out with more than what they came in with. He entered an organization where the norm among prisoners was feelings of hopelessness. He wanted to transform hopelessness to hopefulness.

Interestingly the path from hopelessness to hopefulness marked my own transition teaching corrections. I taught the introductory corrections class for eight years during the 1990s. I always included a class tour to a medium-security facility. Year after year I saw the facilities become more and more oriented toward security and control. There was little if any place for purposeful activity. The prisons were clean and fairly new, but each time I visited with my students over the years, I noticed the facilities transforming into something resembling dog kennels. The public was fed up with rehabilitation and liberal solutions to crime problems. What was next? The situation seemed hopeless.

I was exposed to the restorative approach during a sabbatical in 2000. I observed mediations between juvenile offenders and their victims. What I witnessed in the mediation process encouraged me. The victim was clearly the center of the process and stood on the moral high ground. The juvenile offender owned up to what he did and was prepared to make amends. In this setting no excuses for exoneration were made for the crime. Neither divorce, nor poverty, nor child abuse could exempt the offender from the harm caused by his or her actions. Not all of the mediations worked out, but the ones that did were unforgettable. When I returned to the university, I developed courses on the subject. I wanted to apply my newfound knowledge in the community and discovered there was a faith-based restorative justice honor dorm about an hour's drive from my university.

I discovered Holman's honor dorm offers relative safety and respect. Opportunities exist for purposeful activity. While inspired by a deeply devout Christian, the dorm provides comfort for men of many denominations and faiths. And the restorative approach links their spiritual beliefs with values, principles, and a plan of action involving all those affected by crime. Edgar and Newell, who work with English prisons, point out that the majority of prisoners have never experienced social integration in the first place.[2] For those willing to change, involvement in restorative processes holds the promise for more effective social inclusion. Edgar and Newell observe

> The focus on the needs of the offender looked at through the restorative prison places them in the context of their crimes within communities, families, and their victims. It seeks solutions to their needs through working with those stakeholders in meeting their needs as well. Within all the arenas of action in the plan, the restorative justice focus provides a wider vision of the person, their life and the reality of the sentence experience for them.[3]

The conflict between security values and what one author refers to as harmony values is a major obstacle to introducing restorative justice in prison.[4] Security values include self-protection, rule of law, authority, competitiveness, and tough law enforcement. Harmony values include peaceful coexistence, mutual respect/human dignity, sharing of resources, development of individual potential, and wealth redistribution. The social order clearly depends on both. Prisons will always favor ideas for implementing security measures, although security implementation does not need to be totally controlled by punishment and domination.[5]

HONORS

In Holman's honor dorm rules are enforced more strictly than among the general population because its culture demands a higher standard of behavior. At the same time, peacemaking circles encourage harmony, personal growth, and community accountability. Honor dorm residents prefer their living arrangements because they are safer. Residents also favor the honor dorm because it fosters respectful relationships. They say there are no expectations for good behavior outside the honor dorm. One resident comments, "In general population you don't even have to make your bed." The bottom line is that security values and harmony values coexist in the honor dorm. There is simply more attention given to their balance.

When Mike Haley introduced honor dorms he was serving his first term as corrections commissioner. He wanted to create an entire faith-based prison but served only one term when the governor's office changed parties. Currently the director of the jail in Mobile, Alabama, he says support from the governor is crucial for prison reform.[6] In addition, the cooperation of wardens, the commitment of the security staff, support from chaplains, and support from free world volunteers is necessary. There is more than one restorative honor dorm in Alabama, although most honor dorms in the state are not formally based on restorative principles. Faith-based and restorative justice values are congruent, however. As Zehr points out, "restorative justice can be seen as a *compass* pointing a direction."[7] One does not need to use the word "restorative justice" for it to take place.

Still, faith-based dorms with no emphasis on restorative values evolve differently. A faith-based dorm at a level-six institution in Alabama, Donaldson Correctional Facility, is very different from Holman.[8] At Donaldson most courses are religiously based. The men in the dorm are more isolated from the rest of the prison—in part because the prison has more space and partly because the inmates hold themselves above the men in general population. In addition to religion, rules and regulations are a major focus in the life of the dorm. All manner of rule violations are more strictly enforced. One Holman honor dorm resident who used to live in the honor dorm at Donaldson prefers this way of life. He comments, "At Donaldson you took your punishment like a man." An inmate expelled from the honor dorm at Donaldson cannot return.

Like members of the public, some inmates clearly prefer retributive values. In contrast, the warden at Holman favors restorative ones. Warden Culliver thinks the men in the honor dorm should share what they have with other men in the prison. In other words, they should help them heal. He says the inmates in general population behave differently than they did before the honor dorm opened. Because the honor dorm is relatively open to free world visitors, the men in general population have become more used to them and behave more respectfully when they tour the facility. There are fewer fights and stabbings, although this might be due to the opening of a segregation unit for troublemakers.

RESTORATIVELY SPEAKING

Expanding restorative justice in prison may require compromise.[9] That is certainly the case at Holman. Other than the warden, the prison staff for the most part does not know what restorative justice is, and when there is a conflict between restorative values and tradition security measures, the latter prevails. Risk is avoided, and it is difficult to make decisions without going through the chain of command. My association with the honor dorm is seen positively by some and negatively by others. Those who don't appreciate the efforts of volunteers think we are "coddling criminals." Referring to my university affiliation, one officer said, "The University of West Florida runs the honor dorm. We don't need it in the hallways."

Restorative justice may not exist in the pure model visualized by its organizers who worried that restorative justice goals could be subverted to achieve coercive ones. Nevertheless, its presence lessens the harshness of the prison system.[10] As Johnstone says, giving "restorative justice a foothold in the criminal justice system from which it can grow" is more likely an indicator bringing into sight a fundamental shift in how crime and justice are viewed.[11]

It is morally responsible to give inmates who want to change a safe place to do so. The honor dorm at Holman provides a model for how restorative justice principles and practices can be integrated into a prison environment. There are several ways that restorative justice at Holman could be strengthened. First, the opportunity for victims to meet with their offenders is not available in Alabama. The honor dorm compromises by incorporating victim impact education, mock letter writing exercises with victims, and victim impact panels. These victim impact opportunities have a profound impact on some residents. In addition, residents hold each other accountable to the honor dorm community.

Second, honor dorm residents need more interaction with the free world community. Like most prisons, Holman is geographically isolated. Many of the men are from urban areas and do not share small-town values. No one from Atmore volunteers at Holman. The owner of Annie's Community Café says that many of the people who work at the prison live in the community, and what the staff shares about prisoners is largely negative. No churches from Atmore have prison ministries. Church involvement is largely from Mobile, which is sixty miles away. The University of West Florida is equally distant from the prison.

Inmates benefit from interaction with free world people. They see new faces, learn new perspectives, and receive hope for the future. At the same time, honor dorm residents give back by empathizing and sharing their experiences with victims, volunteers, and students. In particular, university students enrolled in corrections, restorative justice, victimology, and race, gender, ethnicity courses benefit when inmates share information with them. As former prison commissioner Haley observes, prisoners show tremendous gratitude to anyone who treats them with dignity.[12] But negotiating visits with volunteers and student groups is time consuming and difficult. Prisons shut out the rest of the world. Allowing greater interaction with free world people would help normalize a stagnant and oppressive environment.

Honor dorm residents would like to give back to the community—whether it be a project in their hometown, working with local schools, or providing donations to local charities. So far the avenues for community service have not been identified. The dorm substitutes by emphasizing community service within the dorm and occasionally attempting to provide service to the prison at large. Many in the honor dorm are no longer the same persons they were when they committed their crimes ten, twenty, or thirty years ago. Yet they are classified as dangerous criminals who have nothing to give back to society. After experiencing substantial transformation, it is frustrating to be prohibited from giving something back, even if it is from behind the walls

Prisons are hostile places for introducing restorative justice. Still, the honor dorm at Holman is a success. The honor dorm is a success because it contains a solid four-semester curriculum based on restorative justice principles. It is a success because the men manage the dorm and participate meaningfully in their community. It is a success because the men do not cause problems for corrections officers. It is a success because it is supported by the warden and supervisory officers who would like to see it expanded. It is appreciated by many corrections officers for its clean and relatively problem-free environment. It is a success because a group of men have begun to make amends to their victims in their classroom work. It is a success because the honor residents are loved and appreciated by a solid core of free world volunteers. It is a success because some men have changed their attitudes and behaviors including violence and drug and alcohol abuse. Would these changes have occurred without the honor dorm? Possibly. But they are much more difficult to sustain and advance in environments based on fear, dominance, and survival.

The restorative justice approach outlined in this book is not a panacea. It does not work for all offenders. Men *volunteer* to join the honor dorm. It is important to remember that no rehabilitative or recovery program works without the willingness to change. The honor dorm continues to attract new people, and many of them don't make it through the first two years. But most of those who do remain in the dorm successfully transfer to other institutions, are paroled, or reach the end of their sentences.

Holman's honor dorm offers a more positive environment for men who have committed very serious crimes. It will be interesting to track the experiences of honor dorm "graduates" in the future. Will the honor dorm help men transition to society? Will it expand its commitment to restorative principles with a more victim-centered approach? Will the residents have the opportunity to contribute meaningfully to free world communities? The restorative justice honor dorm is a work in progress. As of this writing it is eight-and-a-half years old. As a reform effort, it has clearly survived a hostile environment. And for many men it is an opportunity to learn new ways of living.

NOTES

1. Personal interview with Mike Haley, former Alabama corrections commissioner, April 30, 2008.

2. Kimmett Edgar and Tim Newell, *Restorative Justice in Prisons: A Guide to Making It Happen* (Winchester, U.K.: Waterside Press, 2006), 106.

3. Edgar and Newell, *Restorative Justice in Prisons*, 109.

4. Alison Liebling with Helen Arnold, *Prisons and Their Moral Performance: A Study of Values, Quality and Prison Life* (Oxford: Oxford University Press, 2004), 438.

5. Edgar and Newell, *Restorative Justice in Prisons*, 62.

6. Personal interview with Mike Haley.

7. Howard Zehr, *The Little Book of Restorative Justice* (Intercourse, Pa.: Good Books, 2002), 10.

8. This section is based on interviews with four Holman honor dorm inmates who formerly lived in the honor dorm at Donaldson Correctional Facility, May 15, 2008.

9. Gerry Johnstone, *Restorative Justice: Ideas, Values, Debates* (Devon, U.K.: Willan Publishing, 2002), 168.

10. Johnstone, *Restorative Justice: Ideas,* 169.

11. Johnstone, *Restorative Justice: Ideas,* 169.

12. Personal interview with Mike Haley.

Bibliography

Abbott, Jack Henry. *In the Belly of the Beast.* New York: Random House, 1981.

"ADOC Escapes." Alabama Department of Corrections. www.doc.state.al.us/escape.asp.

Alcoholics Anonymous. 4th ed. New York: Alcoholics Anonymous World Services, Inc. 2001.

Ali, Muhammad. Daily Celebrations. www.dailycelebdrations.com/service.htm.

Allard, Pierre, and Wayne Northey. "Christianity: The Rediscovery of Restorative Justice." In *The Spiritual Roots of Restorative Justice,* edited by Michael L. Hadley, 119–42. Albany: State University of New York Press, 2001.

Allen, Jennifer M. "Planning and Design in Restorative Justice: A First Look at Four Victims of Crime Impact Panels in the Midwest." *American Association of Behavioral Social Science On-Line Journal,* 2004. aabs.org/journal2004/AABSS_76-88.pdf.

Altschuler, David M., and Troy L. Armstrong. "Intensive Aftercare for High-Risk Juveniles: Policies and Procedures." Office of Juvenile Justice and Delinquency Prevention, U.S. Department of Justice, 1994. www.ncjrs.gov/pdffiles/juvpp.pdf.

Ammar, Nawal H. "Restorative Justice in Islam: Theory and Practice." In *The Spiritual Roots of Restorative Justice,* edited by Michael L. Hadley, 161–80. Albany: State University of New York Press, 2001.

Andrews, Don A. "The Principles of Effective Correctional Programs." In *Correctional Contexts: Contemporary and Classical Readings*, 3rd ed., edited by Edward J. Latessa and Alexander M. Holsinger, 250–59. Los Angeles: Roxbury Publishing, 2006.

Baker, J. E. "Inmate Self-Government." *The Journal of Criminal Law, Criminology, and Police Science* 55, no. 1 (March 1964): 39–47.

Banerjee, Neela. "Court Bars State Effort Using Faith in Prisons." *New York Times*, December 4, 2007. www.nytimes.com/2007/12/04/us/04evangelical .html?ex=1197435600&en=f5bb0d0a68340127&ei=5070&emc=eta1.

Banks, Cyndi. *Criminal Justice Ethics*. Thousand Oaks, Calif.: Sage Publications, 2004.

Bazemore, Gordon, and Lode Walgrave, eds. *Restorative Juvenile Justice: Repairing the Harm of Youth Crime*. Monsey, N.Y.: Criminal Justice Press, 1999.

Beck, Allen J., Paige M. Harrison, and Devon B. Adams. "Correctional Violence Reported by Correctional Authorities, 2006." Bureau of Justice Statistics Special Report 2007. www.ojp.usdoj.gov/bjs/abstract/svrca06.htm.

Ben-David, Sarah, Peter Sifen, and David Cohen. "Fearful Custodial or Fearless Personal Relations: Prison Guards' Fear as a Factor Shaping Staff-Inmate Relation Prototype." *International Journal of Offender Therapy and Comparative Criminology* 40, no. 2 (June 1996): 94–104.

Bender, Kimberly, and Marilyn Armour. "The Spiritual Components of Restorative Justice." *Victim and Offenders* 2, no. 3 (July 2007): 251–67.

Berg, Mark T., and Matt DeLisi. "The Correctional Melting Pot: Race, Ethnicity, Citizenship, and Prison Violence." *Journal of Criminal Justice* 34, no. 6 (November–December 2006): 631–42.

Binswanger, Ingrid A., Mark F. Stern, Richard A. Dayo, Patrick J. Heagerty, Allen Cheadle, Joann G. Elmore, and Thomas D. Koepsell. "Release from Prison: A High Risk of Death for Former Inmates." *The New England Journal of Medicine* 356, no. 2 (January 2007): 157–65.

Birthways Child Resource Center, Inc. www.empathybelly.org/home.html.

Blue, Arthur W., and Meredith A. Rogers Blue. "The Case for Aboriginal Justice and Healing: The Self Perceived through a Broken Mirror." In *The Spiritual Roots of Restorative Justice*, edited by Michael L. Hadley, 57–80. Albany: State University of New York Press, 2001.

Blumstein, Alfred, Jacqueline Cohen, and David Farrington "Criminal Career Research: Its Value for Criminology." *Criminology* 26, no. 1 (February 1988): 1–35.

Bottoms, Anthony. "Compliance and Community Penalties." In *Community Penalties: Change and Challenges*, edited by Anthony Bottoms, Lorraine Gelsthorpe, and Sue Rex, 87–116. Devon, U.K.: Willan Publishing, 2001.

Boss, Judith A. "The Anatomy of Moral Intelligence." *Educational Theory* 44, no. 4 (December 1994): 399–416.

Braithwaite, John. *Crime, Shame, and Reintegration.* Cambridge: Cambridge University Press, 1989.

Britton, Dana M. "Perceptions of the Work Environment among Corrections Officers: Do Race and Sex Matter?" *Criminology* 35, no. 1 (February 1997): 85–105.

Brueggemann, Walter. "Covenant as a Subversive Paradigm." www.religion-online .org/showarticle.asp?title=1727.

Bureau of Justice Statistics. *Correctional Populations in the United States, 1997.* www.ojp.usdoj.gov/bjs/abstract/cpus97.htm.

———. "Prison Statistics, Summary Findings." www.ojp.usdoj.gov/bjs/prisons .htm#publications.

Burnside, Jonathan, with Nancy Loucks, Joanne R. Adler, and Gerry Rose. *My Brother's Keeper: Faith Based Units in Prisons.* Devon, U.K.: Willan Publishing, 2005.

Bush, George W. "Transcript of State of the Union, January 20, 2004." CNN.com. www.cnn.com/2004/ALLPOLITICS/01/20/sotu.transcript.7/index.html.

Centre for Justice and Reconciliation. "Growing Interest in Innovative Prison Management System." Prison Fellowship International News, 2006. www.pficjr.org/newsitems/apac1/.

Chih Lin, Ann. *Reform in the Making: The Implementation of Social Policy in Prison.* Princeton, N.J.: Princeton University Press, 2000; Oxford: Oxford University Press, 2000.

"Circles of Support and Accountability." Center for Peacemaking and Conflict Studies. Fresno Pacific University. peace.fresno.edu/cosa/.

"Circles of Support and Accountability: An Evaluation of the Pilot Project in South-Central Ontario." Correctional Services of Canada. 2005. www.csc-scc.gc.ca/ text/rsch/resports/r168/r168_e.pdf.

Claassen, Ron. "An Introduction to Discipline That Restores." Center for Peacemaking and Conflict Studies. Fresno Pacific University. disciplinethatrestores .org/IntroDTR.pdf.

Claassen, Ron, and Dalton Reimer. *Basic Institute in Conflict Management and Mediation.* Center for Peacemaking and Conflict Studies. Fresno Pacific University, 1999.

Claassen, Ron, Charlotte Tilkes, Phil Kader, and Douglas E. Noll. "Restorative Justice: A Framework for Fresno." Center for Peacemaking and Conflict Studies, 2001. peace.fresno.edu/docs/.

Clear, Todd R., Patricia L. Hardyman, Bruce Stout, Karol Lucken, and Harry R. Dammer. "The Value of Religion in Prison: An Inmate Perspective." In *Behind Bars: Readings on Prison Culture,* edited by Richard Tewksbury, 333–35. Upper Saddle River, N.J.: Pearson Prentice Hall, 2006.

Clemmer, Donald. *The Prison Community.* Boston: Holt, Rinehart, Winston, 1940.

Community Service. Ohio Department of Rehabilitation and Correction. www.drc.state.oh.us/web/commserv.htm.

Coyle, Andrew. *The Prisons We Deserve.* London: Harper Collins, 1994.

———. "Restorative Justice in the Prison Society." Paper presented at the International Prison Chaplains' Association Conference, Drubergen, Holland, May 2001.

Cressey, Donald. "Contradictory Directives in Complex Organizations: The Case of Prison." *Administrative Science Quarterly* 4, no. 1 (June 1959): 1–19.

Cullen, Francis T. "Social Support as an Organizing Concept for Criminology: Presidential Address to the Academy of Criminal Justice Sciences." *Justice Quarterly* 11, no. 4 (December 1994): 527–59.

Cullen, Francis T., Jody L. Sundt, and John F. Wozniak, "The Virtous Prison: Toward a Restorative Rehabilitation." In *Contemporary Issues in Crime and Criminal Justice: Essays in Honor of Gilbert Geis,* edited by Henry N. Ponetell and David Shichor, 265–86. Saddle River, N.J.: Pearson, 2001.

Culliver, Grant. *The Key.* W. C. Holman Correctional Facility. Atmore, Alabama.

Dali Lama. Daily Celebrations. www.dailycelebdrations.com/service.htm.

DiIulio, John J., Jr. *Governing Prisons: A Comparative Study of Correctional Management.* New York: Free Press, 1987.

Doerner William G., and Steven P. Lab. *Victimology.* 4th ed. Cincinnati, Ohio: Lexis Nexis/Anderson Publishing, 2005.

Doob, Anthony N., and Cheryl Marie Webster. "Sentence Severity and Crime: Accepting the Null Hypothesis." *Crime and Justice* 30 (2003): 143–96.

Edgar, Kimmett, and Tim Newell. *Restorative Justice in Prisons: A Guide to Making It Happen.* Winchester, U.K.: Waterside Press, 2006.

Farkas, Mary Ann. "Correctional Officer Attitudes toward Inmates and Working with Images in a 'Get Tough' Era." *Journal of Criminal Justice* 27, no. 6 (November–December 1999): 459–506.

———. "A Typology of Correctional Officers." *International Journal of Offender Therapy and Comparative Criminology* 44, no. 4 (August 2000): 431–39.

Feasey, Simon, Patrick Williams, and Rebecca Clark. "An Evaluation of the Prison Fellowship Sycamore Tree Programme." Sheffield Hallman University, 2005. www.restorativejustice.org.uk/rj_&_the_CJS/pdf/Sycamore_tree_evaluation.pdf.

Frederiksen, Erica A. "Rethinking Justice in a Post Colonial World." Paper presented at the annual meeting of the Canadian Political Science Association, London, Ontario, June 2–4, 2005.

Furst, Gennifer. "Prison-Based Animal Programs: A National Survey." *The Prison Journal* 86, no. 4 (December 2006): 407–30.

Gates v. Coller, 349 F. Supp. 881, 896 (ND Miss. 1972).

Gendreau, Paul. "The Principles of Effective Intervention with Offenders." In *Choosing Corrections Options That Work: Defining the Demand and Evaluating the Supply*, edited by Alan T. Harland, 117–30. Thousand Oaks, Calif.: Sage, 1996.

Gendreau, Paul, Claire E. Goggin, and Moira A. Law. "Predicting Prison Misconducts." *Criminal Justice and Behavior* 4, no. 4 (December 1997): 414–41.

Goodnough, Abby. "In a Break with the Past, Florida Will Let Felons Vote." *New York Times*, April 16, 2007. www.nytimes.com/2007/04/06/us/06florida.html?ex= 1176523200&en=a94a840f40d89ca0&ei=5070&emc=etal.

Hadley, Michael J. "Introduction: Multifaith Reflection on Criminal Justice." In *The Spiritual Roots of Restorative Justice*, edited by Michael L. Hadley, 1–30. Albany: State University of New York Press, 2001.

Harris, Nathan. "Reassessing the Dimensionality of Moral Emotions." *British Journal of Psychology* 94, no. 4 (November 2003): 457–73.

Helfman, Harold M. "Antecedents of Thomas Mott Osborne's 'Mutual Welfare League' in Michigan." *Journal of Criminal Law and Criminology* 40, no. 5 (January–February 1950): 597–600.

Hepburn, John R., and Celesta Albonetti. "Role Conflict in Correctional Institutions." *Criminology* 17, no. 4 (February 1980): 445–59.

Hirschi, Travis. *Causes of Delinquency.* Berkeley: University of California Press, 1969.

Homel, Ross, and Carleen Thompson. "Causes and Preventions of Violence in Prison." In *Corrections Criminology*, edited by Sean O'Toole and Simon Eylands, 101–8. Sydney: Hawkins Press, 2005.

Hughes, Timothy, and Doris James Wilson. "Reentry Trends in the United States." Bureau of Justice Statistics, U.S. Department of Justice. ojp.usdoj.gov/bjs/reentry/reentry.htm.

Inciardi, James A., Dorothy Lockwood, and Judith A. Quinlan. "Drug Use in Prison: Patterns, Processes, and Implications for Treatment." *Journal of Drug Issues* 23, no. 1 (Winter 2003): 119–29.

"Inside Prison Fellowship." www.pfm.org/Bio.asp?ID=43.

Irwin, John. *The Felon.* Englewood Cliffs, N.J.: Prentice Hall, 1970.

———. *The Warehouse Prison: The Disposal of the New Dangerous Class.* Los Angeles: Roxbury Publishing, 2005.

Irwin, John, and James Austin. *It's About Time: America's Imprisonment Binge.* 2nd ed. Belmont, Calif.: Wadsworth, 1997.

Jackson, Lisa F. "Meeting with a Killer." *Court TV.* Broadcast fall 2001.

James, Doris J., and Lauren E. Glaze. "Mental Health Problems of Prison and Jail Inmates." Bureau of Justice Statistics Special Report 2006. www.ojp.usdoj.gov/bjs/abstract/mhppji.pdf.

Johnstone, Gerry. *Restorative Justice: Ideas, Values, Debates.* Worchester, U.K.: Willan Publishing, 2002.

Jurik, Nancy C. "Individual and Organizational Determinants of Correctional Officer Attitudes toward Inmates." *Criminology* 23, no. 3 (August 1985): 523–40.

Juvenile Awareness Program. www.wild-side.com/scaredstraight.html.

Karmen, Andrew. *Crime Victims: An Introduction to Victimology.* 5th ed. Belmont, Calif.: Wadsworth/Thomas Learning, 2004.

King, Ryan S. "Changing Direction: State Sentencing Reforms 2004–2006." *The Sentencing Project Releases: News Report.* sentencingproject.org/Admin/ Documents/publications/sentencingreformforweb.pdf.

Lambert, Eric G., Nancy L. Hogan, and David N. Baker. "Gender Similarities and Differences in Correctional Staff Work Attitudes and Perceptions of the Work Environment." *Western Criminology Review* 8, no. 1 (April 2007): 16–31.

Lambert, Eric G., Nancy Hogan, and Shannon M. Barton. "Satisfied Correctional Staff: A Review of the Literature on the Correlates of Correctional Staff Job Satisfaction." *Criminal Justice and Behavior* 29, no. 2 (April 2002): 115–43.

Langan, Patrick A., and David J. Levin. *Recidivism of Prisoners Released in 1994.* www.ojp.usdoj.gov/bjs/abstract/rpr94.htm.

Latessa, Edward J., Francis T. Cullen, and Paul Gendreau. "Beyond Correctional Quackery: Professionalism and the Possibility of Effective Treatment." In *Correctional Contexts: Contemporary and Classical Readings,* 3rd ed., edited by Edward J. Latessa and Alexander M. Holsinger, 337–47. Los Angeles: Roxbury Publishing, 2006.

Latimer, Jeff, Craig Dowden, and Danielle Muse. *The Effectiveness of Restorative Practice: A Meta-analysis.* Ottawa, Canada: Department of Justice.

Liebling, Alison, with Helen Arnold. *Prisons and Their Moral Performance: A Study of Values, Quality and Prison Life.* Oxford: Oxford University Press, 2004.

Lindahl, Nicole, with Debbie A. Mukamal. *Venturing Beyond the Gates: Facilitating Successful Reentry with Entrepreneurship.* New York: Prisoner Reentry Institute John Jay College of Criminal Justice, 2007.

Lindsay, William R., Jacqueline Law, Kathleen Quinn, Nicola Smart, and Anne H. W. Smith. "A Comparison of Physical and Sexual Abuse: Histories of Sexual and Non Sexual Offenders with Intellectual Disability." *Child Abuse and Neglect* 25, no. 7 (July 2001): 989–95.

Lindsay-Hartz, Janice. "Contrasting Experiences of Shame and Guilt." *American Behavioral Scientist* 27, no. 6 (July 1984): 689–704.

Lipton, Douglas, Robert Martinson, and Judith Wilkes. *The Effects of Correctional Treatment: A Survey of Treatment Valuation Studies*. New York: Praeger, 1975.

Logan, Charles H., and Gerald G. Gaes. "Meta Analysis and the Rehabilitation of Punishment." *Justice Quarterly* 10, no. 2 (June 1993): 245–63.

Long, Bridget T. "Attracting the Best: The Use of Honors Programs to Compete for Students." Chicago: Spencer Foundation, 2005. Eric Reproduction Service No. ED465355.

Loy, David R. "Healing Justice: A Buddhist Perspective." In *The Spiritual Roots of Restorative Justice*, edited by Michael L. Hadley, 81–98. Albany: State University of New York Press, 2001.

Maguire, Mike, and Peter Raynor. "How Resettlement of Prisoners Promotes Desistance from Crime. Or Does It?" *Criminology and Criminal Justice* 6, no. 1 (February 2006): 19–38.

Marshall, Liam. "Development of Empathy." In *In Their Shoes: Examining the Issue of Empathy and Its Place in the Treatment of Offenders*, edited by Yolanda Fernandez, 36–52. Oklahoma City: Woods N Barnes, 2002.

Marshall, W. L. "Historic Foundations and Current Conceptualizations of Empathy." In *In Their Shoes: Examining the Issue of Empathy and Its Place in the Treatment of Offenders*, edited by Yolanda Fernandez, 2–8. Oklahoma City: Woods N Barnes, 2002.

Martinson, Robert. "What Works? Questions and Answers about Prison Reform." *Public Interest* 35, no. 4 (Spring 1974): 22–54.

———. "New Findings, New Views: A Note of Caution Regarding Sentencing Reforms." *Hofstra Law Review* 7, no. 2 (Winter 1979): 243–58.

Maslow, Abraham. "A Theory of Human Motivation." *Psychological Review* 50, no. 4 (1943): 370–96.

Mauer, Marc. *Race to Incarcerate*. New York: Free Press, 1999.

———. "What Wave?" *The American Prospect*, 2007. www.prospect.org/cs/articles?articleId=12601.

Maxwell, Gabrielle, and Allison Morris. "What Is the Place of Shame in Restorative Justice?" In *Critical Issues in Restorative Justice*, edited Howard Zehr and Barb Toews, 133–42. Monsey, N.Y.: Criminal Justice Press, 2004.

McCarthy, Belinda R. M., Bernard J. McCarthy Jr., and Matthew C. Leone. *Community-Based Corrections.* 4th ed. Belmont, Calif.: Wadsworth, 2001.

McCarthy, Phil. "Prisoner Reintegration–Looking Forward." New Zealand Department of Corrections, 2006. www.corrections.govt.nz/public/news/prison-fellowship-conference/phil-mccarthy-speech.html.

McClelland, David C., and Carol Kirshnit. "The Effect of Motivational Arousal through Films on Immunoglobulin A." *Psychology and Health* 2, no. 1 (1998): 31–52.

McCold, Paul. "Evaluation of a Restorative Milieu: Replication and Extension of 2001–2003 Discharges." Paper presented at the annual meeting of the American Society of Criminology, Nashville, Tenn., Nov. 13–16.

McCold, Paul, and Benjamin Wachtel. "Community Is Not a Place: A New Look at Community Justice Initiatives." In *Repairing Communities through Restorative Justice,* edited by John G. Perry, 39–53. Lanham, Md.: American Correctional Association, 2002.

McKnight, John. *The Careless Society: Community and Its Counterparts.* New York: Basic Books, 1995.

McRoberts, Omar M. "Religion, Reform, Community: Examining the Idea of Church-Based Prisoner Reentry." Urban Institute, Reentry Roundtable, 2002. www.urban.org/uploaded pdf/410802_Religion.pdf.

Miller, Jerome G. "The Debate on Rehabilitating Criminals: Is It True that Nothing Works?" www.prisonpolicy.org/scans/rehab.html.

Mirsky, Laura. "Albert Eglash and Creative Restitution: A Precursor to Restorative Practices." *Restorative Practices E Forum.* 2003. www.iirp.org/libarary/eglash.html.

———. "New Research Shows that Social and Emotional Learning Improves Academic Achievement." *Restorative Justice E-Forum.* 2008. www.safersanerschools.org/library/caselstudy.html.

Muhammad, S., and M. J. Tehrani. "Prison as a Growth Community: A Prison Reform Project in Iran." *The Journal of Humanistic Psychology* 37, no. 1 (Winter 1997): 98.

Mumola, Christopher J. "Medical Causes of Death in State Prison, 2001–2004." Bureau of Justice Statistics, 2007. www.ojp.usdoj.gov/bjs/pub/ascii/mcdsp04.txt.

Nathanson, Donald L. *Shame and Pride: Affect, Sex, and the Birth of Self.* New York: W. W. Norton, 1992.

Newell, Tim. "Restorative Practice in Prisons: Circles and Conferencing in a Custodial Setting." Restorative Justice On-Line. www.restorativejustice .org/search?SearchableText=Newell.

New York Times editorial, "A Smoother Re-entry." www.nytimes.com/2007/03/27/ opinion/27tue4.html?_r=1&ex=1175659200&en=a83a3e7f547c8cef&ei=5070& emc=eta1&oref=slogin.

Paluch, Jack, Jr. *Life without Parole: Living in Prison Today.* Los Angeles: Roxbury Publishing, 2004.

Park, Jerry Z., and Christian Smith. "Too Much Has Been Given . . . : Religious Capital and Community Volunteerism among Churchgoing Protestants." *Journal of the Scientific Study of Religion* 39, no. 3 (Sept. 2000): 272–86.

Pepinsky, Harold E., and Richard Quinney, eds. *Criminology as Peacemaking.* Bloomington: Indiana University Press, 1991.

Petersilia, Joan. *When Prisoners Come Home.* Oxford: Oxford University Press, 2003.

Petersilia, Joan, Susan Turner, James Kahan, and Joyce Peterson. *Granting Felons Probation: Public Risks and Alternatives.* R-3186-NIJ The RAND Corporation, 1985.

Pogrebin, Mark, and Burton Atkins. "Organizational Conflict in Correctional Institutions." *Journal of Offender Counseling, Services, and Rehabilitation* 7, no. 1 (Fall 1982): 23–31.

Potter-Efron, Ronald, and Patricia Potter-Efron. *Understanding How Shame Affects Your Life.* San Francisco: Harper/Hazelden, 1989.

Pranis, Kay. *The Little Book of Circle Processes: A New/Old Approach to Peacemaking.* Intercourse, Pa.: Good Books, 2005.

———. "Healing and Accountability in the Criminal Justice System as a Workplace: Applying Restorative Justice Processes." Presentation at the National Conference on Restorative Justice, Kerrville, Texas, June 24–June 27, 2007.

———. "Restorative Justice, Social Justice, and the Empowerment of Marginalized Population." In *Restorative Community Justice: Repairing Harm and Transforming Communities,* edited by Gordon Bazemore and Mara Schiff, 287–306. Cincinnati, Ohio: Anderson Publishing, 2001.

"Reentry." Office of Justice Programs, U.S. Department of Justice. www.reentry.gov/.

"The Reentry Mapping Network." Urban Institute. www.urban.org/projects/reentry-mapping/index.cfm.

"Reentry Update." Alabama Department of Corrections.

Reid, Francis, and Deborah Hoffmann, directors. *A Long Night's Journey into Day.* 2001.

Reisig, Michael D. "Rates of Disorder in Higher-Custody State Prisons: A Comparative Analysis of Managerial Practices." *Crime and Delinquency* 44, no. 2 (April 1998): 229–44.

"Restorative Justice FAQ." Victim Offender Mediation Association. voma.org/rjfaq.shtml.

Richards, Stephen C., and Richard S. Jones. "Beating the Perpetual Incarceration Machine: Overcoming Structural Impediments to Re-entry." In *After Crime and Punishment: Pathways to Offender Reintegration,* edited by Shadd Maruna and Russ Immarigeon, 201–32. Devon, U.K.: Willan Publishing, 2004.

Sabol, William J., Heather Couture, and Paige M. Harrison. *Prisoners in 2006.* www.ojp.usdoj.gov/bjs/abstract/p06.htm.

Sabrina, John, and Maury Silver. "In Defense of Shame: Shame in the Context of Guilt and Embarrassment." *Journal for Theory of Social Behavior* 27, no. 1 (March 1997): 1–15.

Schmalleger, Frank, and John Ortiz Smykla. *Corrections in the 21st Century.* 2nd ed. New York: McGraw Hill, 2005.

Shults, F. LeRon, and Steven J. Sandage. *The Faces of Forgiveness: Searching for Wholeness and Salvation.* Grand Rapids, Mich.: Baker, 2003.

"Standard Operating Procedures." Holman Correctional Facility, Faith-Based Restorative Justice Honor Community. November 15, 2004.

Stohr, Mary K., Nicholas P. Lovrich, and Marcia J. Wood. "Service versus Security Concerns in Contemporary Jails: Testing General Differences in Training Topic Assessments." *Journal of Criminal Justice* 24, no. 5 (1996): 437–48.

Sullentrop, Chris. "The Right Has a Jailhouse Conversion." *New York Times,* December 24, 2006. www.nytimes.com/2006/12/24/magazine/24GOP.t.html.

Swanson, Cheryl, Grantt Culliver, and Chris Summers. "Creating a Faith-Based Restorative Justice Community in a Maximum-Security Prison." *Corrections Today* 69, no. 3 (June 2007): 60–63.

Swanson, Cheryl, and Michelle Owen. "Building Bridges: Integrating Restorative Justice with the School Resource Officer Model." *International Journal of Restorative Justice* 3, no. 2 (September 2007): 68–92.

Sykes, Gresham M. *The Society of Captives: A Study of a Maximum Security Prison.* Princeton, N.J.: Princeton University Press, 1958.

Sylvester, Douglas J. "Myth in Restorative Justice History." *Utah Law Review*, no. 1 (2003): 471–522.

Taxman, Faye S., Douglas Young, and James M. Byrne. "With Eyes Wide Open: Formalizing Community and Social Control Intervention in Offender Reintegration Programmes." In *After Crime and Punishment: Pathways to Offender Reintegration*, edited by Shadd Maruna and Russ Immarigeon, 233–60. Devon, U.K.: Willan Publishing, 2004.

Toch, Hans. "Inmate Involvement in Prison Governance." *Federal Probation* 59, no. 2 (June 1995): 34–39.

Toews, Barb. *The Little Book of Restorative Justice for People in Prison: Rebuilding the Web of Relationships.* Intercourse, Pa.: Good Books, 2006.

———. "Restorative Justice: Building the Web of Relationships, Resources for Restorative Justice in Prison." Pennsylvania Prison Society. www.prisonsociety .org/progs/rj.shtml.

Tyson, Katherine. "Developing Compassionate Communities through the Power of Caregiving Relationships." *Journal of Religion and Spirituality in Social Work* 24, no. 1/2 (April 2005): 27–33

Uggen, Christopher, Jeff Manza, and Angela Behrens, "'Less Than the Average Citizen': Stigma, Role Transition and the Civic Reintegration of Convicted Felons." In *After Crime and Punishment: Pathways to Offender Reintegration*, edited by Shadd Maruna and Russ Immarigeon, 261–93. Devon, U.K.: Willan Publishing, 2004.

Umbreit, Mark S., Betty Vos, and Robert B. Coates. "Restorative Justice in the 21st Century: A Social Movement Full of Opportunities and Pitfalls." *Marquette University Law Review* 89, no. 2 (Winter 2005): 251–304.

Umbreit, Mark S., Betty Vos, Robert B. Coates, and Katherine A. Brown. *Facing Violence: The Path of Restorative Justice and Dialogue.* Monsey, N.Y.: Criminal Justice Press, 2003.

Van Ness, Daniel. "Restorative Justice in Prisons." Paper presented at the Symposium on Restorative Justice and Peace, Cali, Colombia, February 9–12, 2005.

Van Ness, Daniel W., and Karen Heetderks Strong. *Restoring Justice: An Introduction to Restorative Justice.* 3rd ed. Cincinnati, Ohio: Anderson Publishing, 2006.

Victim Services. Vermont Department of Corrections, Agency of Human Services. www.doc.state.vt.us/victim-services/vodp/vod-faq#difference.

Volpe, Maria R., and Staci Strobl. "Restorative Justice Responses to Post–September 11 Hate Crimes: Potential and Challenges." *Conflict Resolution Quarterly* 22, no. 4 (Summer 2005): 527–35.

Wachtel, Ted, and Paul McCold. "Restorative Justice in Everyday Life." In *Restorative Justice and Civil Society*, edited by Heather Strang and John Braithwaite, 114–29. Cambridge: Cambridge University Press, 2001.

Werner, Emily. "Resilient Offspring of Alcoholics: A Longitudinal Study from Birth to 18." *Journal of Studies on Alcohol* 47, no. 1 (1986): 34–40.

Wilkinson, Reginald A. "The Impact of Community Service Work on Ohio State Prisoners: A Restorative Justice Perspective and Overview." *Corrections Management Quarterly*, 2000. www.drc.state.oh.us/web/Articles/article63.htm.

Wooldredge, John D. "Inmate Experiences and Psychological Well-Being." *Criminal Justice and Behavior* 26, no. 2 (June 1999): 235–50.

Workman, Kim. "Prisoner Reintegration—Toward a Model of Community Fellowship." www.rethinking.org.nz/images/pdf/2006%20Conference/ 19%20Kim%20Workman.pdf.

Wuthnow, Robert. *Acts of Compassion: Caring for Others and Helping Ourselves.* Princeton, N.J.: Princeton University Press, 1991.

Youness, James, and Miranda Yates. *Community and Social Responsibility in Youth.* Chicago: University of Chicago Press, 1997.

Zehr, Howard. *Changing Lenses: A New Focus for Crime and Justice.* Scottsdale, Pa.: Herald Press, 2005.

———. *The Little Book of Restorative Justice.* Intercourse, Pa.: Good Books, 2002.

————. *Transcending: Reflections of Crime Victims.* Intercourse, Pa.: Good Books, 2001.

Ziolkowski, Theodore. *The Mirror of Justice.* Princeton, N.J.: Princeton University Press, 1997.

Index

Second Chance Act, 172
sentencing, 5–6, 9
sentencing circles, 29
shame, 91, 106, 111–14
Stuart, Barry, 78
Sullentrop, Chris, 3
Summers, Chris, ix, 49, 187, 189
Sycamore Tree Project, 34, 108–9

Tewksbury, Richard, 127
therapeutic forgiveness, 24
Toews, Barb, 21, 36, 37, 127
Tomkins, Sylvan, 90
Truth and Reconciliation Commission,
    26, 167
Tyson, Katherine, 167–8

Van Ness, Daniel, 27, 33
victim offender reconciliation programs
    (VORPs), 26, 34, 103
victims: needs of, 102–4; restorative
    justice on, 30; rights organizations,
    102; victim impact panels, 106–8. See

also victim offender reconciliation
    programs; victim's rights movement
victim's rights movement, 28
violence: culture of, 78–80, 82–84; and
    prisoners, 7
Violent Crime Control Act of
    1994/1995, 125
the virtuous prison, 10, 11
VORPs. *See* victim offender
    reconciliation programs

Wachtel, Ted, 91
W. C. Holman Correctional Facility, xii,
    8, 47
W. C. Holman Faith-Based Restorative
    Justice Honor Dorm. *See* honor
    dorm
Werner, Emmy, 175–76
Workman, Kim, 181, 186

Zehr, Howard, 24, 29, 34, 39, 102, 105,
    112, 140, 217–18

About the Author

Cheryl Swanson is an associate professor and former chair of the Department of Criminal Justice and Legal Studies at the University of West Florida in Pensacola, Florida. She serves as vice chair of the corrections section of the Academy of Criminal Justice Sciences, as a volunteer instructor with the Faith-Based Restorative Justice Honor Dorm at W. C. Holman Correctional Facility, as cochair of the Friends of Holman Faith-Based Restorative Justice Honor Dorm, and as a volunteer with the Trauma Intervention Program, a victim-based service. She served as past cochair of the Restorative Justice Section of the Association for Conflict Resolution and past director of the Center for Alternative Dispute Resolution at the University of West Florida. She is a member of the Academy of Criminal Justice Sciences and the Southern Criminal Justice Association.

Among other works, Professor Swanson is the author of a book chapter—"Should Victims Have the Right to Meet with Their Offenders?"—in the second edition of *Issues in Victimology*; an article with Michelle Owen on "Incorporating Restorative Justice into the School Resource Officer Model," in the *International Journal of Restorative Justice*; and she contributed to an article in *Corrections Today*, "Evaluating a Faith-Based Restorative Justice Honor Dorm from the Perspectives of a Warden, a Chaplain, and a College Professor." She has written articles on restorative justice applications to the crime of embezzlement, AIDS in prison, children of incarcerated parents, and using electronic monitoring as an alternative to incarceration. She contributed an entry to the *Encyclopedia of Criminology* on intermediate sanctions.